It was a great honour for us to have our book presented at SPRU.

May 2018

Rodrigo Arocena

Judith Sutz

Developmental Universities in Inclusive Innovation Systems

CONTENTS

About the Authors

Rodrigo Arocena holds PhD degrees in Mathematics and in Development Studies from Venezuela's Central University. He is Professor of Science and Development, Faculty of Sciences, University of the Republic, Uruguay (since 1994). Former positions in the same University include being its Rector (2006–2014) and Full Professor of Mathematics in the Faculty of Sciences (1986–1996). He organized the Unit of Science and Development in the Faculty of (natural and exact) Sciences as an interdisciplinary space for fostering academic collaboration between natural sciences and social sciences. His teaching and research are related to Higher Education, Science, Technology, Innovation, and Development.

Bo Göransson is Senior Research Fellow at the Research Policy Group at the Lund University School of Economics and Management, Sweden. He holds a PhD in International Economics from Aalborg University, Denmark. His research work focuses on how knowledge and learning systems drive economic development and growth. Much of the research deals with issues related to innovation policies, capacity building, and the impact of new technologies in developing countries, particularly the role of universities in innovation systems and development. He is coordinator of the UniDev research network.

Judith Sutz is the Academic Coordinator of the University Research Council of the University of the Republic, Uruguay, and Professor of Science, Technology and Society in the Faculty of Social Sciences. She holds a PhD in Socio-Economics of Development from the University of Paris. Her research work is related to the specific conditions for innovation in developing countries and with problems associated with the production and social use of knowledge in such countries. She is a member of the Advisory Editorial Board of Research Policy, Science and Public Policy, Innovation and Development and Revista Iberoamericana de Ciencia, Tecnología y Sociedad.

LIST OF FIGURES

LIST OF TABLES

CHAPTER 1

General Introduction and An Overview of the Book

We live in a very unequal world. Striking and persistent disparities in development between macro regions, countries, and even regions within countries are apparent. Differences in income, health, education, and other basic aspects of life are often considerable even between families inhabiting the same geographical location. The possibilities human beings have for living valuable lives are highly dependent on where they are born, geographically and socially. The spectacular expansion of scientific and technological knowledge that has taken place during the last centuries has been a source of great benefits. Many of these benefits have largely been denied to large parts of the world population where social ills and inequalities remain unabated in the face of scientific progress. This is the starting point of this book.

We want to explore paths that have already been pursued or that may be opened in the future for better contributions of advanced knowledge to improving living conditions, particularly where and for whom it is more urgent. That is the significance of the subtitle of the book, in search of alternatives for knowledge democratization in the Global South.

Advanced knowledge is not referred to here implying that other types of knowledge are less important or relevant. Advanced knowledge denominates the outputs of academic work and its applications. It is not "Western knowledge" anymore, even if it started developing some centuries ago in a very small part of the Western world. Today, advanced knowledge is cultivated in the whole world, albeit with expressive differences in intensity. This consideration is important because the knowledge involved in

© The Author(s) 2018
R. Arocena et al., *Developmental Universities in Inclusive Innovation Systems*, https://doi.org/10.1007/978-3-319-64152-2_1

grassroots innovations, those innovations done by people who themselves modify different facets of their ways of life, are in a sense much more democratized than advanced knowledge. Such knowledge is widely shared and is focused on the problems that people themselves identify as problems. In contrast, advanced knowledge is relatively concentrated and generally weakly oriented toward solving those kinds of problems. Democratizing advanced knowledge means then to broaden its scope by taking on board a wide set of research problems and innovation projects that until now have been below its radar. It means putting the might of advanced knowledge—a might nobody would deny, even if fearing its consequences—at the service of people until now underserved by it. In this book, "knowledge" will be used mainly referring to "advanced knowledge". Our main purpose is to explore the possibilities for its democratization. But this delimitation of our topic does not imply in the least a pretension of completeness or a tacit assumption of an exclusionary importance of advanced knowledge.

Knowledge generation and utilization take place in diverse social processes that involve many actors. The set of such actors and their interactions can be thought of as the Innovation System of a given country or region. Power relations within an Innovation System define who gains and who loses from innovation broadly understood as the effective incorporation of new knowledge to social and economic practices. We contend that prevailing policies for science, technology, and innovation foster rather than hamper knowledge-based inequality. If a goal of an efficient Innovation Systems is to favor social inclusion, different policies are needed.

The increasing role of advanced knowledge implies that universities are ever more important actors in the context of Innovation Systems. Combining higher education, research, and knowledge utilization is what universities do or should do. They can do it more or less efficiently and also in ways that restrict or expand the benefits of knowledge. When they efficiently contribute to knowledge democratization, thus cooperating in overcoming inequality and underdevelopment, they may be considered to be Developmental Universities. They can function and work not in solitude or connected only with privileged elites but in the highly integrated contexts of Inclusive Innovation Systems.

So this book is about Developmental Universities in Inclusive Innovation Systems.

AN OVERVIEW OF THE BOOK

The book is divided into two interrelated parts. The first part focuses on the relationship between development and knowledge production. The second part considers the contribution of universities to development.

Chapter 2 starts the first part by discussing the concept of development and how it has been interpreted by different schools of thought in the developmental discourse. For that a sequential analytical model is proposed that considers values, facts, trends, and policies as a coherent whole. The model features four approaches and their interlinkages—the normative, the factual, the prospective, and the propositional approaches—and uses them as analytical tools in the following chapters to explore alternative paths to development. Taking a point of departure in Amartya Sen's characterization of development as the expansion of capabilities and freedoms as well as paying special attention to environmental issues, the normative notion of Sustainable Human Development is summarized. The core of the factual and prospective approaches is the increasing role of knowledge as the main resource in power relations. That is one of the most relevant processes concerning possibilities and obstacles for Sustainable Human Development. Advanced knowledge becomes directly related to inequalities and even to social exclusion. Consequently, democratization of knowledge appears as a main component in the propositional approach. It exemplifies the main connection between the normative approach and proposed policies given by Sen's assertion that the expansion of capabilities and freedoms not only characterizes the ends of development but also is its fundamental tool.

Chapter 3 focuses on inequalities related to knowledge, which have been rising during the last decades. What knowledge is generated and how it is used greatly influence the amount and distribution of power in society. Such influence is seen in who are the winners of scientific expansion and economic growth. It is also seen in who are the losers of such fundamental processes that have been changing the human landscape and also the natural landscape. The highly unequal consequences of those processes become apparent by looking at who are less or more damaged by environmental degradation. The notion of learning divides summarizes the description and explanation of knowledge-based inequalities.

Given the power of knowledge, its production should be oriented, above all, to contributing to Sustainable Human Development. In order to translate such a normative assertion into proposals, a factual study of the social processes of learning and innovation is needed. That is the task of Chapter 4. Generating and using knowledge involve many actors and their interactions, a set often called the Innovation System. Innovation processes are shaped by who these actors actually are, what they do, in which ways they relate (or do not relate) to each other, and how power is distributed among them. A key aspect of innovation is how knowledge is incorporated in social practices. Analyzing those issues helps gauging the possibilities of knowledge democratization. When the power of knowledge is apparent in facts and trends, learning processes deserve special attention. They take place in different contexts, more often than not stemming from interactions between several actors, and are closely related to innovation. Democratizing knowledge requires generalizing learning activities. Regions where this does not happen tend to be peripheral; social groups with weak learning opportunities risk exclusion.

Our understanding of the problems of development suggests that a fundamental question concerning social inclusion is what kind of knowledge is being produced and diffused in the innovation system and for whom. This question is not very relevant when social inclusion is expected to result from the trickle-down effect of productivity enhancement and economic growth. But such an effect is quite weak in a world deeply shaped by knowledge-based inequality and by environmental damage. Thus, knowledge-based inclusive policies that foster frugal innovation are central for the propositional approach presented in this book. They are specifically discussed in Chapter 5, in the context of the trends and possibilities considered in the prospective approach. Their aim is to curtail environmental and social threats by making Sustainable Human Development–friendly scenarios more feasible. Fundamental among such scenarios are what can be called Inclusive Innovation Systems.

Universities are usually relevant actors in Innovation Systems. Universities that give priority to the democratization of knowledge as a strategy for development in the context of Inclusive Innovation Systems may be considered developmental universities. Elaborating this notion is the task of the second part of the book. It starts in Chapter 6. There some factors that shape the evolution of universities in the long run are taken into account, particularly in connection with the rise of the so-called Humboldtian University, which was the dominant model up to recent times. Then actual debates and contrasting proposals for transforming universities are discussed. The following questions are considered: which are the main differences among current proposals for the third mission of universities? How are the demands for social responsiveness of universities expressed and by whom? How do universities react and answer to such demands? The currently dominant model of the "entrepreneurial university" is briefly analyzed.

Chapter 7 introduces the normative idea of developmental universities as an alternative to the dominant models of the recent past and of the present. It starts by characterizing the situation of academic institutions in the Global South. This situation is mainly shaped by the actual traits of underdevelopment. One of them is the comparatively weak commercial demand of advanced knowledge stemming from the economic dynamics of underdeveloped countries and related to national producers of such knowledge, universities above all. Universities should pay attention to social demand of knowledge in general, particularly when it is potentially related to the needs of deprived sectors. Developmental universities expand and democratize knowledge by combining teaching, research, and cooperating with other collective actors in fostering development. This notion and related ones have in common a view of considering knowledge and education as public goods. The possibilities of contrasting models for transforming universities are discussed in connection with their potential stakeholders.

In Chapter 8, the possibilities of fostering developmental universities are examined. First, it discusses the actual role of universities in Innovation Systems. A main aspect of the relation between universities and society at large consists of the type and degree of autonomy that universities have; a notion of connected autonomy is proposed. Particular attention is given to describing prevailing academic evaluation systems, showing that they are detrimental from the point of view of Sustainable Human Development, and trying to understand why they are nevertheless kept in place. Some alternatives are suggested for elaborating metrics and evaluation systems that do not hamper but foster the contribution of universities to improving the quality of life for everybody.

Chapter 9 looks to the future. First, it attempts to answer the question: how can universities contribute to knowledge democratization? Then it considers how to gauge whether progress is being made; for that, seven "indicators of the developmental role of universities" are elaborated. They are related to the generalization of advanced lifelong learning, the modes and links shaping knowledge production and use, and the ways of governing universities. These issues are looked at from a prospective approach that highlights the rising role of knowledge in power relations as well as related environmental and social risks. Shaping innovation policies as a part of social policies (and vice versa) is suggested as a type of productive specialization. It is a telling example of the general task of knowledge democratization which is urgent in the South and perhaps also in the North.

PART I

Development and Inclusive Innovation Systems

CHAPTER 2

An Integrated Conception of Development

A MODEL FOR STUDYING DEVELOPMENT PROBLEMS: VALUES, FACTS, TRENDS, AND PROPOSALS

In order to study development problems in general and particularly their relation with knowledge, we propose a sequential analytical model that considers values, facts, trends, and policies as a coherent whole. We assume that concrete policy proposals should be based on some way of combining an interpretation of facts and trends with a choice of ends.

Development Studies include both descriptive and prescriptive dimensions. Descriptions of situations and problems must at the same time be differentiated from and combined with prescriptions for solving such problems in the context of the situations under consideration. But further distinctions are needed. Prescriptions should be based not only on factual descriptions but also on ethical options; a normative approach is required.

Descriptions are really useful when they include explanations; the factual approach gives insights by means of empirical and theoretical elements. Theory must be based on observations, but it is theory that orients and even allows meaningful observations, to a point that it can be said that the latter would not really exist without the former. From that viewpoint, the factual approach is both theoretical and empirical.

A prospective approach should complement the factual approach. Arguably, a minimally satisfactory comprehension of a given phenomenon or process requires some understanding of its possible evolutions. Moreover, policies are not really intended to influence the present but the future.

© The Author(s) 2018   9
R. Arocena et al., *Developmental Universities in Inclusive Innovation Systems*, https://doi.org/10.1007/978-3-319-64152-2_2

To connect policy instruments with normative ends in an acceptably rational way, not only present facts but also main trends and alternative possibilities must be taken into account.

The propositional approach should, of course, include suggestions for public policies but also for orienting actions of a wide variety of agents. Development Studies aim at formulating proposals that are knowledge-based and value-oriented. They must be based on normative, factual, and prospective approaches.

Development policies cannot be fruitfully discussed without clear statements about their normative ends, their factual assumptions, and their hypothesis concerning probable futures.

So, we shall try to combine four approaches—normative, factual, prospective, and propositional—without confusing them. It seems natural to start by the normative approach and end by the propositional approach. Policy proposals and proposals in general should stem from combining a choice of values with an interpretation of facts and trends.

Several difficulties stem from confusing those approaches. For instance, to qualify normatively certain facts, if not differentiated from their analysis, may jeopardize the comprehension of the dynamics that led to those facts. Difficulties also stem from isolating each approach from the others: propositions that do not consider facts and trends that indicate present and possible future barriers to what is intended will probably led to failures. In the same vein, normative approaches may become merely declamatory if propositional approaches do not foster the aims they involve, perhaps due to the theoretical choices taken to explain facts or to identify trends.

Values should not mold the description and interpretation of facts and trends but they should legitimately influence the choice of problems to be studied (that is, the research agenda). The normative approach must not only shape the propositional approach but also influence the selection of processes to be considered by the factual and prospective approaches. Normative guidance acts as Fayerabend (1988) says theory acts: it unearths directions of concern, illuminating a workable zone of problems around which facts and trends can and should be thoroughly studied.

The four approaches sketched in this chapter can be graphically depicted as shown in Fig. 2.1.

The four approaches have important levels of autonomy, being at the same time mutually influential. Some influences are direct and almost self-evident: from normative positions stem what is desirable in terms of ends and in terms of means; they act as well as a focusing device that highlights

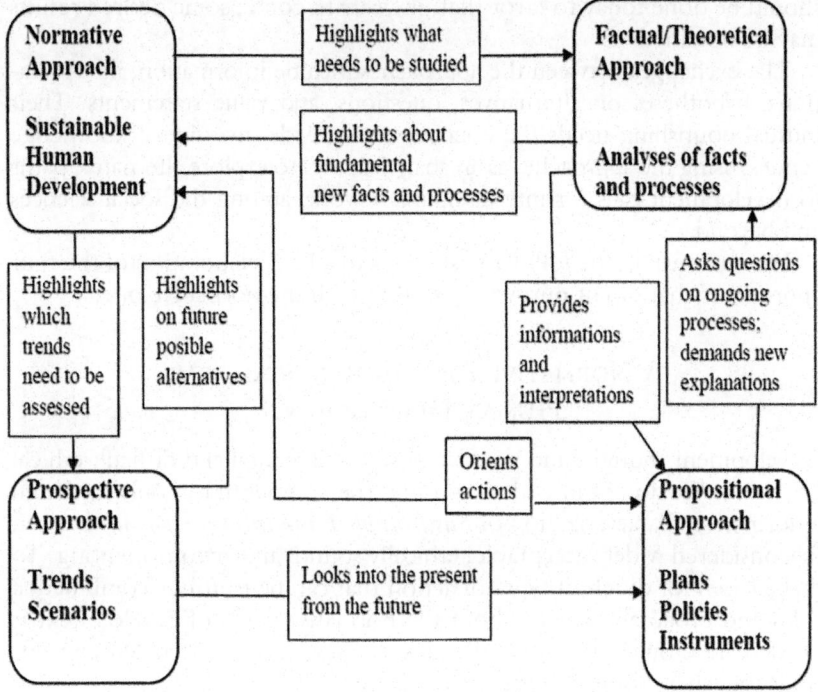

Fig. 2.1 The four approaches and their interlinkages
Source: Adapted and translated from (Arocena and Sutz 2016: 86)

relevant facts and trends to be analyzed; they also orient actions. But normative approaches are not immutable. For instance, the transformation of sustainability into a normative aim followed the accumulation of empirical facts signaling a dangerous situation whose trends heralded, if no change was produced, a catastrophic outcome. Normative aims are not a wishful-thinking list. To be a lighthouse for action, they should point to the impossible only in Weber's sense, when he posited that "man would not have attained the possible unless time and again he had reached for the impossible" (quoted in Gerth and Wright 1991: 128). Therefore, reasoned alternatives stemming from the prospective approach are a useful input to the normative approach.

Trends are a fundamental input for the propositional approach. In a sense, they act as a focusing device from the future into the present: what should be done today to favor that, in years to come, some desired results may be obtained?

The exchanges between the approaches include information, interpretations, hypotheses on alternatives, questions, and value statements. Their mutual nourishing needs the concourse of a wide diversity of knowledge venues; using the approaches as an analytical tool to explore alternative paths to development calls for interdisciplinary work, among the social sciences and beyond.

We now turn in the following sections to a brief elaboration of the four approaches that orient our work, starting with the normative one.

A NORMATIVE APPROACH: SUSTAINABLE HUMAN DEVELOPMENT

Development thought and practice pose fundamental and difficult ethical problems. We do not intend to consider them in depth but only to sketch a normative characterization of *Sustainable Human Development* that can be considered widely acceptable, ethically sound, and action-orienting. To make room for different types of action that can be fruitfully combined, a solid and broad agreement about the normative goals of development is needed. It should offer a plural space for several more detailed conceptions that share some general orientations.

With such a purpose, a good starting point is the already-famous characterization of "Development as Freedom" (Sen 1999). It inspires the notion of Human Development that was elaborated when it became apparent that economic growth was not sufficient for improving the quality of life. A synthetic and widely accepted formulation of such a notion is the following: "[H]uman development is the expansion of people's freedoms and capabilities to lead lives that they value and have reason to value" (UNDP 2011: 1).

Another fundamental notion that should be included in the normative approach is the concept of Sustainable Development, which is understood as fulfilling the needs of the present generations without compromising the possibilities of future generations to fulfill their own needs. Such a notion was elaborated when it became apparent that prevailing styles of economic growth were damaging the environment to such a degree that future generations may face increasing difficulties to attend to their fundamental needs.

Despite the strong evidence that led to the elaboration of the notions of Human Development and Sustainable Development, it is still usual to equate development with growth and, moreover, to equate growth with the increase of GDP (gross domestic product), which is a defective measure even of economic growth (Stiglitz et al. 2010).

Such fundamental notions stress that the ethical imperatives linked with development are about both the present and the future: "[N]ot working toward guaranteeing the basic capabilities to the future generations would be scandalous, but in the same way, not working toward bringing those elementary capabilities within the reach of the deprived in the present generation would also be outrageous" (Anand and Sen 2000: 2030).

Environmental damage requires that the aim be to expand capabilities and freedoms of actual and future generations. Thus, Sustainable Human Development has been characterized by the expansion of substantive freedoms and capabilities of people today without compromising those of future generations (UNDP 2011: 2; Sen 2013: 11). It can be presented as a natural expansion of Sen's conception that has generated a major change in development theory (Evans and Heller 2015). A really new paradigm is needed. In such a perspective, some comments may be useful.

The valuable core of the original idea of development was its commitment to improving the quality of human life. A revised version of such commitment is Sen's characterization of development as the expansion of freedoms and capabilities of people to live lives they have reason to value. In that direction, some remarkable progress has been accomplished in recent decades, particularly concerning health, life expectancy, and education. Such progress has been highly dependent on the quantitative and qualitative expansion of the production of some goods and services (certainly not of all of them). That expansion in turn has been strongly fostered by technological innovation. In this sense, Human Development is related to economic development, briefly seen as the combination of economic growth and technological innovation.

Now, the demand for sustainability arises precisely because the prevailing types of production have already damaged the environment in such a way that the quality of life today is seriously affected and it looks like it will be more so tomorrow. Thus, the normative goal should be not only preserving but expanding the possibilities for future generations. In fact, we could define the self-sustainability of development by the expansion in the present of individual and collective freedoms and capabilities that will help people to live valuable lives in the future. It points to social and environmental conditions as well as to knowledge, skills, and, more generally, human agency.

The emphasis on agency is related to a fundamental trait of Sen's characterization of development: the normative approach is also the starting point of the propositional approach. In fact, the expansion of freedoms and capabilities not only defines the goals of development but also constitutes the fundamental means of development; the link between ends and means is stressed by the normative view of people not as patients but as agents (Sen 1999). Values should guide policies.

Let us stress that both individual agency and collective agency are considered: "we need a vision of mankind not as patients whose interests have to be looked after, but as agents who can do effective things—both individually and jointly" (Sen 2013: 7). From another strand of literature comes a convergent assertion: "[W]e argue that collective-action situations lie at the core of development. A *collective action situation* (...) occurs whenever a desired joint outcome requires the input of several individuals" (Gibson et al. 2005: 15).

Such an agency-based characterization of development seems to be fully compatible with ethical approaches stemming from the triple demand of liberty, equality, and fraternity. Understanding it in such a way, we adopt the following working definition.

Sustainable Human Development is (i) the expansion of people's freedoms and capabilities, both individual and collective; (ii) in order to lead lives that they value and have reason to value; (iii) in ways that preserve and enlarge the possibilities of future generations for living such lives; (iv) assuming that the expansion of freedoms and capabilities is both the defining aim of development and its main tool, which (v) implies treating people as agents, not as patients.

Beyond the "Place and Ladder" Paradigm

Prevailing conceptions of development belong to what can be called the "place and ladder" paradigm. It has been the dominant paradigm for almost seventy years and it still holds that position although it is at odds with the notion of Sustainable Human Development.

This dominant paradigm sees the process of development as the so-called developing countries "catching up" with the so-called developed countries. More specifically, it assumes that innovations and socio-technical system change will come from the Global North; in these conceptions, as Schot and Steinmueller put it, the rest "need to play catch-up with those innovations" (Schot and Steinmueller 2016: 21).

Developed countries, by definition, do not need to develop themselves: their situation characterizes the "place" of development. In turn, catching up means something akin to climbing a "ladder" that starts in backwardness and ends in the place where developed countries are located.

If we take Human Development à la Sen seriously, developed countries just do not exist: where has the task of expanding freedoms and capabilities arrived at its end? People are not ensured to be able to live valuable lives anywhere.

The United States has been the major example of development as a place at least since the late 1940s. It was recently described in the following terms: "[T]here are no shortage of social ills to address: that, as one Princeton academic study found, the US resembles an oligarchy more than a democracy; that wages have been stagnating or falling for many years, fuelling resentment that Trump feeds on; a racist judicial system; an inefficient private healthcare system; extortionate university fees; a younger generation facing a future of insecurity; the likelihood of further disastrous military interventions in the coming years; and so on" (Owen Jones, *The Guardian*, July 26, 2016).

Such statements are surely controversial but it is not easy to deny that they have a grain of truth that is sufficient to discard such a place as a successful example of the normative goals of development. Even stronger statements can be made when environmental sustainability is taken into account: the so-called developed countries are the main polluters to such a degree that, if the rest of the world climbs the ladder that leads to that place, an environmental catastrophe is unavoidable. That can be seen by looking to what is happening in China, probably the most successful example of "catching up" in world history. It is also a telling example of unsustainable and unequal economic growth. The Economic Commission for Latin America and the Caribbean concludes that "China has become the world's largest emitter of greenhouse gases because its rapid economic growth has been fuelled by an energy mix that is heavily dependent on coal. At the same time, structural change has generated significant territorial imbalances and a highly uneven income distribution. [...] Income inequality has soared since the economic reforms: by 2012 the Gini coefficient stood at almost 0.55, higher than in any country of the Organization for Economic Cooperation and Development" (ECLAC 2016: 43).

Taking the notion of Sustainable Human Development seriously entails that development cannot be equated with catching up and that developed countries simply do not exist.

Of course, more or less powerful and rich countries, as well as more or less poor and powerless countries, do exist. The first set of countries is usually called the North. There, it is quite difficult to expand the freedoms and capabilities of large groups of people. The second set of countries can be termed the Global South. There, the normative goals of development pose much more difficult problems than in the North. Those are facts that should be analyzed as such.

A Factual Approach: The Structural Change of Our Time

Differences in wealth and power between groups and countries arise from interactions between technology and social relations. The power of technology, fostered by its close combination with science, has increased.

In order to gauge possibilities and difficulties for expanding capabilities and freedoms, it is necessary to describe and explain the ever-increasing social role of advanced (scientific and technological) knowledge. The opportunities and risks it generates, as well as the benefits and damages to which it is related, need to be given priority in a research agenda ethically oriented by the engagement with Sustainable Human Development. Such a focus is warranted because of the extraordinary impact new knowledge has and continues to have on every aspect of our lives. Or as Mokyr (2002: 2) puts it, "[T]he central phenomenon of the modern age is that as an aggregate we know more. New knowledge developed in the past three centuries has created a great deal of social conflict and suffering, just as it was the origin of undreamed-of wealth and security. It revolutionized the structures of firms and households, it altered the way people look and feel, how long they live, how many children they have, and how they spend their time. Every aspect of our material existence has been altered by our new knowledge".

But what does "knowing more" mean exactly? Is it just an issue of scientific knowledge accumulation on the one side and technological knowledge accumulation on the other, issued by the self-reinforcing process of new questions–new answers–new questions in each of those realms? Apparently, there is something more. The additional ingredient has been dubbed so important as to give birth to a very big revolution: "[T]he second economic revolution, the wedding of science to technology which began in the last half of the nineteenth century, is the source of modern economic growth and entails enormous specialization, division of labor, urban societies and global markets" (North 1997: 10).

This wedding emerges as something new, issued from the slow rapprochement of science and technology. As Kranzberg (1967) puts it, it was not too harmonious a wedding, but it provided steady scientific advancements through technological instrumentation as well as science-based new technologies and, no less important, based on the latter, totally new industries. The "mild flirtations" (Kranzberg 1967: 48) were fueled by conscious efforts to provide—in some parts of the world—spaces for intellectual exchanges between the future couple. Mokyr speaks of the "Industrial Enlightenment" as a sort of social movement of importance for the flirt: "[T]he Industrial Enlightenment realized instinctively that one of the great sources of technological stagnation was a social divide between those who knew things ('*savants*') and those who made things ('*fabricants*'). To construct pipelines through which those two groups could communicate was at the very heart of the movement" (Mokyr 2005: 1138). "The wedding of science and the useful arts" is the way in which Noble (1977) describes the efforts, in the United States, to systematically instill science in the engineering profession; such efforts were born from the increasing complexity of the engineering problems associated with the new industries of the late nineteenth century.

Those weddings and its antecedents did not occur everywhere. Economic historians have coined a famous expression, "great divergence", to give account of the differentiation between Europe and the rest of the world in terms of sustained growth. Many of those economic historians put issues related to science and technology at the core of the great divergence, even if explaining these issues by different social processes and historical conditions. An illustration of the divergence is a table compiled by Paul Bairoch, showing the evolution of the industrial output of several countries from 1750 to 1913. Just to give some figures, taking as level 100 the industrial output of the United Kingdom in 1900 as a point of reference, it is asserted that:

In 1750, the total industrial output of the regions of what would become the Third World was 93; the corresponding figure for the Developed World (at that time Europe) was 34;

By 1830, the United States slowly entered the scene; the figures differed from those of 1750 but the difference was still favorable to the Third World, 172–73;

By 1860, the trend changed: 83–143;

By 1880, the differences became dramatic: 63–223;

By 1900, the figures were 60–481; the United States overcame the United Kingdom, and Germany did the same a decade later (Bairoch 1982: 296).

Except for a few countries, mainly Japan and the East Asia "four dragons", the situation had not changed substantially a century later.

There are several explanations proposed for this evolution. Bairoch includes among them the huge increase in productivity of the developed countries' industry due to technical advances. It is interesting to tentatively explore the timing of the divergence by means of a typology of knowledge proposed by Joel Mokyr. "Useful knowledge", Mokyr asserts, can be classified in two types: "omega knowledge", related to the answers given to questions like "what" and "why", and "lambda knowledge", related to "how". "Omega knowledge" is broader than science, even if it contains science: it includes observations and explanations of all kinds, not only those that are "purposefully shared (...) and tested by consensuality" (Mokyr 2002: 5). "Lambda knowledge", also named "prescriptive knowledge", includes "the set of executable instructions or recipes for how to manipulate nature" (Op. cit.: 10). A further differentiation relates to aggregation: whereas an addition to "omega knowledge" is a discovery, for "lambda knowledge" it is an invention (Op. cit.: 12). "Lambda knowledge" cannot exist without some amount of "omega knowledge", but the amount of the latter (that is, the epistemic base of the former) has deep consequences on the scope and evolution of prescriptive knowledge. If it is known that something works but not why it works, improvements can be made, but only by trial and error, which is unreliable and costly, hampering extensions and new applications. The wider and deeper the epistemic base "on which a technique rests, the more likely is that a technique can be extended and find new applications, product and service quality improved, the production process streamlined, economized and *adapted to changing external circumstances, and the techniques combined with others to form new ones*" (Mokyr 2002: 14, emphasis added). The well-known fact that science contributed little to the techniques that were at the base of the Industrial Revolution is related to the narrow epistemic base of such techniques.

Things started to change in this regard in Western Europe and the United States during the nineteenth century. "Electric technology, much like organic chemistry, represents a new kind of lambda knowledge that emerged in the nineteenth century, and in which the minimum epistemic base is much larger than ever before" (Op. cit.: 93). And then, in a great break with what usually happened before, old techniques did not stall in their evolution but expanded rapidly and impacted on different productive sectors, and new techniques emerged that gave rise to new productive sectors. Mokyr asks: "...why did (technical progress) accelerate and accumulate rather than slow down and then fade out..." (Op. cit.: 95).

The "wedding of science and technology" in North's words seems to be the answer. In Mokyr's terms, "...the co-evolution of omega and lambda knowledge by this time had settled on a different dynamic, one that eventually led to a fundamental instability of the set of useful knowledge" (Ibid).

It can be suggested that part of the explanation of the figures of the divergence in industrial output presented by Bairoch lies in the characteristics lambda knowledge had until the mid-nineteenth century and those it acquired after. A narrow epistemic base for the techniques used when such techniques were widely known put a premium on those regions with a high volume of population. When the epistemic base of lambda knowledge widened through the wedding with omega knowledge—a wedding that did not occur in the countries of the Third World—the gains in productivity of old industries and the turmoil of opportunities to create new industries contributed to the reversal the figures show.

The wedding has not happened even today in the countries of the Third World that remained underdeveloped. It is sufficient to look at actual figures of investments on research and development (R&D) to see how the efforts for creating knowledge as well as new or improved products, processes, and services from new knowledge continue to be concentrated in the countries that were at the forefront of the "second economic revolution", with a few, albeit important, new Asian entrants. The United States and Western Europe accounted in 2013 for half the world expenditure on R&D (51.3%); East and Southeast Asia accounted for 36.8%, and China reached almost three quarters of the United States expenditures on R&D in 2013 and so accounted for 20% of the world R&D expenditure (NSF, Science and Engineering Indicators 2016: 454).

Following from the previous remarks, our factual approach starts by stressing that, in some comparatively restricted areas of the world, a knowledge-based and innovation-driven economy (de la Mothe and Paquet 1996) emerged during the last decades of the twentieth century and can be considered as consolidated by now. That is the main structural change of our time and the main engine of globalization. It does not take place all over the planet but its impacts are truly global, though quite different concerning different regions and social groups. It is the first clue to understanding the actual role of knowledge and particularly its relation with inequality. This relation is clearly seen in the contemporary aspects of underdevelopment, which will be described below.

Today the expansion of a knowledge-based and innovation-driven economy shaped by capitalist-type relations has a differentiated but global influence that is even more extensive and intensive that the influence exhibited yesterday by the expansion of the industrial economy. In that sense, we may speak of a globalized capitalist knowledge economy. Telling aspects of that economy are the roles of multinational corporations in world R&D, global value added, and international trade that make them the principal agents of market integration and globalization in general (Dahlman 2009).

The possibilities opened by the increasing role of knowledge and related benefits are highly concentrated in some social groups and in some regions, comparatively wide groups in the North and more or less narrow groups in the Global South. Thus, advanced knowledge becomes directly related to inequalities and even to social exclusion. And so, it poses a fundamental challenge for the expansion of capabilities and freedoms of many people.

Paying due attention to such reality is a starting point in the search for new alternatives for development.

UNDERDEVELOPMENT TODAY

The above-sketched factual approach can be applied to the analysis of the relations between the North and the Global South, which were some time ago called the West and the Rest.

The emergence during the nineteenth century of industrial economies had global consequences that can be roughly and partially described as the divide between "centers" and "peripheries", the former being the industrialized countries of the West and the latter the non-industrialized countries and regions of the Rest.

For the Rest, that entailed a specialization in primary goods that sometimes was the result of forced deindustrialization (Rodrik 2011: 136, 141; Bairoch 1993: 54). In the decades following the crisis of the 1930s, some levels of industrialization were reached in several peripheral countries, including many in Latin America, where nevertheless production still shows on average low complexity and diversification. In the long run, that is a source of relative poverty. As Reinert reflects: "[P]oor countries are stuck in poverty, among other reasons, because they specialize in activities that are devoid of learning potential" (Reinert 2007: xxviii). During the same period, a quite small number of countries escaped from their peripheral situation by upgrading the knowledge and innovation content of their productive activities.

The old, new, or just-emerging "centers" of today are the sites of the new knowledge-based and innovation-driven economy. They are characterized as those countries that have been able to generate and use knowledge in ways that strongly upgrade their capabilities for producing increasingly complex goods and services. Such is the set of countries usually called the North.

Other countries have been less successful in that task and their economies are characterized by specializing in comparatively less complex activities, where indigenous capabilities do not add much knowledge to what is produced. Such characteristics define the "peripheral condition" of today.

The "non-central" countries can be called semi-peripheries, peripheries, or marginalized regions according to their economic relations with knowledge and innovation. This Rest of today, as defined by not being where the structural change we are considering takes place, is even more heterogeneous and susceptible of quick change than the Rest of yesterday defined by not being industrialized. In some big countries, we find marginalized regions, peripheries, semi-peripheries, and even emerging centers. But the Rest of today is no less real than the Rest of yesterday. It is usually called the Global South.

That division between North and Global South is as schematic and useful for understanding and acting as the classic division between industrialized and non-industrialized countries. The latter is a relevant but historical transient special case of the former, which is defined by the (high or low) content of advanced knowledge in the production of goods and services.

The great structural change of today is driven by the incorporation of first-rate knowledge and highly qualified people to a permanently widening set of productive activities. This in turn is a double source of inequality or, better perhaps, of two types of inequality that may be called the social one and the regional one. In the centers, many people do not have opportunities for studying at an advanced level or of working in contexts that foster permanent learning. This is the source of what we call the social inequality stemming from the increasing role of knowledge. If its effects are serious in the centers, they are much more so in the peripheries where they are aggravated by the regional inequality stemming from the comparatively weak demand of advanced knowledge that is a direct consequence of the "peripheral condition" (Arocena and Sutz 2010). The weak demand means that science, technology, and innovation are on average not very relevant for productive activities. It implies that, in peripheral regions, comparatively few people have access to Higher Education and even fewer people have opportunities to work in contexts that foster permanent and advanced learning. Since the fundamental productive factors of today are not strong in the peripheries, high-quality jobs are not abundant, incomes and productivity are on average low, and informal activities are the only possibilities open for many people.

Now, knowledge generation and use are fundamental factors of economic and military power. Their influence extends to the political realm and even to the ideological sphere. Differences of power are used to consolidate asymmetries concerning knowledge. A main example of that is given by how central countries use their superior power to "kick away the ladder" (Chang 2002) by building international regulations that do not allow peripheral countries to make use today of productive policies that yesterday were profitably used by central countries.

In this way, we arrive at an old concept that yesterday was essential in the heterodox conceptions of development: underdevelopment. For the orthodox dominant views in the "place and ladder" paradigm, underdeveloped countries just do not exist; only developed countries and (more or less) backward countries exist; the latter are diplomatically called developing countries. For some heterodox versions of the "place and ladder" paradigm (for example, the Latin American structuralism), underdevelopment is a fundamental reality. It is generated precisely because asymmetries of power between central and peripheral countries entail that the latter cannot simply climb the ladder as the former did in the past. They are not only backward but also underdeveloped countries. To catch up with developed countries, they have to climb different ladders.

In the emerging paradigm inspired by the notion of Human Development, it seems that underdevelopment is an issue of no importance. At least it is almost neglected in "Development as Freedom" (Sen 1999). Working with a similar perspective, Nussbaum (2011) does not pay attention to underdevelopment as such. She explains why Human Development is needed above all in poor countries but also in the so-called developed countries. The last confirms that development as a place does not exist. Nevertheless, it is not the same to foster development in powerful and rich central countries than in dependent and poor peripheral countries. The concept of underdevelopment helps to keep differences in mind.

In the context of a factual approach to development issues, underdevelopment can be briefly characterized by the combination of the peripheral condition with external subordination. It is a really existing phenomenon that fosters inequality and, as such, a major obstacle for the normative goals of Sustainable Human Development. It should not be ignored.

ELEMENTS FOR A PROSPECTIVE APPROACH: SOME MAIN TRENDS

Having considered values and some fundamental facts, we now attempt to sketch a prospective approach to development.

We present, as an introduction, "some shifts and tensions" stressed by Hodgson (2015): "there is a consensus that the center of gravity of the global economy is going to shift to the east, especially with the rise of China and India. [...] capitalism is a highly dynamic and complex system that is vulnerable to financial instability. [...] global human population is still rising rapidly, the world is facing shortages of usable water and other important physical resources, pollution in some countries is rising to spectacular levels, and the possibility of dramatic climatic change brings the threat of large-scale population movements, famines, and severe sociopolitical disruption" (Hodgson 2015: 349–350).

Among several global trends, the following five strike us as very important.

1. *Expanding role of scientific and technological knowledge in social relations.*

It is quite clear that "big science and large technological systems [...] transform the extrasocial world, nature and the environment—and *with it* the social world" (Schroeder 2007: 49). The impacts of advanced knowledge in health, violence, production, communication, work, and everyday life in general are apparent. So "at their widest extent, the consequences of science and technology cause 'instability'" (Schroeder 2007: 135). This happens for good and for bad, as can be seen by looking at the curative power of some health technologies and at the destructive power of science-based weapons. It fosters some other trends in our list.

This process leads to a "knowledge-intensifying scenario" with "a high level of plausibility" (Hodgson 2001: 182). It is characterized in the following terms: "[I]nitially, the following broad and interlinked developments within modern capitalism will be assumed: a. In core sectors of the economy, the processes of production and their products are becoming more complex and sophisticated. b. Increasingly advanced knowledge or skills are being required in many processes of production. Skill levels in many sectors are being raised to cope with the growing degrees of difficulty and complexity" (Hodgson 2001: 181). Moreover, "[T]he economy becomes relatively less 'machine-intensive', and more 'knowledge-intensive'. An important feature of the knowledge-intensive economy is the dematerialization of much production, and the shift from action-centred to intellective skills" (Hodgson 2001: 184).

2. *Growth and, more so, diversification of production of goods and services.*

With the Industrial Revolution, "modern economic growth" started. Persistent depressions and recessions notwithstanding, it is still a major factor of change. Examples of that are the increasing proportion of the world population that lives above a monetary-defined poverty line and the expansion during the last decades of the so-called global middle classes, a phenomenon apparent in China and India.

Growth became increasingly based on the expansion of scientific and technological knowledge. This combination of growth and knowledge is, in the long run, the main factor promoting well-being, especially concerning health and education (Roser 2015; Roser and Ortiz-Ospina 2016). Economic growth, in general, needs a healthy population; knowledge has made a major positive impact on this dimension. Economic growth also allows for a quantitative expansion of education. Knowledge-based growth, in turn, needs more educated people and educated in ways that allow for a deeper comprehension of the functioning of the natural and social world and oriented to problem-solving. The improvements in health and education—which are both consequences and enablers of knowledge-based growth—enhance, in principle, the freedoms people have to live lives they have reasons to value.

Expanded access to a bigger and more diversified supply of goods and services, widely known by everyone through global advertising and mass communication, has remarkably fostered not only consumption but even more aspirations to consume more. In this way, economic growth became an often decisive issue concerning political options in general and the legitimacy of many quite different governments in particular. As Kohli (2003) recalls, "...democratization has created expectations that cannot be easily satisfied without sustained economic growth and some redistribution" (Kohli 2003: 56). This is also valid in places—like China—where a democratic opening has been resisted by "the use of well-organized coercion but also by presiding over a buoyant economy (thus by maintaining some performance-based legitimacy)" (Kohli 2003: 50).

Increasing production and consumption are the main causes of another trend—the degradation of the global environment—which was acknowledged only a few decades ago but which has already changed the world landscape and is most worrisome for the future.

3. *Environmental and climatic degradation.*

In any given day, the media furnishes information related to actual damage and future risks associated with this trend. It has opened the possibility of a catastrophe. Worries about such a possibility have fostered engagements to change that nevertheless look insufficient. Reflecting on the Paris Agreement of 2015, a document by the Economic Commission of Latin America and the Caribbean (ECLAC) posits that "...the sum of the pledged country targets is insufficient to meet the objective of avoiding a global temperature rise of 2°C above pre-industrial levels: it is estimated that annual emissions will reach 55 gigatons in 2030, which would lead to a temperature rise of closer to 3°C" (ECLAC 2016: 149).

Deep changes would be necessary to avoid the catastrophe: "the people demand more and more economic growth in order to consume more, as a citizen right. Ordinary citizens will have to change their lifestyles to avert disaster" (Mann 2013b: 95).

That will not be easy. Moreover, even if economic growth could be halted, that could be an undesirable solution: "[E]conomic growth will still matter a great deal in the coming century: it is the most powerful tool for reducing global poverty and inequality (as it is, also, for reducing national poverties). One can hardly overestimate its importance in poorer countries as a means of making the lives of ordinary people better" (Milanović 2016: 232).

What are the most probable outcomes concerning this trend? Mann (2013a: 403) speculates that "[G]lobal warming and greater weather variability might result in either of two extremes: geopolitically negotiated reforms on a global level to reduce emissions, or the collapse of much of modern civilization. Perhaps more likely is a muddling through sundry disasters toward an intermediate solution, favoring some classes, macroregions and nations more than others—the normal outcome [...]". More frugal consumption is needed for this trend to be weakened. Concerning production, rather than simply diminishing it, what seems to be needed are different types of production, with less environmental costs and improved results. For example, frugal innovation, already under way in some contexts (Bound and Thornton 2012), could expand as a combination of an ideological shift against unbounded consumption and a priority in the research and innovation agenda to doing better things with less natural resources, in particular by a wider use of advanced science and technology, giving priority to deprived sectors. Moreover, frugal innovation typically benefits lower- and middle-income groups of the economy whereas commercial innovation, through its direct impact on income distribution, tends to benefit higher-income groups to a larger extent (OECD 2013).

In 2016, the Danish Agency for Science, Technology and Innovation published an OECD study on megatrends, from which it is worth quoting a lengthy passage directly related to Mann's earlier quoted remark on ordinary citizens having to change their lifestyles in the face of disaster: "[W]hile the concept of the circular economy means different things to different people, many would nonetheless agree that it implies a systemic change, moving to a zero- or at least low-waste, resource-efficient society and involving big changes to our methods of both production and consumption. Looking beyond the potential for materials savings and a smaller footprint on the environment that a move away from the established "take, make and dispose" model could bring, a circular economy would create huge economic opportunities as new services and business models emerge and the relationship between producer and consumer, and between a product and its user, undergoes radical transformation. Repair, re-use, re-distribution and re-manufacture would increase, as well as recycling rates; materials technology would evolve and enable a move from non-renewable materials to the production and use of high levels of renewable materials in finished products" (Danish Agency for Science, Technology and Innovation 2016: 31).

Perhaps this is too rosy a picture, but besides the recognition that our global culture is one that promotes "take, make and dispose" in productive terms and "take and dispose" in consumption terms (our addition), the hailing of repairing and re-using seems to echo what environmentalists have been saying for a long time. Fear may, perhaps, bring change.

4. Increasing influence of financial capital.

It is asserted that "financial markets have become the main drivers of the world economy" (Hodgson 2015: 136). Usually, the ways in which that influence has been translated into facts are seen as a main culprit of the great recession of 2008. Nevertheless, the benefits going to the top positions of financial capital are still unbelievably big: that is a proof of its power and, also, a motive to conjecture that this trend will probably become stronger. Financial capital is closely related to governments, particularly in the North, as well as to international financing institutions. Such relations are apparent when Free Trade Treaties and related agreements are promoted. As a rule, such agreements erode the regulation of financial capital activities and diminish states' sovereignty. This happens, for example, when the relations between states and transnational corporations are located out of reach of national courts. Free Trade–type agreements foster opening every sector to foreign investment, deregulation of trade in services, strict enforcement of intellectual property, and limitations to public procurement policies. That means that the usually knowledge-weak countries in the Global South are prevented from promoting the expansion and use of indigenous knowledge generation by tools that have been widely used by central countries. Thus, this trend hinders the overcoming of underdevelopment as previously characterized.

5. *Rising inequality.*

It is usually accepted that in the 1980s a momentous "inequality turn" (Atkinson 2015) took place.

A celebrated book by Thomas Piketty shows that such a turn indeed happened in the whole world and asserts that it will shape the future (Piketty 2014: 23, 25, 233). Moreover, "the fact that wealth is noticeably less concentrated in Europe today than it was in the Belle Époque is largely a consequence of accidental events (the shocks of 1914–1945) and specific institutions such as taxation of capital and income" (Piketty 2014: 376). That meant that income inequalities were reduced in the West, but when the effects of such exceptional events were over, "inequality began to rise sharply again since the 1970s and 1980s" (Idem: 237). In this view, the trend will be fostered in the rich countries of the West by long-term slow national income growth (Idem: 121). That would imply that the economy as a whole has a rate of growth that is smaller than the rate of return on capital and consequently that the share of capital in national income increases, which would mean a relative loss for the non–capital-owning majority of the population.

The current situation is depicted as "the unlimited growth of global inequality of wealth, which is currently increasing at a rate that cannot be sustained in the long run and that ought to worry even the most fervent champions of the self-regulated market" (Idem: 399).

The expanding role of knowledge adds to the growth of inequality. In fact, knowledge can be seen as a resource with increasing returns to use. That means that when a country or a social group makes strong use of knowledge during a relatively extended period, one of the results is that it usually has more knowledge at the end than at the beginning. The contrary tends to happen to a country or social group with a weak use of knowledge. Thus, inequality related to knowledge tends to be self-reinforcing. This correlates directly with innovation: "[W]hen the issue of inequality has been investigated, we often find that the diffusion of innovation widens the gap between the higher and the lower status segment of a system. This tendency for the diffusion of innovations to increase socioeconomic inequality can occur in any system, but it has specially been noted in Third World countries" (Rogers 1995: 125).

In the next chapter, we shall explore more closely the connections between the expanding role of knowledge and the rise of inequality. The interactions in general between knowledge and (in)equality are a fundamental dimension of the contemporary world. They can be seen as the starting point for a strategy oriented to cooperate with Sustainable Human Development, and particularly with the pursuit of equality, by promoting knowledge democratization.

On Alternative Futures

As we look toward the future, the consolidation of the knowledge-based economy seems very probable, the persistence of high inequality (which is also partially knowledge-based) looks quite probable, and the aggravation of environmental degradation and climatic damage is perhaps the most probable of these phenomena.

Now, it is difficult to imagine a more or less stable scenario shaped by those three trends, because of the social problems and, even more, the environmental problems that would characterize such a scenario. So we may say that the persistence of the three trends characterizes the *unstable probable scenario*.

Inequality and lack of sustainability are not independent phenomena. When people do not have better opportunities, they are forced to accept jobs of low quality that affect their basic rights, their health, and the environment. When countries do not have better productive opportunities, they often accept and even foster activities that damage people and environments. Thus, polluting activities are being increasingly located in underdeveloped contexts. But that does not mean that deprived people are the main polluters; on the contrary: "I[ ]t suffices to look at the amounts of air conditioning, driving, and meat consumption that is being done by the global top 1 percent or global top 10 percent to realize that the rich are the main contributors to climate change" (Milanović 2016: 233).

A quite evident contradiction may challenge the actual distribution of power as well as prevailing ways of generating and using knowledge. On the one hand, the globalization pushed by the emergence of a capitalist knowledge society in the North fosters production and consumption in such ways that, in the world at large, wealth expands and average poverty diminishes, thus closely connecting the strength of governments with the levels of economic growth. On the other hand, that same process seems to deepen inequality within most countries while natural resources are used in ways that systematically increase environmental damage and open the possibility of a climatic catastrophe.

This would arise as a result of the collision of prevailing types of production with environmental and social sustainability. Such a possibility can be called the *collision scenario*. It will not be easy to avoid it.

Prevailing types of economic growth generate environmental damage, but its absence does not by itself prevent such damage and aggravates social problems. Mann (2013a: 387) says that "[i]t is simply impossible to avoid a major loss of GDP all over the world, given present technologies, if we are serious about climate change. Indeed, the main goal of effective climate change policy has to be a move to a permanently lower level of GDP". But a closer analysis suggests that the two perspectives are not completely contradictory. GDP is a very defective measure of socially satisfactory production of goods and services. The former could be increased while the latter is diminished; an outstanding example of this is the contribution to GDP of producing weapons. For example, if the production of weapons is halved while a quarter of the resources previously dedicated to weapons are assigned to health, GDP would diminish while production could become more socially satisfactory. What is needed is "a permanently lower level" of use and, especially, damage of natural resources as well as improving food production, health services, and the like. That includes technological and social shifts, oriented in particular to more efficient, frugal, and inclusive types of innovation. It entails a move in the realm of knowledge production and use as well as in the realm of policies and habits. Powerful interests should be overcome: "[I]t isn't just a question of overcoming business opposition. It is also necessary to overcome the short-term interests of the mass of northern citizens and of richer citizens everywhere" (Mann 2013a: 388).

In any case, it looks very difficult to combine specific interests and global sustainability because, as Geels (2010: 507) puts it, "...sustainability is a normative goal and a collective good problem (with associated prisoner dilemmas and free rider problems). The former means that sustainability transitions will be full of debates about the relative importance of various environmental problems, which entail deep-seated values and beliefs. The latter means that private actors have no immediate incentive to address sustainability problems. Public authorities and civil society will therefore be crucial drivers for sustainability transitions. Their actions will need to change economic frame conditions and/or consumer practices, which subsequently incentivize private actors to reorient their innovation and commercial activities".

It is apparent that to avoid the *collision scenario* substantial changes are needed. In any case, the almost universal aspiration to consume more—that became more or less feasible due to "modern economic growth" based on science and technology—should be checked in the realm of ideas, in ways that at the same time open alternative paths for diminishing poverty and inequality.

Max Weber taught that "[N]ot ideas, but material and ideal interests, directly govern men's conduct. Yet very frequently the 'world images' that have been created by 'ideas' have, like switchmen, determined the tracks along which action has been pushed by the dynamic of interest" (quoted in Gerth and Wright 1991: 280).

During the last decades, the "world image" offered by neoliberal individualism has been dominant. Its ideological power and the economic power of financialization back each other. Both foster consumerism as well as the unchecked expansion of market relations that erodes cooperation (Heyer et al. 2002), setting humanity on a track that leads to disaster.

Perhaps, as already suggested, fear will open the way to alternative views. Mann (2016: 286) sees "regulation as likely to make a comeback, especially to combat climate change and if there is a populist reaction against the rising inequality and exploitation that neoliberalism brings. If climate change is effectively combatted, the regulation of capitalism and consumerism would be considerable. If it is not, the ensuing last-minute regulation of market forces amid disastrous times would be much more punitive domestically and probably often vicious geopolitically".

Better perspectives need to overcome "three major obstacles": first, "a high emissions consumer culture"; second, "the autonomous power of capitalism, driven on the treadmill of short-term profit to destroy the environment"; and, third, the prevailing dynamics "of the individual nation-state and its politicians, who are driven on two treadmills, one of GDP growth, the other of the electoral cycle (or the authoritarian regime's equivalent). What politician would advocate severe rationing or taxing of fossil fuels?" (Mann 2013a: 396)

Maybe acute environmental and social challenges will switch tracks toward alternative combinations of ideology and technology that protect life and counter inequality. That would point to changes in knowledge production and use, in order to produce better rather than more, for the many, in sustainable ways. In such a case, a *Sustainable Human Development–friendly scenario* would become feasible.

THE BEDROCK OF THE PROPOSITIONAL APPROACH

In this section, we argue that the normative, factual, and prospective approaches presented above converge to show that democratization of knowledge should be a fundamental strategy in the propositional approach to Sustainable Human Development. In the following chapters, we shall elaborate and exemplify that strategy.

A good starting point is to go back to the defining purpose of the original heterodox conceptions of development: to overcome underdevelopment. Above, we characterized underdeveloped regions by the combination and mutual reinforcement of the peripheral condition with external subordination. Thus, underdevelopment is rooted in a productive structure where weak value added stems from advanced knowledge and high qualifications. Consequently, improving the quality of life and protecting the environment are hindered while external subordination is fostered. A sine qua non requisite for overcoming such a situation is to incorporate highly qualified people as well as advanced science and technology to every socially valuable production of goods and services. As an upgrading process, it means increasing the use of knowledge in each component of an expanding set of activities. For that, expanding the generation of knowledge and broadening its agenda are also needed. In such a process, thresholds are crossed whenever doing something relevant and valuable becomes in some sense knowledge-based and innovation-driven. In a nutshell, more knowledge becomes useful for more people. Thus, to democratize knowledge is necessary for transforming the productive structure in ways that go beyond the peripheral condition.

What is being said here can be related to the search of a "new developmentalism" as presented, for example, by Chang (2011: 55): "[T]he 'humanistic' dimension of development, which has been highlighted by approaches like the human development approach of the UNDP and Amartya Sen's capability approach, should be more explicitly incorporated into the 'new developmentalist' approach, while without losing the emphasis on the 'productionist' view. Development in the humanistic sense cannot be taken too far and made sustainable without a robust transformation in the underlying productive structure and capabilities".

What Chang calls "development in the humanistic sense" belongs to the normative approach while the emphasis on productive transformation is a part of the propositional approach. Understood in such a sense, they are not contradictory notions of development but complementary aspects of an integrated conception.

The normative aim of expanding capabilities and freedoms stresses the relevance of inclusive policies that see people not as patients. The general orientation of such policies is to collaborate with the agency of usually excluded social groups in processes that redistribute incomes and power in general in their favor.

The factual approach characterized the increased power stemming from knowledge as the core of the structural transformation of our time. It is deeply related to inequality in ways that will be specifically considered in the following chapter, highlighting the connections between knowledge and democracy.

References

Anand, S., & Sen, A. (2000). Human Development and Economic Sustainability. *World Development, 2812*, 2029–2049.

Arocena, R., & Sutz, J. (2010). Weak Knowledge Demand in the South: Learning Divides and Innovation Policies. *Science and Public Policy, 37*(8), 571–582.

Arocena, R., & Sutz, J. (2016). Innovación y Sistemas Nacionales de Innovación en procesos de desarrollo. In A. Erbes y D. Suárez (comp.), *Repensando el desarrollo: una discusión desde los sistemas de innovación* (pp. 69–102). Argentina: Universidad Nacional de General Sarmiento. Available at: http://www.ungs.edu.ar/ms_publicaciones/wp-content/uploads/2016/08/9789876302449-completo.pdf. Accessed 11 May 2017.

Atkinson, A. B. (2015). *Inequality: What Can Be Done?* Cambridge, USA: Harvard University Press.

Bairoch, P. (1982). International Industrialization Levels from 1750 to 1980. *Journal of European Economic History, 11,* 269–333.

Bairoch, P. (1993). *Economics and World History. Myths and Paradoxes.* Chicago: The University of Chicago Press.

Bound, K., & Thornton, I. (2012). *Our Frugal Future: Lessons from India's Innovation System.* Available at: https://www.nesta.org.uk/sites/default/files/our_frugal_future.pdf. Accessed 11 May 2017.

Chang, H.-J. (2002). *Kicking away the Ladder: Development Strategy in Historical Perspective.* London: Anthem Press.

Chang, H.-J. (2011). Hamlet Without the Prince of Denmark: How Development Has Disappeared from Today's 'Development' Discourse. In S. Khan & J. Christiansen (Eds.), *Towards New Developmentalism: Market as Means rather than Master* (pp. 47–58). Abingdon: Routledge.

Dahlman, C. (2009). Growth and Development in China and India: The Role of Industrial and Innovation Policy in Rapid Catch-Up. In G. Dosi, M. Cimoli, & J. E. Stiglitz (Eds.), *Industrial Policy and Development. The Political Economy of Capabilities Accumulation* (pp. 303–335). Oxford: Oxford University Press.

Danish Agency for Science, Technology and Innovation. (2016). *An OECD Horizon Scan on Megatrends and Technology Trends in the Context of Future Research Policy.* Available at: http://ufm.dk/en/publications/2016/files/an-oecd-horizon-scan-of-megatrends-and-technology-trends-in-the-context-of-future-research-policy.pdf. Accessed 10 May 2017.

de la Mothe and Paquet, G. (Ed.). (1996). *Evolutionary Economics and the New International Political Economy.* London: Pinter.

ECLAC (Economic Commission for Latin America and the Caribbean). (2016). *Horizons 2030: Equality at the Centre of Sustainable Development* (LC/G.2660(SES.36/3). Santiago de Chile: Economic Commission for Latin America and the Caribbean.

Evans, P., & Heller, P. (2015). Human Development, State Transformation and the Politics of the Developmental State. In S. Leibfried, E. Huber, M. Lange, J. Levy, F. Nullmeier, & J. Stephens (Eds.), *The Oxford Handbook of Transformations of the State* (pp. 691–713). Oxford: Oxford University Press.

Fayerabend, P. (1988). *Against Method.* London: Verso.

Geels, F. W. (2010). Ontologies, Socio-Technical Transitions (to Sustainability), and the Multi-Level Perspective. *Research Policy, 39*(4), 495–510.

Gerth, H., & Wright, C. (1991). *From Max Weber.* Oxford: Routledge.

Gibson, C., Andersson, K., Ostrom, E., & Shivakumar, S. (2005). *The Samaritan's Dilemma: The Political Economy of Development Aid.* Oxford: Oxford University Press.

Heyer, J., Stewart, F., & Thorp, R. (2002). *Group Behaviour and Development. Is the Market Destroying Cooperation?* Oxford: Oxford University Press.

Hodgson, G. M. (2001). *Economics and Utopia. Why the Learning Economy Is Not the End of History*. Hoboken: Taylor and Francis e-Library.

Hodgson, G. M. (2015). *Conceptualizing Capitalism. Institutions, Evolution, Future*. Chicago: The University of Chicago Press.

Kohli, A. (2003). Democracy and Development: Trends and Prospects. In A. Kohli, C.-I. Moon, & G. Sørensen (Eds.), *States, Markets and Just Growth : Development in the Twenty-First Century* (pp. 39–63). New York: The United Nations University.

Kranzberg, M. (1967). The Unity of Science. *American Scientist, 55*(1), 48–66.

Mann, M. (2013a). *The Sources of Social Power. Vol. IV Globalizations, 1945–2011*. Cambridge: Cambridge University Press.

Mann, M. (2013b). The End May Be Nigh, but for Whom? In I. Wallerstein, R. Collins, M. Mann, G. Derluguian, & C. Calhoun (Eds.), *Does Capitalism Have a Future?* (pp. 71–97). New York: Oxford University Press.

Mann, M. (2016). Response to the Critics. In R. Schroeder (Ed.), *Global Powers. Michael Mann's Anatomy of the Twentieth Century and Beyond* (pp. 281–322). Cambridge, UK: Cambridge University Press.

Milanović, B. (2016). *Global in Equality: A New Approach for the Age of Globalization*. Cambridge, MA: Harvard University Press.

Mokyr, J. (2002). *The Gifts of Athena. Historical Origins of the Knowledge Economy*. Princeton: Princeton University Press.

Mokyr, J. (2005). Long-Term Economic Growth and the History of Technology. In P. Aghion & S. Durlauf (Eds.), *Handbook of Economic Growth, Vol. 1, Part 2* (pp. 1113–1181). Amsterdam: Elsevier.

Noble, D. (1977). *America by Design. Science, Technology and the Rise of Corporate Capitalism*. New York: Knopf Books.

North, D. (1997). *Some Fundamental Puzzles in Economic History/Development*. Indiana University Working Paper Series. Available at: http://econwpa.repec.org/eps/eh/papers/9509/9509001.pdf. Accessed 10 May 2017.

NSF, Science and Engineering Indicators 2016: 454.

Nussbaum, M. (2011). *Creating Capabilities. The Human Development Approach*. Cambridge, MA: Harvard University Press.

OECD. (2013). *Organization for Economic Cooperation and Development, "Innovation for Inclusive Growth: Conference Discussion Report"*. Paris: OECD Publishing.

Piketty, T. (2014). *Capital in the XXI Century*. Cambridge, MA: Harvard University Press.

Reinert, E. S. (2007). *How Rich Countries Got Rich and Why Poor Countries Stay Poor*. New York: Public Affairs.

Rodrik, D. (2011). *The Globalization Paradox: Democracy and the Future of the World Economy*. New York/London: W.W. Norton.

Rogers, E. M. (1995). *Diffusion of Innovations* (4th ed.). New York: Free Press.

Roser, M. (2015). Life Expectancy. *Published online at OurWorldInData.org*. Accesible at: http://ourworldindata.org/data/population-growth-vital-statistics/life-expectancy/. Accessed 10 May 2017.

Roser, M., & Ortiz-Ospina, E. (2016). Literacy. *Published online at OurWorldInData. org*. Available at: http://ourworldindata.org/data/education-knowledge/literacy/. Accessed 10 May 2017.

Schot, J., & Steinmueller, E. (2016). Framing Innovation Policy for Transformative Change: Innovation Policy 3.0. SPRU Draft. Available at: http://www.johanschot.com/wordpress/wp-content/uploads/2016/09/Framing-Innovation-Policy-for-Transformative-Change-Innovation-Policy-3.0-2016.pdf. Accessed 10 May 2017.

Schroeder, R. (2007). *Rethinking Science, Technology, and Social Change*. Stanford, CA: Stanford University Press.

Sen, A. (1999). *Development as Freedom*. New York: Anchor Books.

Sen, A. (2013). The Ends and Means of Sustainability. *Journal of Human Development and Capabilities, 141*, 6–20.

Stiglitz, J., Sen, A., & Fitoussi, J. (2010). *Mismeasuring Our Lives: Why GDP Doesn't Add Up*. New York: The New Press.

UNDP. (2011). *Human Development Report 2011, Sustainability and Equity: A Better Future for All*. New York: United Nations Development Program.

CHAPTER 3

Knowledge-Based Inequalities

The Issue of Inequality

The world is highly unequal in many aspects, particularly concerning incomes of individuals. An indication of this is the global Gini value, which is "slightly under 70 [and] significantly greater than the national Gini value in even the most unequal countries in the world, such as South Africa and Colombia" (Milanović 2016: 132).

This quote deserves, for the purposes of this chapter, some comments. The first is the resilience of individual income inequality as measured by the Gini Index. Latin America, the region with the worst historical record of inequality, has also been the region that witnessed the most important drop in inequality between 2006 and 2010, even though this has not changed its relative situation: it continues to be the worst in inequality terms, with a regional Gini of over 50 (Tsounta and Ouseke 2014). The observed drop in Latin American inequality is attributed to a great extent to a series of targeted social policies that increased the incomes of individuals and households in the lowest rungs of the economic ladder (Cornia 2010). Such policies were politically and financially possible due to the double conjuncture of more attention given to social policy at the government level in several countries of the region and very high prices of the commodities that are the main source of regional exports. To a good extent, these two sides of the conjuncture have been redressed. If the income inequality drop is tied to conjunctures and not to structural change (that may need much more time to materialize), income inequality may well come back with all its strength.

© The Author(s) 2018
R. Arocena et al., *Developmental Universities in Inclusive Innovation Systems*, https://doi.org/10.1007/978-3-319-64152-2_3

The second comment relates to the new political importance given to the issue of inequality. It is not just that inequality is not seen any more as a temporary price to be paid for economic growth. It is not seen either as a secondary target, the main one being poverty reduction. The inclusion of inequality reduction as one of the seventeen aims of the Sustainable Development Goals illustrates the latter while the former Millennium Development Goals included only poverty reduction. Probably the sharp rise in income inequality in most Organization for Economic Cooperation and Development (OECD) countries, particularly in the USA—so eloquently shown by the work of Piketty—explains why inequality "…has hit the front pages" (Lazonick and Mazzucato 2012: 6). Part of the explanation of this media impact refers to a "…seemingly inexorable concentration of income at the top of the distribution chain…" (Ibid). Atkinson (2015: 21) indicates, for the UK, that "[T]o get back to where we were when the Beatles were playing, we have to reduce the Gini coefficient by some 10 percentage points". As for the USA, it is asserted (Ibid: 19) that "The top 1 per cent in the US now receives close to one-fifth of total gross income—meaning that, on average, they have twenty times their proportionate share" and, moreover, "the share of the top 1 per cent of those within the top 1 per cent (that is, the top 0.01 per cent) is also around one-fifth of the total income of this group. This means that 1/10,000 of the population receives 1/25 of the total income". In any case, income inequality has become a scandal and a political issue.

The third comment relates to a very important question highlighted in the inequality literature: inequality of what? People are unequal in so many different aspects and for so many different reasons that it seems impossible to encompass the whole in a single definition followed by a single indicator. It is true, though, that several of the different aspects in which inequality manifests itself are interrelated, and it is generally accepted that income inequality is of paramount importance in terms of triggering other forms of inequality. Moreover, income inequality has been thoroughly measured for a long time, allowing us to follow its evolution and to explore its relationships with a wide range of social, economic, and political events and processes.

However, income inequality is far from being accepted as the main manifestation of inequality. "Income may be the most prominent means for a good life without deprivation, but it is not the only influence on the lives we can lead. If our paramount interest is in the lives that people can lead—the freedom they have to lead minimally decent lives—then it cannot but be a mistake to concentrate exclusively only on one or other of the means to such freedom. We must look at impoverished lives, and not just at depleted wallets" (Sen 2000: 9). Impoverished lives relate to— among other issues—health, housing, education, public participation, and influence on societal decisions. All of them may be traced back at least to some extent to income deprivation, but the last of these offers an insufficient explanation of inequality in terms of differences in the opportunities people have to live lives they have reason to value. Social organization and state involvement, for instance, can make huge differences in people's lives.

A telling example is the following. One of the possible sources of the radical impoverishing of a family life is what is called "catastrophic" spending in health, meaning that a health problem appears that can be solvable but only through out-of-pocket high-spending that puts that family in a bankruptcy situation. Income makes a difference, given that what for some families is a catastrophic spending may not be so for another. But more importantly, in some societies, out-of-pocket spending in health—a proxy for being exposed to catastrophic spending—is much lower than in others because the financial burden of providing health services is taken by public policies or collective insurance schemes. For instance, in the first decade of the twenty-first century, private spending in health was 28% in the OECD countries while it averaged 42% in the world and peaked at 45% in Latin America, of which 38% was out of pocket (ECLAC 2010: 183). Particularly in the case of health, but not only there, lowering income inequality may be far from enough for fostering better lives.

With all of these caveats, income inequality, particularly at the present levels of accumulated wealth by a tiny minority, matters: "[W]hen measuring inequality, we are concerned not just with the consumption of the rich— important though this may be—but also with the power that wealth can convey. This power may be exercised over one's family, as with the passing on of wealth to heirs, or more generally in such ways as control of the media or influence with political parties" (Atkinson 2015: 37).

This chapter deals with the influence of knowledge, particularly the influence of the prevailing orientation of knowledge production and use, on some manifestations of inequality. As we shall see, some influences operate by action whereas others by inaction. By highlighting the role of knowledge in present inequalities, we will argue that, at least in some cases, knowledge may be turned into a tool to fight them.

THE RISE OF INEQUALITY

The normative approach highlights the issue of (in)equality. The factual approach focused on knowledge and innovation. It sees them as main factors both for fostering and for fettering Sustainable Human Development.

On the one hand, the following quotation describes a process of paramount relevance: "[A]s a result of technological developments in medicine and the improved average standard of living, between 1800 and 2000 life expectancy at birth rose from a global average of about thirty years to sixty-seven years, and to more than seventy-five years in several developed countries" (Hodgson 2015: 1). Technological developments in medicine—for the sheer fact of increasing the global life expectancy—have indeed made impressive impacts on the lives people are able to live. However, averages hide huge disparities in life expectancies: "[A] girl born in Sierra Leone can expect to live 50 fewer years, on average, than her Japanese counterpart" (Ruger 2006: 998).

On the other hand, the role of advanced knowledge in widening inequality has been described as follows in relation to the most technologically advanced country, the United States: "the past couple of decades, we've seen changes in tax policy, greater overseas competition, ongoing government waste, and Wall Street shenanigans. But when we look at the data and research, we conclude that none of these are the primary driver of growing inequality. Instead, the main driver is exponential, digital, and combinatorial change in the technology that undergirds our economic system" (Brynjolfsson and McAfee 2014: 61).

The connections between technical change and social relations deserve paramount attention. In particular, they are often the main causes of inequality, as stressed by the previous quotation. It is taken from a book entitled *The Second Machine Age*, a characterization of present times supported by the following assertion: "The introduction of reliable low-cost electronic computers into the economy was the most revolutionary technical innovation of the twentieth century" (Freeman and Soete 1997: 158).

We will come back to this issue more than once. Here, we just want to stress again that knowledge is a resource that, generally speaking, tends to increase when it is widely used and to decrease when it is seldom used. That trend favors regions and social groups that can be considered to be knowledge-strong but damages those that are knowledge-weak. It has very concrete effects, expanding the capabilities of the people who have opportunities to study at an advanced level and to work in contexts that demand permanent learning and where innovation is required. The opposite happens to people without such opportunities: on average, when you do not keep learning you get to know less than before.

That process is akin to the "Matthew effect" detected by Merton (1968) in the academic reward system, because it frequently expands differences in resources and prestige between academic groups. The name come from a verse in the Gospel of Matthew that says that he who has plenty will be given abundance and he who has little will have it taken from him. Perhaps a "generalized Matthew effect" can be detected in society at large as a consequence of the increasing role of knowledge, learning, and innovation. It is a way to refer to a pervasive aspect of knowledge-based inequality.

Increasing returns to use of knowledge probably constitute one of the main causes of the increasing income inequality that has been detected in most places in recent times (Held and Kaya 2007; Milanović 2011, 2016; Deaton 2013; Atkinson 2015; OXFAM 2016). Atkinson (2015: 82) summarizes the major factors contributing to inequality by stating that "credit should be given to the economists who have focused on rising inequality and identified a number of contributing factors, including globalization, technological change (information and communications technology), growth of financial services, changing pay norms, reduced role of trade unions, and scaling back of the redistributive tax-and-transfer policy".

The assertion concerning the rise of inequality in recent decades has to be qualified in at least two aspects. First, as already recalled, during the first decade of this century, inequality diminished in Latin America (Atkinson 2015). Second, in the world as a whole, inequality seems to have diminished since 1988 and at least up to 2011 (Milanović 2016), a relevant phenomenon due mainly to accelerated growth in very populous and, at least up to yesterday, very poor countries such as China and India.

Nevertheless, in those countries as in most others, particularly those where the economy is knowledge-based and innovation-driven, inequality has been growing. The Economic Commission for Latin America and the Caribbean (ECLAC) states that "[I]ncome distribution inequality rose sharply between the early 1980s and the year 2000, and still slightly more thereafter. In the developed world and in several developing regions, inequality is at its highest level in more than three decades. The Gini coefficient of the member countries of the ... OECD ... increased from 0.29 in the 1980s to 0.32 in 2013, and this trend is found both in developed countries that have traditionally recorded higher levels of inequality (such as the United States, whose coefficient rose from 0.34 in 1985 to 0.39 in 2013), and in countries with a strong egalitarian tradition, such as the Scandinavian countries" (ECLAC 2016: 19). In wealth terms, "[A]ccording to Credit Suisse (2015), the richest 1% of the population of Western Europe owns 31% of all wealth, while the poorest 40% owns just 1%" (Op. cit.: 71).

Inequality in its diverse manifestations recognizes knowledge as one of its drivers. However, it is not knowledge per se but knowledge as the outcome of a social process driven by interests, conflicts, and asymmetries of power which counts when analyzing its relationships with inequality. The latter is often forgotten: science and particularly technology and innovation are often taken as given, as an ineluctable expression of a rationality that escapes from the intervention capacity society has in other realms. This issue is discussed in the next section.

ON THE EXISTENCE OF TECHNOLOGICAL ALTERNATIVES

When we face statements—like those of Brynjolfsson and McAfee or Freeman and Soete in the previous section—that refer to the revolutionary impact of some technologies, there may be a temptation to accept the stated facts as if nothing different could have happened. A sort of technological inevitability, derived perhaps from the tacit hypothesis that if a technology prevails it is because of its techno-economic superiority, tends to obscure the nature, deeply embedded in social and power situations, of a good deal of the technology that shapes our lives. The latter has been highlighted, more or less directly, by a vast body of scholarly literature on economic history, sociology, socio-economics of technical change, and the field of science, technology, and society. One formulation, among several, on this issue is the following: "...innovation is socio-technical in nature: innovations are created through interaction between technological, social, economic, cultural and political aspects. At the same time, policy also forms a part of innovation: while it cannot completely determine the direction of this innovation, it can certainly influence it" (Maclaine Pont et al. 2016: 29).

However, unearthing these interactions and influences may be hard work, particularly when the pace of technical change accelerates, as has been happening in several key technologies during the last one hundred years. In the preface to a book on the history of computing in the twentieth century, this difficulty is clearly stated: "[T]echnological advances appear as sudden, discontinuous leaps that cover all previous work with an impenetrable cobweb of obsolescence. (...) There is a point at which the study of the technological past turns into paleontology, and in the history of computation that point is uncomfortably close, and moving closer" (Metropolis et al. 1985: xv). The "impenetrable web of obsolescence" and the lack of historical track due to the speed of change notwithstanding, the fact remains that the technology we have is not here by a natural necessity but as an outcome of a complex set of interactions, as recalled earlier. This does not mean that all types of options, particularly those of the past, are open nowadays. Coming back to the abacus or to smoke signals is not a realistic prospect, even if we fear the degree in which the power of computers, coupled with the use of intelligent mobile phones, puts the very notions of individual privacy at risk. What it does mean is that technology is the emergence of choices among what is feasible; some choices may not even be explored, but this is no reason to accept that the choices effectively made are the only ones possible.

Innovation is related, in principle, to the satisfaction of a given need: "[P]erhaps the highest-level characterization that is safe to make about technical innovation is that it must involve the synthesis of some kind of need with some kind of technical possibility" (Langrish et al. 1972: 57). Or as Lundvall puts it, "[W]e shall regard innovations as the result of collisions between technical opportunity and user needs. We acknowledge that single innovations might result from pure accidents, but we do not see this as a normal pattern" (Lundvall 1985: 4). The problem is that concepts like "need" or "solution" are far from univocal. The solutions that would enhance the lives or give power and autonomy to some may imply for others the impoverishment of their lives. The users for which solutions are searched are far from reflecting all of humankind. Accepting this relativization implies considering technological innovations as answers to questions put in determined terms; other questions or the same question put in different terms could eventually lead to other innovations.

Joseph Weizenbaum, the computer scientist who in the 1960s invented the first program able to "maintain" a conversation mimicking natural language, reflected on the massive computerization of the American society in the following terms: "...many of the problems of growth and complexity that pressed insistently and irresistible for response during the postwar decades could have served as incentives for social and political innovation. An enormous acceleration of social invention, had it begun then, would now seem to us as natural a consequence of man's predicament in that time as does the flood of technological invention and innovation that was actually stimulated" (Weizenbaum 1976: 31). Social and political innovations would probably not have led to a less technological society, but possibly to different technical approaches to solve societal problems. What is important in Weizenbaum's message is that the acknowledged inevitability of the use of some technologies is in part the result of the shaping of social and economic processes by those technologies. This is not technological determinism, but the recognition of two-way feedback loops between society and innovation.

Irreversibility takes another denomination in the economics of technical change parlance: it is called lock-in, meaning that it may be very difficult, when one option is made, to change the current way of doing things or of organizing activities. A famous example of technological lock-in is the arrangement of the first row of letters in the usual keyboards or current computers: QWERTY(UIOP). Paul David asserted that "...three features of the evolving production system (...) were crucially important in causing QWERTY to become 'locked in' as the dominant keyboard arrangement. These features were *technical interrelatedness, economies of scale,* and *quasi-irreversibility* of investment. They constitute the basic ingredients of what might be called QWERTYnomics" (David 1985: 334, emphasis in the original). Two aspects deserve attention here because they speak of a much more general trend. First, QWERTY is a quite inferior solution for the speed and accuracy of type writing than the alternatives that were designed, implemented, and defeated. Second, as David put it, "I believe there are many more QWERTY worlds lying out there in the past (...); worlds we do not yet fully perceive or understand, but whose influence, like that of dark stars, extends nonetheless to shape the visible orbits of our contemporary economic affairs" (Ibid: 336).

Technological lock-in stories proliferate. Some analysts believe that a main explanation of their occurrence is related to social power in any of its manifestations. In the case of refrigerators, for instance, "[B]y about 1930, prototypes of both types (gas and electric) were developed, and one might expect that the gas refrigerator, because its overwhelming advantages, would capture the consumer market. It didn't" (Rogers 1995: 138). The reason given by Rogers is that four American big producers of electric appliances with great economic power, particularly General Electric, considered that the electric refrigerator would give them more profits and invested heavily to position it in the market, leaving no room for the competitor design.

A different type of technological irreversibility, directly related to the power some social strata have over others, relates to technologies associated with production. Marc Bloch told the puzzling story of the watermill, an invention that comes from ancient times but whose use was expanded only in the Middle Ages (Bloch 1969: 143). Its late triumph related less to the general technical advantage of using water instead of manpower as an energy source and more to the fact that water resources were transformed into a monopoly of feudal lords and, moreover, that by being denied the use of manual mills the peasants were obliged to resort to the lords' mills, securing in that way the due payment for the obtained harvest. It was indeed a fight, fought over centuries, where the permission to have hand-mills was exacted from the feudal order only to be lost, over and over again. As Bloch puts it, "…by imposing heavy milling dues seigniorial lords, owners of the manorial mills, may sometimes have unintentionally encouraged a fidelity to the past; but in the end they destroyed it by the use of force" (Idem: 168). Stephen Marglin analyzes this example and several others implying the introduction of technological change in production in different socio-political processes, from feudal times to the early days of industrial capitalism and the Soviet Union socialism. His main point is that what we usually see as the "winning technology" around which the organization of work is established, making it irreversible, is not a technical imperative but a result of asymmetries of power: "…the primary determinant of basic choices with respect to the organization of production has not been technology—exogenous and inexorable—but power—endogenous and resistible" (Marglin 1974: 112).

An example of this assertion can be found in David Noble's account of the rise of one of the most revolutionary technologies introduced in production: numerically controlled machine tools. More than one competing technology was devised in early times (late 1940s) to automate the operation of machine tools, some of which were based on machinist skills. Numerically controlled technology was pushed onto machine-tool manufacturers by the US Air Force even if it proved highly unreliable for several years because of the difficulties in translating into equations and algorithms the thousands of relevant variables, some of them contingent on the operation ambiance and others related to the machine tools parts' imperceptible changes due to use (that experienced machinists were tacitly able to consider). This technology was pushed forwards in part by power struggles around who was in control over production, with management wanting full control from the desk (Noble 1979).

Hess puts cases like this in a more general framework: "[T]he problem of the flexibility of efficiency definitions and criteria, or more generally definitions of what constitutes a design improvement, is solved by an alignment of efficiency criteria with other criteria, such as who will benefit from the technological change and who will lose. Efficiency criteria such as saving labor can shift power relations among workers along lines of skill, class, and gender. Likewise, shifts in the definition of what counts as a more efficient technology can alter power relations between workers as a whole and managers or between one industry and another. *Not only can a new technology change power relations, but power relations can change definitions of efficiency and evaluations of technological design"* (Hess 2007: 73, emphasis added).

In the case of numerically controlled machines, management was supported by a new "common sense" of engineers guiding technological change which Noble calls the "ideology of automation" (Noble 1979: 35). It qualified human intervention as human error and oriented design toward denying the operators of the technology any autonomous interaction with the control system. It is interesting to note that the significant difference between a "breakthrough" approach, based on abstract principles, and a "tinkering" approach based more on people's on-the-job experience has been identified in other sectors. It is the case, for instance, of the design differences in wind turbines in the US and in Denmark, the latter an example of "tinkering" that was successful in international market terms (Garud and Karnøe 2003).

Of course, as in the case of "QWERTYnomics", once a technological design option has been sufficiently hammered by money, ideology, or sheer power, a lock-in in investment occurs and a "veil of obsolescence" renders any other option hardly visible. The point to be made from this example is that true as it is that technology influences the power relations among production actors, the latter influence technology. And so, the technology that won preeminence at any point in time is not an indisputably more rational way of solving problems or organizing production, but one way of solving problems or organizing production that may admit equally if not better technical solutions, able as well to satisfy other criteria. Moreover, "[E]qually in knowledge, technology and institutions, innovation in any given area does not face a single track, but a branching array of evolutionary pathways. An illusion of linearity is conferred by a spectrum of positive feedback processes. Some blindly reinforce contingent emergence. Others are actively driven by incumbent interests and concentrated power. That 'progress' can be so often and prominently represented as a 'race' along a preordained track—erroneously and yet so little challenged—is but one example of the potent political forces at work" (Stirling 2013: 1).

From the 1960s onwards, the Scandinavian countries experimented with alternatives to the prevalent technologies of automation. Two main examples relate to car-making—mainly the Volvo experience—and to graphic interfaces in newspaper production. The spirit of the alternative is captured in the name of a project related to the latter: UTOPIA, an acronym in Scandinavian language for "Training, Technology, and Product in the Quality of Work Perspective". In both cases, the search for alternatives was a complex socio-technical process, shaped by conflicts between the different actors involved, in the car-making case even between workers in different production premises using different technological approaches (Granath 1998) and always struggling with the established ways of doing things. Eventually, they failed as full-fledged alternatives, but not for offering inferior technological solutions. The flexibility they allowed in the automated processes and the capacity of rapid intervention to avoid the accumulation of errors they provided were considered superior technological features (Granath 1998; Lundell 2005; Howard 2005). There is not a unique account of why this technological design, which was superior from a human-centered point of view as well as from a technical point of view, failed to impose itself as a new standard. Part seems to be due to technological investment lock-ins, given that in the Swedish graphic industry it was considered difficult to make the old and new automation philosophy compatible while too much was already invested in the old one, moreover a world standard, which made it difficult to think about exports (Leydesdorff and Van Den Besselaar 1987). In the car industry, association with international car-making companies with no interests whatsoever in the human-centered heuristics to design explains in part the non-scaling-up of the experiment. Indeed, alternative design and implementation of advanced technology in production are extremely complex socio-technical endeavors, systemic in nature, and moreover constrained nowadays by the standards imposed by globalization. In such a context, the fate of technology is explained as much by asymmetries in power as by technical considerations.

An important point in common of all these alternatives in automation design was the cognitive dialogues between engineers and workers, with mutual recognition of and respect for the knowledge each brought to the design table. As an engineer of the UTOPIA project puts it, "[T]he catchwords were *quality of work and product*, and by that we emphasized that the quality of the product was an interest of the producers and an interest of the trade unions and also that a just as important goal was the quality of work, the work organization, the skills of the workers and that there was a connection between the two. So, the technology that should be produced should be skill enhancing tools rather than deskilling automation" (Pelle Ehn, in the UTOPIA Project, 1981–1986). Without a social and cognitive alliance between workers and scientists and engineers, no alternative design may even be imagined. For that, an attitude like the one fostered by Elinor Ostrom would be needed: "[I]nstead of presuming that some individuals are incompetent, evil, or irrational, and others are omniscient, I presume that individuals have very similar limited capabilities to reason and figure out the structure of complex environments" (Ostrom 1990/2008: 25). This attitude is behind what, based on experiences like the ones just sketched, has emerged as Participatory Design, related mainly to information and communication technologies but also beyond. This is deeply entrenched with a normative preference for democratizing technology by recognizing and encouraging users' participation in the design of technological systems.

When knowledge is power (as it is now more than ever before), countervailing the de facto oligopoly of knowledge-related decisions becomes a main component of democratizing knowledge. This has been particularly difficult to implement in the production realm both in capitalist economies as well as in the past State-led socialist economies. For quite different reasons (even if also intimately related to power), it has been difficult to diffuse technological alternatives aimed at stopping the chemical damages to the environment. But again, the issue at stake is the origin of the difficulty. There is evidence, a glimpse of which we have presented here, suggesting that workable technological alternatives may be designed if new cognitive/political alliances can be formed. Given that cognitive/political alliances are steered by power relations, the difficulty seems to lie with the latter. This does not make the building of alternatives any easier, quite the contrary, but at least it does not accommodate any technologically false pretenses of the inevitability of the prevailing technology systems. The following quotation is telling in this regard: "[I]f we accept the argument that developing technological capabilities does involve a complex, endogenous process of change, negotiated and mediated both within organisations and at the level of society at large, it is obvious that policies cannot and should not be limited to addressing the economic integration of technological change, but must include all aspects of its broader social integration. We thus reject the notion of technology as an external variable to which society and individuals, whether at work or in the home, must adapt" (European Commission 1997: 18).

SCIENCE, TECHNOLOGY, SOCIAL RELATIONS, AND INEQUALITIES

In this section, we will further elaborate our interpretation of the rise of inequality, discussed above, by connecting it with the facts and trends discussed in Chapter 2.

It is useful to keep in mind a general account of the turbulent megatrends influencing the impact of science, technology, and innovation on society and economic inequality: "[T]he 1980s ushered in a new (second) technological revolution, characterized by remarkable changes in information technology, globalization, and the rising importance of heterogeneous jobs in the service sector. This revolution, like the Industrial Revolution of the early nineteenth century, widened income disparities. The increase in inequality happened in part because the new technologies strongly rewarded more highly skilled labor; drove up the share of, and the return to, capital; and increasingly opened the economies of rich countries to competition from China and India [...]. The structure of demand, and thus of jobs, moved toward services, which in turn were staffed by less qualified and worse- paid labor. On the other hand, some service sector jobs, as in finance, were extremely highly paid. This widened wage, and ultimately income, distribution. In addition, pro-rich policies reinforced these trends" (Milanović 2016: 54).

In terms of the quality of jobs, a 2016 International Labour Organization (ILO) report indicates that "[S]ome of the technological developments have also allowed business to manage their labor demand minute by minute, leading to increased need for short-term, part-time and on-call jobs" (ILO 2016: 49). That type of demand strongly disrupts the countervailing power of labor vis-à-vis employers. Already in the mid-1990s, Wilkinson (1996) showed the notable differences in life expectancy derived from differences in stress related to job positions; what the ILO calls "non-standard employment" may develop in the near future not only in income inequalities but in much wider manifestations of unequal "unhealthy societies".

Inequality is furthered by dominant economic and political relations, as eloquently argued by OXFAM (2016). The combination of economic, political, and ideological power in ways that foster inequality can be detected in the USA by looking at "the vicious cycle where the political domination of the top leads to beliefs and policies that enhance economic inequality and reinforce their political domination" (Stiglitz 2012: 267).

Such a combination entails great perils for democratic policies: remember Atkinson stressing "the power that wealth can convey". It is interesting to note that another scholar of inequality expresses the same type of concerns: "Since it is in the interest of the rich to promote the current process of globalization, from which they are [...] strong beneficiaries, and since the middle class and the poor can at least formally derail that process, the focus of the rich is on democracy suppression (even though some of the measures are not consciously implemented as such)" (Milanović 2016: 200).

Given that the first trend in the list discussed in the prospective approach is the increasing role of knowledge in social relations, its connection with inequality deserves closer consideration. We have already quoted the assertion of Brynjolfsson and McAfee, who consider that technological change is the main driver of growing inequality as an "...underlying trend (...) similar worldwide across sometimes markedly different institutions, government policies, and cultures" (Brynjolfsson and McAfee 2014: 61). In that view, technological change fosters inequality in three main ways. First, the role of new knowledge favors highly educated people in relation with the rest. Second, it gives more power to capital in relation to labor. Third, "exponential, digital, and combinatorial change in the technology" gives rise to a "winner-takes-all" economics characterized by cheap replication and little cost of global delivery, a combination fostered by the digitalization of markets that allows top-quality providers to capture an immense share of its respective markets (Brynjolfsson and McAfee 2014: 69).

Up to now, concerning this trend toward increased inequality, it has been argued on the one hand that it is fostered by prevailing economic, political, and even ideological relations and on the other hand that it is also fostered by some main patterns of actual technological change based on advanced knowledge. It can also be asserted that a cause of rising inequality lies in the connection between those two causes (that is, in the connection between social relations and knowledge): "In recent decades, the combination of financial capital and scientific-technical knowledge has gained unparalleled potency in the production of inequality between those who control the combination and those who do not" (Tilly 2005: 115). Moreover, "[U]nequal access to knowledge and unequal control over its production or distribution matter in the 21st-century world not only because of knowledge's intrinsic value but also because its unequal distribution causes other sorts of inequality. Knowledge gives political, financial, and existential advantages to its holders. Returns from knowledge allow its holders to reproduce the institutions and relations that sustain their advantages. In such areas as public health, food supply, environmental quality, and lethal combat, applications of knowledge strongly affect who survives and who lives comfortably" (Tilly 2005: 122).

The potential of knowledge for fostering inequality in the midst of markedly unequal social relations is particularly clear, as we have already seen, in labor relations. The workers' fight against the inequality bias introduced by technological changes that curtailed their freedoms, their income, and their learning opportunities is an old phenomenon. Today, technologies that allow the recollection, storage, and analysis in real time of huge amounts of personal data reconfigure social relations of a very unequal nature among business or institutions and the laymen. Sherry Turkle, an analyst of the relationships that people establish with digital devices, from computers to mobile phones, reflects in this way: "...digital communication makes surveillance easier. The corporations that provide us with the means to talk in the net (to text, email, and chat) take our online activity as data. They declare ownership of it and use it, usually to better sell things to us. And we now know that our government routinely makes a copy or our communications as well. The boundaries have blurred between private communication and routine surveillance, between private communication and its repackaging as a commodity. So, in addition to the question *What is intimacy without privacy?* I consider another *What is democracy without privacy?*" (Turkle 2016: 50, emphasis in the original).

ON LEARNING DIVIDES

Every human society is based on knowledge. Moreover, learning is ubiquitous: "[A]ll knowledge is partial and provisional. Society, and the individuals within it, are involved in an interactive and mutually interdependent process where all are learning on the basis of conjecture, error, experience and experiment" (Hodgson 2001: 79).

Nevertheless, opportunities for learning have always been asymmetric. That is more important today than ever before. It has rightly been asserted than when knowledge becomes the crucial resource in the economy, learning is the most important social process (Lundvall and Johnson 1994). In our view, even more can be said, because advanced knowledge is nowadays crucial not only for the economy but for collective activities and power asymmetries in general, so learning opportunities and processes shape social relations, particularly concerning inequality.

Learning takes place by studying and by working in innovative contexts, where the knowledge acquired by studying may be applied creatively in solving problems, producing in this way new knowledge and, no less important, posing new questions that lead to further knowledge explorations. In some contexts, many people are able to keep learning in both ways at an advanced level. In other contexts, only small or even tiny minorities have such opportunities. Such divides can be called learning divides. They separate privileged groups from deprived groups almost everywhere. They are a fundamental example of knowledge-related inequality that hampers the expansion of capabilities and freedoms of many human beings.

It is worth analyzing a bit further the two types of components of learning processes. It seems clear that learning by creatively solving complex problems using the most up-to-date resources cannot be done without learning by studying. However, it is possible to have capacities to solve problems built upon learning by studying and not using them: if the production of goods and services does not demand such capacities, the learning opportunities derived from the problem-solving challenge associated with such production will be lost. As Erik Reinert puts it, "successful cases of economic development prove the importance of *simultaneously providing* not only a flow of better educated people, but also jobs where their skills are demanded. [...] Nations that only address the supply side of educated people end up educating for migration" (Reinert 2007: 230–231, emphasis in the original).

A main difference between the North and the Global South can be characterized as a learning divide. Such a divide puts on one side societies where a fair proportion of its population are able to study at an advanced level as well as to find places to put at work the capacities acquired, thus being able to keep on learning, and on the other side societies where a tiny minority is offered this double opportunity, the majority being cut off from enhancing their capabilities by continual learning.

We shall try to give a graphic idea of the learning divide. We can characterize the "learning situation" of a country—continuing with the idea that learning is a process with two components—by two coordinates in a pair of Cartesian axes. The difficulty lies in finding good approximations to each component available for a fair amount of countries. We may use the Gross Enrollment in Higher Education (HE) as a proxy for "learning by studying" and the proportion of the gross domestic product (GDP) devoted to research and development (R&D) as a proxy for "learning by problem-solving". Neither of the two proxies is near perfect, but they present the advantage of being available in long series for most countries. The data for

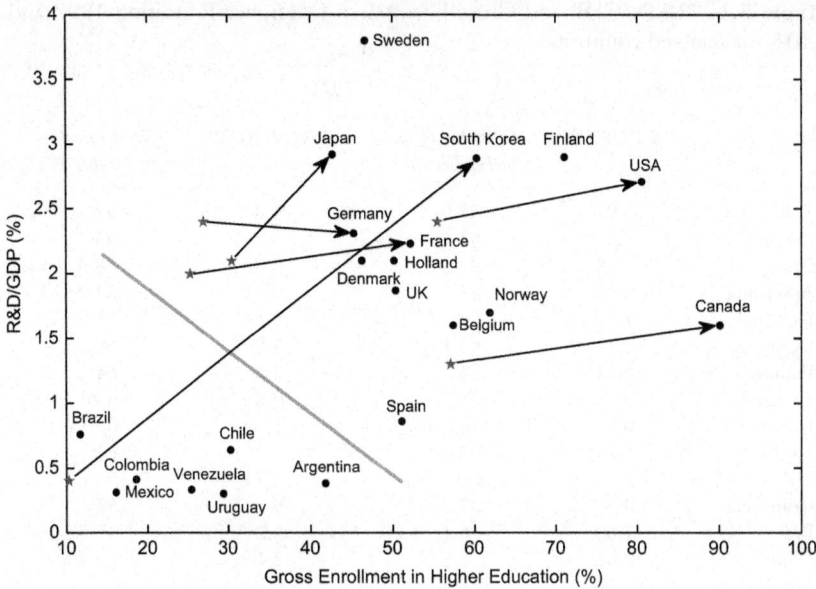

Fig. 3.1 The learning divide in 1997 (and some country positions in 1975)
*country position in 1975
Source: Arocena and Sutz 2000: 9, UNESCO Statistics

1997 clearly showed the divide (Arocena and Sutz 2000), as presented in
Fig. 3.1. This picture also shows the position occupied by some countries
in 1975. The case of South Korea is impressive, crossing the learning divide
in twenty years. For other countries, it is noticeable that whereas significant
improvements were achieved in Gross Enrollment in HE, more modest
ones have been attained in the proportion of GDP devoted to R&D. A
similar trend can be observed when we look at the development during the
following 20 years: data for 2014 confirms an impressive leap forwards in
HE but a very modest change in R&D/GDP for several countries, as
shown in Table 3.1. This trend can be attributed in part to the inaccuracy
of the Gross Enrollment in HE indicator; moreover, for some countries,
the indicator may say very little in terms of the quality of HE because of the
proliferation of low standards in tertiary education with little governmental
control. However, the increase in access to HE is, in some countries, a real
phenomenon, often accompanied by important social struggles, as shown
by the Chilean students' upheaval of 2011.

Table 3.1 R&D/GDP and Gross Enrollment in Higher Education 1997 and 2015 for selected countries

	1997		2015	
	R&D/GDP	Gross Enrollm. in Higher Ed.	R&D/GDP	Gross Enrollm. in Higher Ed.
S. Korea	2.9	73.9	4.3	97
Finland	2.5	81	3.2	93
Chile	0.64	37.3	0.38	88.6
Argentina	0.47	48	0.61	82.9
Denmark	1.81	56	3.1	81
Germany	2.31	45.3	2.8	65
France	2.21	54	2.26	64
Uruguay	0.2	33.7	0.33	63.1
Italy	0.95	48	1.29	63
Sweden	3.2	63	3.2	62
UK	1.71	60	1.71	56
Colombia	0.3	22.2	0.2	55.6
Brazil	1.00	16.1	1.2	49.3
China	0.65	6.5	2.1	43.4
Mexico	0.26	17.9	0.54	28.3
India	0.63	9.6	0.82	25.5

Source: RICYT 2017; UNESCO Statistics 2017

Table 3.1 shows two interesting features. One is the impressive double improvement exhibited by South Korea, continuing its trend since the mid-1970s, and by China. The other is the important improvement in the HE indicator in several countries that at the same time present a modest growth in R&D and even de-growth (Chile and Colombia). Spain and all Latin American countries except Mexico, which had a poor evolution in both indicators, seem to have found it easier to expand the capacities to learn than to expand the opportunities to creatively apply those capacities to problem-solving. This does not come as a surprise. A social policy that promotes educational expansion—like scholarships schemes, positive action to encourage access, and de-centralization—may end up with more young people accessing HE. On the other hand, as already mentioned, the proliferation of tertiary educational options in times of the "social assault on education" may inflate the figures. But expanding the opportunities for having jobs where continual learning is part of the task implies a structural transformation of the productive setting that is very complex to achieve.

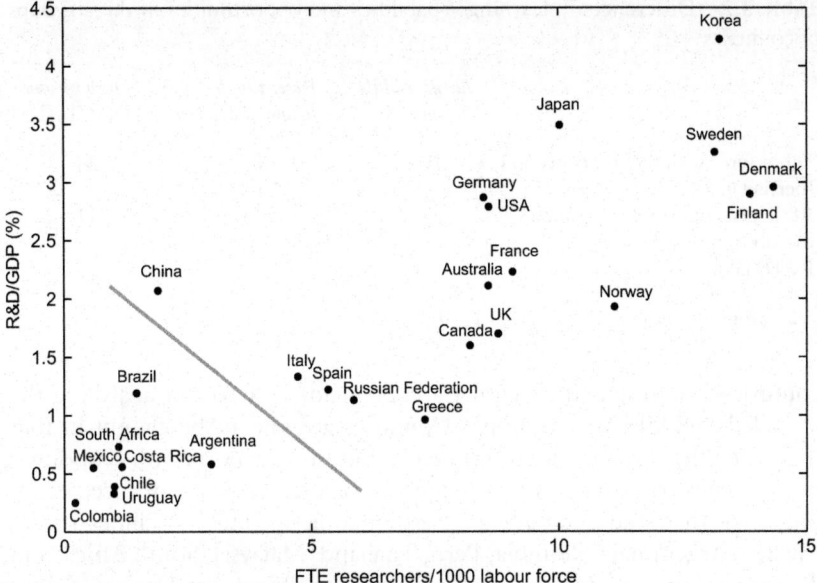

Fig. 3.2 The learning divide in 2015
Source: OECD 2017, Tables 10 and 11; RICYT 2017

This, as we shall see, has important implications for universities engaged with developmental processes.

The poorest countries continue to be well below an imaginary learning divide schematized as in Fig. 3.1. But for other countries where better indicators can be built, it is worthwhile to re-examine the validity of the learning divide concept. The opportunities to learn through creative jobs are reasonably associated with the level of spending in R&D; for the capacities to learn at the country level, we may take as a better proxy than Gross Enrollment in HE the number of full-time equivalent (FTE) researchers per 1000 in the labor force. The latest OECD data allows us to build Fig. 3.2. The notion of a learning divide holds.

Another indicator of available capabilities—alongside the proportion of R&D personnel in the labor force—is the proportion of labor force with tertiary education. Even if data is not available for all the "Southern" countries, it allows a telling comparison between "large middle income countries", "recent high income East Asian countries" and "high income OECD

Table 3.2 Differences in learning capabilities and opportunities in three groups of countries

	Large middle income	Recent high income East Asia	High income OECD
Labor force with tertiary education (percent)	19	34	34
R&D personnel (per thousand in the labor force)	3	11	11
R&D/GDP (%)	0.7	3.1	2.2

Source: Based on Doner and Schneider 2016: 10, 12

countries" as presented by Doner and Schneider (2016) for analyzing the so-called "middle-income trap". Countries are said to be caught in that trap when they are unable to compete in industrial exports with economies where wages are much lower or in innovative activities with advanced economies. In that study, the group ("large middle income") includes Brazil, Mexico, Argentina, Colombia, Peru, Thailand, Malaysia, South Africa, and Turkey. In turn, "recent high income East Asia" includes Korea, Taiwan, Singapore, and Hong Kong (the last excluded when considering R&D). Using Doner and Schneider data, we can present Table 3.2.

Differences concerning capabilities arising from learning and innovation are apparent. From a point of view where such capabilities are stressed, it could be said that countries in the first group are in fact trapped in a neo-peripheral trap: they were able to escape from the "old periphery" of non-industrialized countries, and thus their economic growth was significant for many years, but they were not able to upgrade to knowledge-based and innovation-driven economies.

Mexico is a telling example: "although many Mexican exports are classified as knowledge-intensive, they are in fact intensive in unskilled labour owing to the vertical fragmentation of the respective activities in global value chains" (ECLAC 2016: 114).

Peripheries of today are quite heterogeneous, even more so than yesterday. The large middle-income countries analyzed by Doner and Schneider are much stronger economically than most other countries in the Global South. Their economic growth has been remarkable in the long run (that made them "middle income countries"). But they do not seem to be on a track of self-sustained economic development.

EXCLUSION AND KNOWLEDGE

An especially worrying consequence of the multidimensional and multi-causal phenomenon of inequality is social exclusion. This exclusion is related to knowledge in ways that prevailing innovation policies, as oriented by the market, are perhaps not only failing to address but even reinforcing.

One way of analyzing the type of causality that relates inequality to knowledge production and knowledge use is through the typology of social exclusion proposed by Sen (2000). Social exclusion can be active (when a will to exclude is present) or passive (when exclusion occurs even if not explicitly wanted); it can also be constitutive (with particularly severe and lasting consequences) or instrumental (leading to important inconveniences).

When these types of exclusion are combined, a two-by-two matrix can be presented. Its four cells represent: (I) active and constitutive exclusion, (II) active and instrumental exclusion, (III) passive and instrumental exclusion, and (IV) passive and constitutive exclusion. Each of these "social exclusion cells" is connected to relative deprivation; they have as one of their drivers the type of knowledge that is produced and how knowledge is used and distributed.

Cell I (active and constitutive exclusion) can be exemplified by Trade-Related Aspects of Intellectual Property Rights (TRIPS) and the exclusion it implies to accessing fundamental medicines. As Stiglitz asserts, "[T]he fundamental problem with the patent system is simple: it is based on restricting the use of knowledge. Because there is no extra cost associated with an additional individual enjoying the benefits of any piece of knowledge, restricting knowledge is inefficient. But the patent system not only restricts the use of knowledge; by granting (temporary) monopoly power, it often makes medications unaffordable for people who don't have insurance. In the Third World, this can be a matter of life and death for people who cannot afford new brand-name drugs but might be able to afford generics" (Stiglitz 2007). Moreover, "[T]he economics profession has devoted vast amount of research and textbook space to proving the inefficiency of various forms of protectionism. The basic story in this work is that protectionism causes the price to exceed the marginal cost of production. All of this work is entirely applicable to patents and copyrights, except the impact is at least an order of magnitude larger than with most instances of protectionism in international trade. While tariffs and quotas rarely raise the price of goods by more than 30 or 40 percent, patents on prescription drugs typically raise the price of protected products by 300 to 400 percent, or more, above the marginal cost. In some cases, patent protected drugs sell for hundreds or thousands of times as much as the competitive market price" (Baker 2005). In other words, the TRIPS agreement signed in 1994 "protected the patent rights of inventors and the copyrights of writers, musicians, and artists, but its chief beneficiaries were big pharmaceutical companies. Big Pharma's patented drugs against AIDS were too pricey to be used widely in poor countries, and so hundreds of thousands died. 'Generic' drugs costing a fraction of the price were produced by India and China, but TRIPS prevented their sale. TRIPS also kept a northern lock on creativity in cutting-edge technologies. [...] This offensive reached even natural resources, as monopoly property rights over water, the soil, and plants were increasingly asserted. Natural remedies from the South were being patented by northern corporations" (Mann 2013: 176).

Cell IV (passive and constitutive exclusion) looks into the same type of problems from a "passive" perspective. Usually, when the choice of problems to be researched is made, or when the venues for innovative efforts are decided, nobody explicitly wants to exclude anybody. The point is that without a conscious inclusive perspective, the problems of those without agency, particularly without effective demand, will not be taken into account. In the realm of health, terms like "neglected diseases" or the 90/10 gap, coined by the World Health Organization— meaning that only 10% of the resources for research in health are related to health problems of 90% of the world's population—express the exclusion, not actively pursued but nevertheless present, of a great part of the world's population from the possibilities of a better health offered by new knowledge.

Knowledge-related exclusion in Cell II (active and instrumental exclusion) can be exemplified by the possibilities to choose people—for jobs, for insurance, for fellowships or acceptance in educational institutions— from a wealth of personal data that may include data as intimate as their DNA. The possibility of people becoming like an open book in the face of public and private administrations able to manage in an unregulated way all personal data to make decisions on them, opens the road for active exclusion, perhaps not constitutive in Sen's terminology, but probably instrumental.

Finally, Cell III (passive and instrumental exclusion) includes the "classical" type of social exclusion derived from unequal capabilities that people, organizations, and even whole societies have at their disposal to produce and to use modern knowledge for solving problems. It is passive because it is not exerted by a conscious will to exclude; it is instrumental because it may not be directly life-threatening. But it is structural in the sense that the type of "knowledge inequality" related to this cell stems from the consequences of the productive structure and its relations with knowledge production and use. One such consequence relates to the very low learning opportunities offered by the labor market to workers when the economy is based mainly on products with low local intellectual added value. At a more aggregate level, the international division of labor—which shows little change for the majority of developing countries—continues to put on one side primary producers or "maquila"-type producers and on the other side sophisticated manufacture and services producers, again with all the consequences for the type of employment and associated wages.

Each cell represents a particular feature of prevailing knowledge-based social exclusion or inequality. Behind each cell, different types of power are exerted through different actors and mechanisms: over global or national regulations, over research and innovation agendas, over economic structures, over people's lives. Fighting these knowledge-based inequalities requires building countervailing powers able to redress at least some of the more salient features of the current situation. Or, as Atkinson put it, "[I]t is my belief that the rise in inequality can in many cases be traced directly or indirectly to changes in the balance of power. If that is correct, then measures to reduce inequality can be successful only if countervailing power is brought to bear" (Atkinson 2015: 82).

It can be surmised, with good reasons, that even if the knowledge-based inequality represented in each cell requires some specific countervailing power to fight it, the intertwined nature of social exclusion manifestations will prevent major achievements unless a more systemic and global perspective is pursued.

The different forms of social exclusion stemming from knowledge show that knowledge politics may be a highly conflicting issue. They suggest also that overcoming this type of situations will often require specific research and innovation policies.

In the next chapter, we consider a general framework for studying innovation processes and related power issues. This is a needed step within the theoretical/factual approach if countervailing power strategies are to become part of the propositional approach.

REFERENCES

Arocena, R., & Sutz, J. (2000). *Interactive Learning Spaces and Development Policies in Latin America* (Druid Working Paper 00–13). Denmark: Aalborg University. Available at: http://www3.druid.dk/wp/20000013.pdf. Accessed 10 May 2017.

Atkinson, A. B. (2015). *Inequality: What Can Be Done?* Cambridge, USA: Harvard University Press.

Baker, E. (2005). The Reform of the Intellectual Property, [online] *Post-Autistic Economic Review*, (32), first article. Available at: http://www.paecon.net/PAEReview/issue32/Baker32.htm. Accessed 11 May 2017.

Bloch, M. (1969). Advent and Triumph of the Water Mill. In M. Bloch (Ed.), *Land and Work in Medieval Europe* (pp. 136, 168). New York: Harper and Row.

Brynjolfsson, E., & McAfee, A. (2014). *The Second Machine Age. Work, Progress, and Prosperity in a Time of Brilliant Technologies*. New York: Norton and Co.

Cornia, G. A. (2010). Income Distribution under Latin America's New Left Regimes. *Journal of Human Development and Capabilities, 11*(1), 85–114.

David, P. (1985). Clio and the Economics of QWERTY. *The American Economic Review, 75*(2), Papers and Proceedings of the Ninety-Seventh Annual Meeting of the American Economic Association, pp. 332–337.

Deaton, A. (2013). *The Great Escape. Health, Wealth, and the Origins of Inequality*. Princeton: Princeton University Press.

Doner, R., & Schneider, B. R. (2016). The Middle-Income Trap: More Politics than Economics. *World Politics, 4*, 608–644.

ECLAC (Economic Commission for Latin America and the Caribbean). (2010). *TimeforEquality:ClosingGaps,OpeningTrails:Summary*(LC/G.2433(SES.33/4). Santiago, Chile: Economic Commission for Latin America and the Caribbean.

ECLAC (Economic Commission for Latin America and the Caribbean). (2016). *Horizons 2030: Equality at the Centre of Sustainable Development* (LC/G.2660(SES.36/3). Santiago de Chile: Economic Commission for Latin America and the Caribbean.

European Commission. (1997). *Building the European Information Society for Us All*. Final Policy Report of the High-Level Expert Group, Brussels.

Freeman, C., & Soete, L. (1997). *The Economics of Industrial Innovation* (3rd ed.). Cambridge, MA: The MIT Press.

Garud, R., & Karnøe, P. (2003). Bricolage Versus Breakthrough: Distributed and Embedded Agency in Technological Entrepreneurship. *Research Policy, 32*, 277–300.

Granath, J. (1998). *Torslanda to Uddevalla via Kalmar: A Journey in Production Practices at Volvo*. Presented at Seminário Internacional Reestruturação Produtiva, Flexibilidade do Trabalho e Novas Competências Profissionais COPPE/UFRJ, Rio de Janeiro, Brasil. Accesible at: https://www.academia.edu/5495539/

Torslanda_to_Uddevalla_via_Kalmar_A_journey_in_production_practice_in_ Volvo. Accessed 10 May 2017.

Held, D., & Kaya, A. (Eds.). (2007). *Global Inequality. Patterns and Explanations.* Cambridge, UK: Polity Press.

Hess, D. (2007). *Alternative Pathways in Science and Industry. Activism, Innovation, and the Environment in an Era of Globalization.* Cambridge, MA: The MIT Press.

Hodgson, G. M. (2001). *Economics and Utopia. Why the Learning Economy Is Not the End of History.* Hoboken: Taylor and Francis e-Library.

Hodgson, G. M. (2015). Conceptualizing Capitalism: How the Misuse of Key Concepts Impedes our Understanding of Modern Economies. *BooksandIdeas. net.* Available at: http://www.booksandideas.net/IMG/pdf/20150507_conceptualizing_capitalism.pdf. Accessed 10 May 2017.

Howard, R. (2005). Utopia: Where Workers Craft New Technology. *Technology Review, 88*(3). Reprinted in Z. Pylyshyn & L. Banon (Eds.). (1989). *Perspectives in the Computer Revolution* (pp. 341–350). Ablex Publishing Co.

ILO. (2016). *Non-standard Employment Around the World.* Geneva. Available at: http://www.ilo.org/global/publications/books/WCMS_534326/lang--en/ index.htm. Accessed 10 May 2017.

Langrish, J., Gibbons, M., Evans, W. G., & Jevons, F. R. (1972). *Wealth from Knowledge: A Study of Innovation in Industry.* New York: Halsted/John Willey.

Lazonick, W., & Mazzucato, M. (2012). *The Risk-Reward Nexus. Innovation, Finance and Inclusive Growth.* Policy Network Paper, New York.

Leydesdorff, L., & Van Den Besselaar, P. (1987). What We Have Learned from the Amsterdam Science Shop. In S. Blume, J. Bunders, L. Leydesdroff, & R. Whitley (Eds.), *The Social Direction of the Public Sciences* (pp. 135–162). Dordrecht: D. Reidel Publishing Co.

Lundell, P. (2005). *Designing Democracy: The UTOPIA-Project and the Role of Labour Movement in Technological Change, 1981—1986, Working Paper No 52.* Stockholm: The Royal Institute of Technology, Centre of Excellence for Studies in Science and Innovation.

Lundvall, B. Å. (1985). *Product Innovation and User-Producer Interaction* (Industrial Development Research Series No. 31). Aalborg: Aalborg University Press.

Lundvall, B.-Å., & Johnson, B. (1994). The Learning Economy. *Industry and Innovation, 1*(2), 23–42.

Maclaine Pont, P., van Est, Q., & Deuten, J. (2016). *Shaping Socio-Technical Innovation Through Policy -Essay Commissioned by the Department of Knowledge, Innovation and Strategy of the Dutch Ministry of Infrastructure and the Environment.* The Hague: Rathenau Instituut.

Mann, M. (2013). *The Sources of Social Power. Vol. IV Globalizations, 1945–2011.* Cambridge: Cambridge University Press.

Marglin, S. A. (1974). What Do Bosses Do?: The Origins and Functions of Hierarchy in Capitalist Production. *Review of Radical Political Economics, 6,* 60–127.

Merton, R. (1968). The Matthew Effect on Science. *Science, 159*(3810), 56–63.

Metropolis, N., Howlett, J., & Rota, G. C. (Eds.). (1985). *A History of Computing in the Twentieth Century*. New York: Academic Press.

Milanović, B. (2011). *The Haves and the Have-Nots. A Brief and Idiosyncratic History of Global Inequality*. New York: Basic Books.

Milanović, B. (2016). *Global in Equality: A New Approach for the Age of Globalization*. Cambridge, MA: Harvard University Press.

Noble, D. (1979). Social Choice in Machine Design: The Case of Numerically Controlled Machine Tools. In A. Zimbalist (Ed.), *Case Studies on the Labour Process* (pp. 18–50). New York: Monthly Review Press.

OECD. (2017). *Main Science and Technology Indicators*. Paris: OECD Publishing.

Ostrom, E. (1990/2008). *Governing the Commons. The Evolution of Institutions for Collective Action*. New York: Cambridge University Press.

OXFAM. (2016). *An Economy for the 1%. How Privilege and Power in the Economy Drive Extreme Inequality and How This Can Be Stopped*. Oxford: Oxfam GB.

Reinert, E. S. (2007). *How Rich Countries Got Rich and Why Poor Countries Stay Poor*. New York: Public Affairs.

RICYT. (2017). *Red Iberoamericana de Indicadores de Ciencia y Tecnología*. Available at: http://www.ricyt.org/indicadores. Accessed 10 May 2017.

Rogers, E. M. (1995). *Diffusion of Innovations* (4th ed.). New York: Free Press.

Ruger, J. P. (2006). Ethics and Governance of Global Health Inequalities. *Journal of Epidemiology and Community Health, 60*(11), 998–1002.

Sen, A. (2000). Social Exclusion: Concept, Application and Scrutiny. *Social Development Papers, 1*, Asian Development Bank.

Stiglitz, J. (2007). *Give Prizes Not Patents*. Available at: http://www.project-syndicate.org/commentary/prizes--not-patents. Accessed 4 Jan 2017.

Stiglitz, J. (2012). *The Price of Inequality*. New York: Norton.

Stirling, A. (2013). "Pluralising Progress: From Inclusive Innovation to Innovation Democracy", Contribution to the Dig-IT Workshop on Inclusive Growth, Innovation and Technology: Interdisciplinary Perspectives, University of Sussex.

The UTOPIA Project 1981–1986. Available at: http://www.nada.kth.se/cid/utopia/quality.htm. Accessed 10 May 2017.

Tilly, C. (2005). *Identities, Boundaries, and Social Ties*. Boulder: Paradigm Publishers.

Tsounta, E., & Ouseke, A. (2014). *What Is Behind Latin America's Diminishing Income Inequality?* International Monetary Fund Working Paper 14/124.

Turkle, S. (2016). *Reclaiming Conversation. The Power of Talk in a Digital Age*. New York: Penguin Books.

UNESCO. (2017). *UI Statistics*. Available at: http://data.uis.unesco.org/Index.aspx. Accessed 10 May 2017.

Weizenbaum, J. (1976). *Computer Power and Human Reason. From Judgement to Calculation*. San Francisco: Freeman, and Co.

Wilkinson, R. (1996). *Unhealthy Societies. The Afflictions of Inequality*. New York: Routledge.

CHAPTER 4

Social Processes of Learning and Innovation

Which actors and their interactions are or may become more relevant concerning the power of knowledge? Paying attention to this question leads to further elaborating a substantial part of the factual and prospective approaches presented in the two previous chapters. Even a preliminary answer opens the way for giving substance to the propositional approach because it helps to analyze a second and related question: along which specific social processes is it feasible to promote knowledge democratization? The National Innovation System (NIS) conceptualization offers an inspiring framework for considering both questions, particularly when the so-called Aalborg version of that conceptualization is adopted and combined with some "Southern" intellectual traditions. Such a combination is attempted in what follows.

Before we present that conceptualization, it is useful to recall why innovation policy has become so important: "changes in knowledge production processes have a number of implications for policy. One involves the need to integrate what were often previously separated policies for science, for technology and for industry (an indeed for Higher Education) into a more holistic 'innovation policy'" (Martin 2010: 43).

AN INNOVATION SYSTEMS FRAMEWORK

Generally speaking, a fertile conceptual framework for analyzing the intertwined processes of research, learning, and knowledge use is provided by the NIS academic tradition. The related basic original references usually

© The Author(s) 2018
R. Arocena et al., *Developmental Universities in Inclusive Innovation Systems*, https://doi.org/10.1007/978-3-319-64152-2_4

given are Freeman (1987), Lundvall (1992) and Nelson (1993); a general overview of the approach is offered in the Postscriptum (Lundvall 2010) of the second edition of the second reference.

In a nutshell, this school of thought sees the use of knowledge and especially innovation processes as fundamentally systemic, interactive, and distributed between different actors in such a way that learning is a main feature.

Reformulating the characterization offered by Freeman and Soete (1997: 291), the NIS will be the name given to the set of actors and institutions and the linkages between them that, at the level of a given nation, promote technological innovation; it includes public policies, production activities, generation and diffusion of science and technology, and Higher Education.

As already stressed, a great virtue of Sen's conception of development is the fundamental role given to human agency. That is highlighted in the normative characterization of Sustainable Human Development. It includes an emphasis on collective action that looks essential for strategies based on interactive learning and innovation processes, like those inspired by the NIS approach à la Aalborg: "[B]asically, the theory underlying innovation systems analysis is about learning processes involving skillful but imperfectly rational agents and organizations. It assumes that organizations and agents have a capability to enhance their competence through searching and learning and that they do so in interaction with other agents and that this is reflected in innovation processes and outcomes in the form of innovations and new competences" (Lundvall 2010: 331).

Thus, an agency-oriented normative approach to development can make good use of the NIS framework for discussing facts, trends, and policies.

Such a framework helps to go beyond the schematic opposition between state and market that has sterilized so many discussions concerning development. That is so precisely because the NIS framework highlights the relevance of several collective actors. Its affinity with institutional economics, as well as its focus on several actors and their interactions, leads quite naturally to considering not only economic relations but also political, ideological, and cultural issues. It may be a great help for "trespassing" frontiers of disciplines, going "from economics to politics and beyond", as Hirschman (1981) urged many years ago when considering the limitations of development economics. The idea of trespassing is forcefully stressed in "Development as Freedom" by the recommendation "to investigate the development process in inclusive terms that integrate economic, social, and political considerations. A broad approach of this kind permits simultaneous appreciation of the vital roles, in the process of development, of many different institutions, including markets and market-related organisations, governments and local authorities, political parties and other civic institutions, educational arrangements and opportunities of open dialogue and debate (including the role of the media and other means of communication).

Such an approach also allows us to acknowledge the role of social values and prevailing mores, which can influence the freedoms that people enjoy and have reason to treasure. Shared norms can influence social features such as gender equity, the nature of child care, family size and fertility patterns, the treatment of the environment and many other arrangements and outcomes. Prevailing values and social mores also affect the presence or absence of corruption, and the role of trust in economic or social or political relationships. The exercise of freedom is mediated by values, but the values in turn are influenced by public discussions and social interactions, which are themselves influenced by participatory freedoms" (Sen 1999: 8–9).

It can be said that the NIS framework offers an "actor-centered vision". It is directly inspired by Lundvall's study of the interactions between producers and users of innovation. In his view, while "the classical actors in innovation studies are individual entrepreneurs and the R&D laboratories of big firms", with perhaps "secondary parts […] played by scientists and policy makers", actual or at least potential contributions of other actors should be taken into account; the distributed and interactive nature of innovations processes opens possibilities of agency also to workers, consumers, and the public sector as a whole (Lundvall 1988: 365).

The NIS conceptualization, by its emphasis on the concrete aspects of interactions between organizations and collective actors more generally, also helps to take into account potentially very different outcomes of such interactions without assuming a given type of consequences. Thus, it is a potentially useful conceptual tool for studying the specific aspects of innovation-cum-learning processes in underdevelopment, where available resources are frequently less abundant than in affluent countries and where problems are posed under different conditions.

An expanding body of research links development issues with Innovation Systems theory and social inclusion concerns (i.e., Lundvall et al. 2011; Arocena and Sutz 2012; Johnson and Andersen 2012; Couto et al. 2013; Chataway et al. 2013; Heeks 2013; Cozzens and Thakur 2014; Crespi and Dutrenit 2014; Papaioannou 2014; Srinivas 2014).

The NIS approach helps to pay attention to the historic trajectories of each country or region, the national and international configurations of power, and the evolution of productive structures and their connections with knowledge production and utilization. The national studies reported in Nelson (1993) give early examples of the previous assertion.

In this theoretical framework, the mismatch often seen in underdevelopment, when indigenous knowledge production capabilities are weakly used to produce satisfactory goods and services, is related to failures in the NIS and, particularly, in the strength of the connections (or absence of connections) between different actors.

The mismatch often appears to be related to knowledge asymmetries and communication problems between producers of innovations and users of innovations, such that the solutions provided by the former are unsatisfactory for the latter (Lundvall 1985). When interactions between different actors are considered to be highly influential—as the NIS conceptualization suggests—asymmetries of knowledge and of power in general become part of the explanation of mismatches. Thus, the corroboration that the organization of work greatly influences the actual dynamics of innovation comes as no surprise; we have already stressed the paramount importance of the opportunities to learn, opportunities that are not automatically present simply because the capabilities to learn are present.

Developing new products and services depends critically on the skills developed by employees on-the-job in the process of solving the technical and production-related problems encountered in testing, producing, implementing, and marketing new products and processes. Developing these sorts of skills in turn depends not just on the quality of formal education but on having the right organizational structures and work environments. Work environments need to be designed to promote learning through problem-solving and to encourage the effective use of these skills for innovation. This implies that relevant indicators for innovation need to do more than capture material inputs such as R&D expenditures and human capital inputs such as the quality of the available pool of skills based on the number of years of education. Indicators also need to capture how these material and human resources are used and whether or not the work environment promotes the further development of the knowledge and skills of employees (Lorenz and Valeyre 2007: 227–228).

More generally, "what people do and learn at their workplace is a major factor structuring the national innovation system and affecting its performance. It is certainly more difficult to change than, for instance, R&D

intensity, but it is also more fundamental and more deeply rooted in the industrial history of the country" (Lundvall 2016: 607). This quote supports the idea presented earlier that it is more difficult to expand opportunities to learn through the creative application of what was learnt by studying than to expand the learning capacities at the country level.

We assume that NIS is a useful concept to analyze the social processes of learning and innovation but with two caveats. First, it needs adaptations when used in the Global South, because it was proposed to give account of processes observed mainly in highly industrialized countries. Second, as social interactions are at the heart of the concept, the issue of power needs to be carefully considered, as acknowledged by Lundvall: "[A] weakness of the system of innovation approach is that it is still lacking in its treatment of the power aspects of development. The focus on interactive learning—a process in which agents communicate and cooperate in the creation and utilization of new economically useful knowledge—may lead to an underestimation of the conflicts over income and power connected to the innovation process. In a global context where the access to technical knowledge is becoming restricted (…) by more and more ambitious global schemes to protect intellectual property this perspective gives a too rosy picture" (Lundvall 2010: 340).

The next section will look at NIS from the South, and the one after that will focus on power and Innovation Systems.

NATIONAL INNOVATION SYSTEMS AS SEEN FROM THE SOUTH

A first remark that quite naturally emerges when the NIS conceptualization is considered in connection with underdevelopment is that "National Innovation System" is an "ex post" concept: it has been theoretically elaborated on the basis of empirical findings in the North. When the reality of the Global South is studied in such a framework, the concept becomes rather "ex ante" in the sense that it does not usually describe an actual situation. That is mainly because, while innovation always exists and in some cases can be quite strong, it is seldom truly "systemic". In many countries of the South, really existing innovation remains frequently encapsulated and isolated (Arocena and Sutz 2000).

This issue of innovation not being a systemic process and its translation in non–scaling-up innovations contribute to the (wrong) idea that there are hardly any indigenous innovation capacities in the South. It is worth noting that the canonical way of measuring innovation, which for industry follows the guidance of the Oslo Manual, gives priority to international comparisons over unearthing idiosyncratic innovations and innovation processes in less industrialized countries, contributing to rendering them little visibility (Sutz 2012). The recognition of the differences in the systemic behavior of innovation in Latin American countries and the most developed ones was the root of the attempt to fine-tune innovation measurements there by means of a specific manual, the Bogota Manual, where it is stated that "[A]ll things considered, in both large firms and small or medium-sized firms, the network of links and interactions between any given firm and its 'environment' (…) can be seen to have a low degree of consolidation. The weakness and lack of co-ordination of national and local innovation systems in Latin America is perhaps one of the main elements to be taken into account when analyzing discrepancies between the behavior and performance of regional firms and firms in the more developed countries" (RICYT 2001: 13).

Measurements usually also pay exclusive attention to formalized innovations, while innovation in informal settings is more the rule than the exception in most developing countries. If innovation is a concept related to newness as well as to usefulness, innovations in informal settings cannot be ignored without losing track of reality (Muller 2010; Cozzens and Sutz 2014; Kraemer-Mbula and Wunsch-Vincent 2016). The invisibilization of the innovations that take place in the South is one of the reasons why the NIS framework needs to be adapted while retaining all its useful insights.

A second remark, closely related to the first one, concerns "the problem of interactions", which was stressed by the Latin American thinking about the issue of "science – technology – development—dependency" several decades ago (Sabato 1975). Now, one of the most relevant traits of the NIS concept is its "relational" nature, meaning that it gives utmost importance to the links between a wide set of collective actors, or as Martin (2010: 44) puts it: "[W]here past policies largely focused on building strong actors (firms, government labs, universities) with regard to knowledge production and innovation, now the emphasis has shifted to nurturing and strengthening the links between those actors so that the national (or regional) innovation system as a whole works as effectively as possible".

Another way of expressing the latter is that market failure, one of the main justifications for public intervention in knowledge issues, has shifted to system failure (Woolthuis et al. 2005). This new justification for policies stems precisely from the recognition of the interrelatedness of knowledge issues.

The problem of interactions is precisely the weakness or even absence of such links in the Global South, a situation that entails that NIS is more virtual than real. The consequences for policies deserve attention: if in the North, fostering or improving relations between different actors belonging to the NIS is often a difficult task, in underdevelopment the task tends to be quite different and even more difficult. If in the first case bridges often need to be upgraded, in the second case they frequently have to be built in order to connect actors that may not even be aware of their isolation. It is worth recalling that the problem is not only the random "happening" of the interactions but its "accumulativeness": "[O]ver longer periods, the intensity with which (...) change-related resources are accumulated and applied will influence other variables, such as the strength of backwards and forwards linkages to suppliers and customers..." (Bell and Pavitt 1997: 88). This "accumulativeness", a structural trait of a "well-behaved" NIS, is only in part a "naturally evolutionary" phenomenon; a good deal of it is the result of different types of nurturing mechanisms.

Thus, we are led to a third remark, which starts recalling that NIS is a policy subject. The notion was elaborated in the North as a theoretical and factual approach as well as a propositional approach. The latter means that it is a framework for elaborating innovation policies. Now, the framework is ex post in the North also in this sense because innovation policies (usually called science policies or science and technology policies) already had an important place in the political agenda of central countries, at least since the late 1940s. Concerning such policies, the NIS conceptualization attempted to improve and widen them, a purpose that has been successful in no small measure as can be seen by the amount of money and the type of efforts dedicated to what are now called science, technology, and innovation policies. The last are frequently mentioned in the Global South but in many cases their real position in the political agenda is quite low.

Seeing the NIS as a policy subject does not mean that the Innovation System can be designed and implemented as a whole. Such an illusion nevertheless shapes the verbal formulation of policies in some cases. Not surprisingly, where that happens, the NIS is an ex-ante notion and related policies have traditionally been neglected. Such mistakes notwithstanding, the NIS framework is useful not only for understanding the reality of a given country concerning knowledge generation, learning, and innovation but also for guiding deliberate efforts to improve the actual situation.

A fourth remark stems directly from the previous sentence: if the notion of NIS is useful for trying to improve a given situation, then it has an evaluative content. Generally speaking, that is already a consequence of understanding the NIS framework as a guide for policies. A policy proposal is never a direct deduction from (an interpretation of) facts and trends. Being a prescription, it always carries a normative weight that should not be implicit but explicit. A particular aspect of that general assertion is being highlighted here: the interactive, distributed, and potentially systemic traits of innovation, as stressed by the NIS conceptualization, offer criteria for evaluating how satisfactory innovation processes are. Since the early days of the NIS conceptualization, Lundvall studied the often unsatisfactory innovations stemming from differences in competence between producers and users of innovations. He gave as a good example the Japanese policies for the modernization of mature productive sectors, like textiles and clothing, which can be seen "as an attempt to <u>compensate for the weak channels of information</u> between producers and science based industries, and to <u>break the inertia</u> built into the traditional user-producer relationships" (Lundvall 1985: 37, emphasis in the original). The role of users has been highlighted in the NIS approach as well as in some influential texts on innovation (Lundvall and Borrás 1997; von Hippel 1988). Concomitantly, innovation policies that take into account the point of view of users (user-driven innovation policies) have been fostered in some countries, besides entering the innovation literature as a special branch of demand-side innovation policies (OECD 2011).

From a Southern perspective, combining specific analysis of the concrete situation with explicit evaluative criteria is particularly important to avoid the frequent temptation of just importing—copying or buying—fashionable instruments of policy.

Stressing the evaluative content of the NIS concept does not mean postulating that an optimal NIS exists, not even as an "ideal system". On the contrary, acknowledging diversity is an important strength of the conceptualization. Nevertheless, innovations can be more or less satisfactory for different actors, depending, for example, on the channels of information between them, on the weight of old routines, on asymmetries of knowledge and power. Policies can be better or worse at coping with related problems. Innovation processes are more or less interactive, distributed, and systemic depending in no small measure on such problems and policies. Something similar can be said concerning who benefits from—or is damaged by—innovations and to what extent.

And once again, the last sentence opens the way to the following remark, the fifth and last of this section: NIS describes situations in which conflict is present. Some conflicts have mainly to do with institutional competence and with inter-institutional problems. One example is the relative weight in the setting of research agendas of state organisms, academia, firms, and entrepreneurial organizations. Another source of conflict in the NIS is the extent to which the direct and indirect impacts upon national innovation capabilities are taken into account in decision-making by state organisms. More general or "contextual" conflicts can be seen in different scenarios (for example, those related to education). A relevant and somehow classic example concerns workers' participation in technological decisions on the shop floor. Sources of conflicts stemming from the environmental impacts of innovations are increasingly frequent and acute.

Generally speaking, different configurations and insertions of NIS affect different social groups unequally, opening favorable possibilities for some of them and threatening or directly damaging others. NISs are not socially neutral, because power is at stake in the relations between actors actually or potentially integrated in a given system. Thus, conflict is necessarily one dimension of NIS. Of course, this is equally valid in the North and in the South: here, we are stressing a feature that has been relatively neglected in the received conceptualization of NIS.

Let us summarize the above-mentioned essential aspects of the NIS concept when it is considered in relation to the South. First, it was elaborated in the North as an ex-post concept, whereas in the South it is basically an ex-ante notion. For analyzing facts and policies in the context of underdevelopment, it is particularly important to take into account two usually emphasized aspects of the concept: it is "relational" and it is a policy subject. Not less important in the same context is another aspect of the NIS conceptualization that somehow often seems to be forgotten: it has an evaluative dimension. Last but not least, an aspect of the NIS that can be seen quite easily from the North and cannot be unseen from the South is that it describes situations in which conflict is present.

POWER AND INNOVATION SYSTEMS

One of the purposes that oriented the elaboration of the NIS concept was to understand national economic performance by considering technology and institutions in a unified framework. The book by Freeman (1987), explaining Japan's success by the strength of its NIS, is a clear example of that. The NIS is seen as a potential source of national power. In fact, what the founding fathers of the concept see as an inspiring antecedent of the NIS concept—the elaboration by Friedrich List in the 1840s of the notion of "National System of Political Economy"—was directly oriented to foster German power against industrialized England. It stands to reason that the outcomes of innovation processes are highly dependent on the relative power of the agents and organizations that interact within them. Thus, two dimensions of power should be considered in connection with NIS: one is the "external" dimension (that is, power of the system as such); the other is the "internal" dimension (that is, the distribution of power between the different actors of the system).

Let us pause to recall a characterization of power and of those two dimensions. Concerning power in general, we rely on the theoretical and historic work of Michael Mann (1986, 1993, 2012, 2013a) about the "sources of social power".

A comprehensive definition of power sees it as "the ability to pursue and attain goals through mastery of one's environment" (Mann 1986: 6). Let us note for further reference that "one's environment" can be considered to be both natural and social. The two dimensions of power previously referred to are generally called collective power and distributive power. The first one is the power that an organized group has over nature or other people. The second one is the power within an organized group that is held by those with a major role in coordination and direction over those with a lesser role.

In a very strong sense, distributive power derives directly from collective power: "[I]n most social relations both aspects of power, distributive and collective, exploitative and functional, operate simultaneously and are intertwined. Indeed, the relationship between the two is dialectical. In pursuit of their goals, humans enter into cooperative, collective power relations with one another. But in implementing collective goals, social organization and a division of labor are set up. Organization and division of function carry an inherent tendency to distributive power, deriving from supervision and coordination. For the division of labor is deceptive. Although it involves specialization of function at all levels, the top overlooks and directs the whole. Those who occupy supervision and coordinating positions have an immense organizational superiority over the others" (Mann 1986: 5–6).

To analyze collective and distributive power in NIS, the fundamental sources of power should be recalled: "[T]he pursuit of almost all our motivational drives, our needs and goals, involves human beings in external relations with nature and other human beings. Human goals require both intervention in nature – a material life in the widest sense – and social cooperation" (Mann 1986: 5). That duality points to technology on the one hand and to institutions and organizations on the other. The NIS conceptualization attempts to study both dimensions in a unified framework.

It is useful to combine that conceptualization with Mann's theory of organizational power.

In that theory, power stems from social relations because of the particular "organizational means" each relation possesses for attaining human goals (Mann 1986: 2). The main sources of organizational power are the Ideological, Economic, Military, and Political relations in which human beings become involved. That is so because those relations stem from fundamental human needs and goals, such that their pursuit fosters the emergence of organized interaction networks that are able to coordinate the action of men and their use of resources.

"*Ideological power* derives from the human need to find ultimate meanings in life, to share norms and values, and to participate in aesthetic and ritual practices" (Mann 1993: 7). "*Economic power* derives from the need to extract, transform, distribute, and consume the resources of nature" (Idem). "*Military power* is the social organization of physical force. It derives from the necessary of organized defense and the utility of aggression" (Op. cit.: 8). "*Political power* derives from the usefulness of territorial and centralized regulation. Political power means *state* power" (Op. cit.: 9). Focusing on Ideological, Economic, Military, and Political relations characterizes what Mann calls his IEMP model.

In Mann's theory, organizational power depends to a large extent on available techniques. Tools and weapons are examples of "infrastructures" of power, which also include alphabets, which can be seen as communicative techniques. "The fundamental infrastructure of all four sources of [...] power is communications. Without effective passing of messages, personnel and resources, there can be no power" (Mann 1986: 136). The influence of technological change is stressed not only in the Neolithic (or Agricultural) Revolution or in the First and Second Industrial Revolutions but also in other cases. For example, the application of iron generated changes in tools and weapons, that is, in agriculture and war that "amounted to a technologically unified revolution. Iron inaugurated a social revolution" (Mann 1986: 185).

It can be asserted that power stems to a large extent from specific combinations of technology and social relations. For example, the combination of modern industrial technology and capitalist social relations is such that "[I]ndustrial capitalism may have changed the whole population's lives more than any other power process in human history" (Mann 2006: 386). The NIS conceptualization focuses on the combinations of technology and institutions in order to explain innovation processes. Thus, it makes sense to ask how the sources of organizational power in Mann's IEMP model shape NIS and influence its outputs.

Of course, economic relations are in general paramount: "[E]conomic networks exercise the most massive impact on collective power in the cumulative long term" (Mann 2006: 386). Moreover, an NIS really exists only if relevant economic organized networks foster innovations in the national context because they are benefited by them. Nevertheless, the historical experiences of technological change show that other types of relations are influential. For example, Germany "catching up" with England and "forging ahead" during the Second Industrial Revolution (also known as the wedding of science and technology) owed much to the power of state as well as to ideological elaborations, including those due to List. Perhaps military power was essential in that case as it was in fostering technological change in the USA during World War II and after. Ideological and cultural factors are also greatly influential. For example, the national case studies of innovation systems configurations analyzed in Freeman and Lundvall (1988) and Nelson (1993) include cultural traits and beliefs as main explanatory factors. Culture biases were recognized by Porter (1990) at the root of national preferences for determined products and processes that orient their innovative efforts.

The elaboration of the NIS framework was closely connected with explaining the expansion of economic collective power of some nations of East Asia during the last decades of the twentieth century. A comparison between such success and relative failures in Latin America has also been frequent in that framework (Freeman 1996).

The East Asian developmental state was able to systematically upgrade the knowledge content of indigenous production. As Amsden (1989: 29) recalls in the case of South Korea, "... in Korea's shipyards, steel mills...or electronic factories, the credo has become 'invest now in inhouse technological capability—even if outside expertise is cheaper – to reap the rewards of self-reliance later'". Political power was fundamental, fostered by the ideological power of nationalism at least in some cases. Nationalism fostered technological upgrading, as Nelson wrote in the '90s: "[T]here is clearly a new spirit of what might be called 'technonationalism' in the air, combining a strong belief that the technological capabilities of a nation's firms are a key source of their competitive prowess, with a belief that these capabilities are in a sense national, and can be built by national action" (Nelson 1993: 3).

In Japan and South Korea, success was made possible by an alliance of the organized power network of a quite stable state leadership and top bureaucracy with the networks of big entrepreneurs. But a closer look is needed. For example, Khan and Blankenburg (2009) relate the technological success of South Korea during the '60s, '70s, and '80s to a very specific distribution of internal power: the state could enforce a "classic infant industry strategy" that included productive upgrading and learning by entrepreneurs partly because of the weakness of landed elites, which "denied the chaebol the opportunity of offering to share rents with powerful social forces in exchange for their support in protecting inefficient rents" (Op. cit.: 350).

In Latin America, the state also fostered such an industrialization strategy, but its degree of autonomy from the upper classes was too weak to enforce the transient character of protection and its necessary counterpart in terms of upgrading and learning. In Latin America, "alliances between strong landed elites and emerging industrialists" hampered infant industry strategies (Khan and Blankenburg 2009: 359). That helps to understand the roots of a fundamental distinction made by Fajnzylber (1984) between East Asian "learning protectionism" and Latin American "frivolous protectionism".

In general, "success or failure of rent-management strategies for industrialization is largely determined by the *compatibility* of technological and institutional strategies for late development with political constraints arising from inner-societal power constellations as from transnational—external—influences" (Khan and Blankenburg 2009: 359). That is still valid beyond industrialization. The "strategy that is most likely to be effectively implemented and enforced in a country can depend amongst other things on its internal distribution of organizational power" (Op. cit.: 337). In turn, such a configuration of power influences the outcomes of innovation processes, the collective national power that stems from them as well as the internal distribution of gains and losses generated by innovation.

Given the relevance of organizational power for what really happens with a given Innovation System, when it comes to policies a main issue needs careful consideration: which are the really existing or potentially emergent networks such that their interests are connected with the proposed strategy? That is a particularly difficult question when democratization of knowledge is pursued and inclusive innovations policies are proposed. Democratization in general, understood as empowering "people", can be considered to be the set of processes countervailing distributive power. As already stressed, such processes have to face an intrinsic difficulty because "distributive power derives originally from collective power, i.e. that stratification derives from social cooperation" (Mann 2006: 366). Strong ideological power is surely needed: the ideological power related to democratic values.

UNDERDEVELOPMENT AND THE PROBLEM OF INTERACTIONS

The issue of power was highlighted when looking at NIS from the South, but it is also fundamental in the North. Considering technological and organizational power brings us again to the problem of interactions. It is at the core of the NIS framework: "Perhaps the most basic characteristic of the innovation system approach is that it is 'interactionist'" (Lundvall 2007: 107).

The problem of interactions is a guiding thread for further elaborating the characterization of underdevelopment presented in Chapter 2, in order to go from facts to policies. This section could in some sense be seen as the converse of the previous section (that is, "the South as seen from the NIS framework"). As before, we combine that framework with the Latin American thinking about knowledge and development. The following quote links issues already considered with what follows and is the guiding thread of this section: "[W]hen, why and how does a society create a demand for science in a given historical situation? What internal and external factors determine the science supply? How do the fluxes of supply and demand move across the different socio-economic circuits? Who profits from the results of scientific and technological research? How do the different actors react to external demands? How and why does the productive structure and the scientific and technological infrastructure alienate from each other? What role corresponds to the state, particularly in developing countries?" (Sabato 1975: 129; our translation).

The first question poses the fundamental issue of demand. Weak market demand of advanced qualifications and knowledge addressed to internal sources characterizes the peripheral condition. That fact stems from the prevailing economic structure and shows that "Southern" economies are not knowledge-based and innovation-driven. This constitutes a main obstacle for economic development.

This still characterized Latin America in the beginning of the twenty-first century (Castaldi et al. 2009). Almost fifty years ago, that trait was seen as a major aspect of underdevelopment in general by the Sussex Manifesto: "the 'need' for science and technology in the developing countries is unlikely to take the form of a commercial demand coming from individual producers" (Singer et al. 1970: 20). This is forcefully put forwards by Dani Rodrik, who asserts that it is not the lack of scientists or research laboratories that is the reason why science is not used as a lever for development, but the lack of knowledge demand from production (Rodrik 2007: 101).

A direct consequence of that phenomenon is that advanced indigenous capabilities in research and innovation and advanced training are weakly fostered, a problem much more serious today than half a century ago (Mazzoleni and Nelson 2009: 384).

Since knowledge demand stemming from the economic dynamics is on average scarce in peripheral countries, the links between actors potentially belonging to the NIS are weak and the system itself may be more virtual than real.

To study such problems—as well as the potential contributions of science and technology to development—a model that became known as "the Sabato triangle" was elaborated almost half a century ago (Sabato and Botana 1968). It proposed "as a model of interactions a triangle with its vertexes representing, respectively, the scientific and technological infrastructure, the productive structure and the government, defined as the fundamental protagonists of those interactions" (Sabato 1975: 130). The Sabato triangle can be seen as the core of the Innovation System. The fundamental idea is that "the triangle" and the System as such exist only if the connections between the needed protagonists of innovation processes are real and minimally strong: a triangle has vertexes and sides.

It can be said that the core of the NIS plays a fundamental role in major innovations while incremental innovations stem from a wider set of processes and interactions: "[T]he process of technical change in industry thus takes two main forms: radical innovations in products and processes which have increasingly originated in professional R&D laboratories in universities, industry and government; second, incremental improvements of products and processes associated with increasing scale of investing and learning from experience of production and use" (Freeman and Soete 1997: 103).

Let us pause to stress that globalization does not entail that the nation-states become unimportant. Rather, the opposite can be asserted, particularly when the interests of people who are not privileged are taken into account: "[W]hen the economy, and the forces and patterns of behavior that accompany it, are truly international, the only institution that can effectively interpose itself between those forces and the unprotected individual is the national state. Such states are all that can stand between their citizens and the unrestricted, unrepresentative, unlegitimated capacities of markets, insensitive and unresponsive supranational administrations, and unregulated processes over which individuals and communities have no control. The state is the largest unit in which, by habit and convention, men and women can feel they have a stake and which is, or can be made to appear, responsive to their interests and desires" (Judt 2008: 424).

In particular, the role of the nation-state is one of the motives that explain why the national dimension of innovation systems is so relevant. But it is not the only motive for that, as follows from Sabato's approach. In fact, his point of view leads to the study of three types of interactions: first, between the three "vertexes", second, inside each of them, and third, between the "triangle" as a whole and the external world. Weak endogenous demand of knowledge addressed to indigenous suppliers means that the "side" connecting the productive structure with the national scientific and technological infrastructure is weak. It also means that the knowledge supply mainly connects the national productive structure with knowledge generation abroad. Generally speaking, we can say that peripheral NISs are shaped by an insertion in the international economy based on a specialization in low and mainly imported added value of knowledge and high qualifications. Redressing this dismal structural situation cannot be done without the nation-state. Moreover, the concrete situations where the Sabato's triangle or the NIS works properly from a functioning system point of view have seen the national state, through its diverse organizations, heavily backing the process. This is clear even in countries, like the USA, where apparently the market has the upper hand (Weiss 2014; Block and Keller 2011).

Paying attention to (the level of) demand is inherent to the NIS conceptualization. In fact, "it might be argued that the innovation system perspective came out of a criticism of the relative neglect of the demand side" (Lundvall 2016: 598).

From the quote that we took as a guide for this section, it follows that, in peripheral NISs, it is difficult to avoid that "the productive structure and the scientific and technological infrastructure alienate from each other". The history of economic development shows that, in the few success stories of escaping from the peripheral condition, the role that corresponded to the state—the third vertex in Sabato's triangle—was especially active. A widely commented case—mentioned above—is the developmental state of East Asia.

Now, external subordination, as one of the defining dimensions of underdevelopment, has curtailed the possibilities for developmental policies in development countries. That can be seen in international agreements and treaties that are a direct consequence of power asymmetries. The Economic Commission for Latin America and the Caribbean (ECLAC) points out some of the effects of these agreements on developing countries:

"the WTO Agreement on Trade-Related Investment Measures (TRIMs) has sharply curtailed the ability of developing countries to impose performance requirements on foreign firms, and has prohibited practices such as demanding minimum quotas of domestically produced goods in firms' procurement or exports" (ECLAC 2016: 150). "The policymaking discretion of developing countries can also be reduced by provisions contained in certain North-South free trade treaties (in particular those signed by the United States) that limit their capacity to apply capital controls, even on a temporary basis, in order to preserve financial stability [...]. This is indeed paradoxical, considering that in the wake of the global financial crisis the International Monetary Fund—a traditional apologist of financial account openness—recognized the usefulness of capital controls for coping with speculative capital flows" (ECLAC 2016: 151). "The commitments assumed in trade or investment agreements can also limit developing countries' policy discretion in public procurement, the treatment of State enterprises, and procedures whereby governments prepare their health, environmental or consumer protection regulations" (Idem).

Looking at underdevelopment from the problem of interactions leads naturally to learning processes. As said, the knowledge content of the actual structural change, and the increasing knowledge basis of social relations in general, can be seen as a suggestion stemming from the factual approach to pay central attention to the learning processes in general, without restricting such attention to educational processes or to high-tech activities.

Let us stress again that learning happens when people undertake challenging processes of problem-solving. At the society level, what counts is the collective capacity to learn, which implies to a good extent learning by interacting. We can define interactive learning spaces as those situations in which different actors are able to strengthen their capacities to learn while interacting in the search for the solution to a given problem. Interactive learning spaces foster collective action in knowledge terms. Their appearance, consolidation, and expansion are ways of building innovation systems from below.

The seeds of such spaces are the concrete collaborative initiatives taken by actors with an identified problem and actors able to search for a workable solution; we call these encounters innovative circuits. Detecting innovative circuits is not straightforward, because they do not respond to any previously determined organizational scheme. They are situations, embedded in society and in economic behavior, which may be seen as the seed of virtuous circles of learning, capability building, technological upgrading, and potential growth. These situations, studied at the micro level, are very instructive concerning the reasons why this type of initiatives takes place, the difficulties that appear once the dialogues begin, the ways in which they can be mastered, and, particularly, how the diffusion processes of the related innovations occur—if they occur at all. This issue of diffusion of innovations derived from problem-solving activities at the micro level is of importance from an NIS perspective. If an innovative circuit remains encapsulated (meaning that the solution found does not trespass the boundaries of the first initiative), its innovative impact will be small. If it is amplified by the expanded use of the solution, the new actors involved will contribute to a learning process that may expand further. Interactive learning spaces are formed from these innovative micro-strengths and their diffusion.

The concept of "niche", presented in Geels's (2014) multi-level perspective on innovation, has some features that are useful to characterize innovative circuits, all differences notwithstanding. "Niches are important, because they provide locations for learning processes, e.g. about technical specifications, user preferences, public policies, symbolic meanings"; "Niches also provide space to build the social networks which support innovations, e.g. supply chains, user–producer relationships" (Geels 2014: 912). But even more characteristically, niches allow for "more space to go in different directions and try out variety" (Op. cit.: 913). Moreover, "[C]ompared to dominant regimes the actors in niches are few, their interrelations sparse, the focal technology immature and the guiding rules in constant flux. Niche technologies can then be seen as 'hopeful monstrosities' (Mokyr 1990): promising in potential, meagre in performance. For this reason niche technologies often need to be protected from pressures exerted by the incumbent sociotechnical regimes until they have become mature enough to enter the market" (Schot and Kanger 2016: 14).

All this is related, in the case of Geels's analysis, to the emergence of radical innovations within a given technological regime, but we may consider that it is also related to tailor-made solutions that are sought because existing solutions are not satisfactory for a given actor. We are accustomed to think about radical innovation as alternatives to whole systems of doing things, in energy, health prevention, transport, payment systems, and so on. But the radical character of innovations, as innovation itself, depends on who is judging whether an innovation is so and whether it is radical. When different heuristics to approaching problems are needed to find satisfactory solutions—and innovative circuits often are built from such need—having space for exploring variety is important.

Innovative circuits where people interact around problems and possible solutions may or may not evolve toward interactive learning spaces; this depends on several factors of which the type of innovation policy in place plays no minor role. A point to make here is that, although innovative circuits may be ubiquitous in any society, their scaling-up into interactive learning spaces is a more difficult social process.

It is worth recalling that the concept of interactive learning spaces can be useful in two ways: it can help to focus on actors, interactions, and the search for solutions in a given situation, and it can help to focus on the opportunities that actors have to behave that way. From this point of view, the differences between North and Global South in terms of knowledge and learning can be summarized by saying that the North is rich in interactive learning spaces whereas the Global South is poor in interactive learning spaces. This is a main dimension of learning divides.

On the Historical Roots and Present Challenges of Structural Change

Development policy in the Global South has to face the learning divides between central and peripheral countries. For that, it may be useful to remember some facts concerning how this type of divide appears in history and is—sometimes—overcome. With such an aim, the factual approach to development discussed above and focusing on the role of knowledge as a key structural change will be revisited.

It is assumed that, to a large extent, power stems from specific combinations of technology and social relations. That entails—as Mann asserted about the social revolution fostered by the appearance of iron technologies—that great changes in technology can be the starting point of immense social transformations. A first momentous example is the appearance of agricultural and husbandry techniques. Such innovations constitute what North (2005) calls "The First Economic Revolution". In agrarian-based societies, extracting and managing the surplus of agriculture and husbandry were key issues for the emergence and success or failure of Ideological, Economic, Military, and Political organized networks. Almost all humanity lived in (quite different types of) agrarian-based societies up until to quite recently.

During the eighteenth century, in a tiny corner of the world, social relations opened possibilities for another great technological change that came to be known as the Industrial Revolution. It was a wave of innovations centered on the textile sector and, above all, on the generation of energy. The latter was so relevant that such technological change has been called "The Revolution of Energy", starting the first machine era, because the steam engine gave rise to a steep increase in generation of energy in such a way that it profoundly changed production and transport: "[I]t all started with steam" (Cipolla 1967: 52).

Until the Industrial Revolution, economic "growth was normally not sustainable and remained vulnerable to set-backs and shocks, both man-made and natural" (Mokyr 2005: 286). This situation started to change but the persistence of so-called modern economic growth required more than the technological innovations that characterize the Industrial Revolution.

Such innovations and the ones that followed them substantially increased the economic and political power of what became during the nineteenth century the industrialized West and its domination over almost all the Rest (of the world). Societies with a fundamentally agrarian base became peripheries of the few centers where industry-based societies first emerged. Thus, it is not strange that industrialization was seen as the backbone of different strategies for overcoming backwardness in the peripheries as well as their subordination to the centers when, in the midst of decolonization and Cold War, the problem of development rose to the top of political and ideological agendas. But by then the decisive issue concerning economic growth and technological power went beyond industrial technologies. As observed by Mokyr, "in the early stages of the Industrial Revolution, many of the important advances owed little to science in a direct way. However, had technological progress been independent of what happened at the loftier intellectual level, had it consisted purely of disseminating best-practice existing procedures, standardizing them, and hoping for learning-by-doing effects, the process would eventually have run into diminishing returns and fizzled out. What was it that prevented that from happening in the decades following the burst of macroinventions we identify with the classic Industrial Revolution?" (Mokyr 2005: 289). A brief answer is that the wedding of science and technology became the main propeller of productive capabilities. That means, as already stressed, that the epistemic base for doing things (useful arts) was systematically widened through closer relations with scientific knowledge.

In the second half of the nineteenth century, the industrializing West already showed that knowledge and innovation were becoming the main causes of the new phenomenon of sustained economic growth. There advanced scientific knowledge began replacing practical tinkering, methodical and systematic but with limited cognitive foundation, as the fundamental propeller of innovations. That entailed an accelerated expansion of technological change.

As shown above, a long-range divergence in economic output and power found some fundamental knowledge roots in that period. "The effective deployment of knowledge, scientific or otherwise, in the service of production is the primary—if not the only—cause for the rapid growth of Western economies in the past centuries" (Mokyr 2005: 287). The Second Economic Revolution (North 2005) entailed a clear differentiation between centers—where such revolution was taking place—and peripheries which, great differences notwithstanding, had something in common: the wedding of science and technology was alien to all of them.

It can be said that, with the wedding of science and technology, innovation became "systemic" in the industrialized societies of the West. That is exemplified by the role and connections of two institutional creations of the nineteenth century where this wedding took place. One of them is the industrial laboratory of Research and Development (R&D): "[S]ince the relation is one of interaction, the expression 'science-related' technology is usually preferable to the expression 'science-based' technology with its implication of an oversimplified one-way movement of ideas. Marx spoke of the machine as the 'point of entry' of science into the industrial system, but today this expression might be used with more justification about the R&D department" (Freeman and Soete 1997: 15).

Sabato said that, in such laboratories, the production of technology rose from an artisan phase to an industrial phase. They were to become main sites of advanced knowledge production directly oriented toward innovation; increasing relations with states and the academic sector would characterize their expansion. In the second case, relations were fueled by another institutional creation, the emergence of the research university. It was fostered by what is called the Humboldtian project of including research as a second mission of universities, with similar relevance as teaching and closely connected with it. The ensuing transformation of universities has been called "The Academic Revolution" (Clark 1995: 1). It started in Germany and was creatively imported to the United States, where the involvement of the academy in economic activities was more directly promoted. Around 1900, those two countries had caught up with Britain and forged ahead in technologically based growth. Universities became main generators of knowledge. Their connections with firms and their R&D laboratories were early exemplified in the expansion of chemical industries in Germany. In that country, as already recalled, university transformation, scientific research, and technological innovation were promoted by the state as a way of overcoming English economic (and military) superiority. Other Western states followed that route because of prestige, production, weapons, and political power. Thus, the core triangle of the NIS—productive sector, knowledge generation, and states—emerged in the central countries. It became able to connect—in a quite systemic manner—education, research, innovation, and production. As more actors and organizations became involved in those connections, NISs grew around the "triangle" and were shaped in each country by its specific economic, political, ideological, and military relations as well as by its geopolitical context.

It can be said that economic development takes place when technological innovation becomes a main driver of economic growth, in such a way that the production of goods and services is upgraded to more complex and diversified activities. When industrialization opened the way to the wedding of science and technology, economic development was ensured and the continuity of economic growth characterized a new period in human history. It started in the West. Several attempts to follow suit took place in the Rest. In recent decades, the most successful ones have been in East Asia. There, in very specific internal and external contexts, the upgrading of production was strongly fostered by the so-called developmental state in close, but not always friendly, collaboration with firms.

Following Freeman's (1987) interpretation of Japan's lessons, the NIS intellectual tradition has regarded the systemic way in which a national effort in East Asia to catch up was pursued, as an important factor for success. The relevance for such projects of indigenous innovation and advanced learning was early understood. Contrary to what was said some time ago, in those countries the "third vertex" of the triangle—scientific, technological, and Higher Education structure—was thoroughly considered and strongly connected with the other two: state and production. Thus, productive transformation went beyond industrialization based on high investment and cheap labor, becoming able to systematically add value stemming from advanced knowledge and high qualifications.

The rapidly industrializing countries of East Asia were able to greatly profit from the Revolution of Information and Communication Technologies (ICTs). If the Revolution of Energy centered on the steam engine opened the way to the mechanization of manufacture and thus to the transition to industry-based societies, the ICTs fostered a comparable transformation. Changes go beyond information and have to do with scientific and technological knowledge in general. Its generation, use, and scope have been fostered to such an extent by the ICTs that this Revolution of Information opened the transition, in advanced industrial capitalist countries, to a knowledge-based society where (a restructured) capitalism is the fundamental configuration of social relations.

The emergence of such societies characterizes what is called the North but its very asymmetric consequences in terms of power are seen all over the world. Knowledge-based and finance-dominated capitalism is the main factor that fosters and shapes globalization. Moreover, "[T]he ability of international financial agents to move capital and resources across borders and between currencies constrains governments and effectively gives capital veto power over an array of policies. The fact that capital movements are still unregulated, and that tax evasion continues to undermine States, despite the prospect of a new financial crisis in the making, is a testament to the political power of capital. It is imperative to build up global counterweights, from the public sector, to prevent the current set-up—whereby profits are privatized and losses are socialized—from simply continuing" (ECLAC 2016: 170).

Capitalist power, and especially financial capitalism power, may be a difficult obstacle for Sustainable Development: "[T]he greatest merit of the Paris Agreement is the long-term signal it sends to the effect that economies must move toward decarbonization, even though it makes no provision for reducing the supply of fossil fuels, an idea resisted by the oil industry, by countries that depend on oil exports, and by investor groups with interests in that sector. Banks, including the development banks, are among the most egregious laggards in terms of adjusting their policies: they have maintained their financing practices and their portfolio exposure to carbon-intensive sectors" (ECLAC 2016: 150).

In the old and new "centers" of the global capitalist world, the basic core of the NIS—the triangle with the state, the productive structure, and the knowledge infrastructure as vertexes—becomes stronger, particularly because advanced knowledge is increasingly important both for the political and military power of the first "vertex" and for the economic power of the second one. Since such knowledge becomes incorporated into a wider set of practices, innovation tends to be more distributed and new actors can be seen as connected with the Innovation System. In this context, interactions are diversified and multiplied and become more complicated. When they are strongly systemic, the collective power of the NIS expands. In other words, the aspects of innovation that the NIS framework stresses—its distributed, interactive, and systemic character—are perhaps even more relevant in knowledge-based economies than in industrial economies. Something similar happens with the presence of conflict related to innovation and learning. Examples are related to access to Higher Education and expensive health, to innovation in agriculture and food production, and to environmental impacts of different technologies. Examples can also be seen in less mentioned but no less relevant issues like the agenda of research and innovation (that is, of done and un-done science) (Hess 2007).

For the Global South, and specifically for the world of underdevelopment, the emergence in the North of a knowledge-based society frames in a new way the issue of economic development. Let us consider again Chang's (2011) plea for a new developmentalism. He rightly asserts that "we need to go back to the 'productionist' tradition of old development economics and put the transformation in productive capabilities that go beyond individuals back at the heart of our development thinking" (Chang 2011: 55). This old tradition equated productive transformation with industrialization; now, it has to be seen as the incorporation of advanced knowledge and high qualifications to every socially valuable production of goods and services. The normative approach cannot be neglected: upgrading weapons production can be seen as an example of economic development but it is alien to human development.

Chang (2011: 56) is also right when he says that "development economists of the old vintage did not pay much attention on the process of technological development in the process of productive transformation. Productive transformation was seen mainly in terms of capital accumulation and the transfer of investible surplus and labour force from the traditional sector". The NIS tradition has clearly shown that productive transformation should be seen mainly in terms of learning processes because these are the fundamental social processes when knowledge becomes the main resource. Such a lesson shows how useful it has been that economists working with the NIS framework became interested in development problems. Now, if "development economists of the old vintage" did not concentrate their attention on technological changes and the specific aspects of the peripheral condition, some non-economists (including already-quoted Latin American scholars) did that in ways that partially anticipated the NIS framework and helped to understand the nature of underdevelopment. So we should not go back to the old disciplinary perspective of development economics, something that one of its most famous scholars acknowledged several decades ago: "development economics started out as a spearhead of an effort that was to bring all-around emancipation from backwardness. If that effort is to fulfill its promise, the challenge posed by dismal politics must be met rather than avoided or evaded. By now it has become quite clear that this cannot be done by economics alone. It is for this reason that the decline of development economics cannot fully reversed: our subdiscipline had achieved its considerable luster and excitement through the implicit idea that it could slay the dragon from backwardness virtually by itself or, at least, that its contribution to this task was central. We now know that this is not so; a consoling thought is that we may have gained in maturity what we have lost in excitement" (Hirschman 1981: 23).

Academic contribution to Sustainable Human Development cannot be the task of economics alone. Interdisciplinary Development Studies are required to study the type of productive transformations that is needed, the combinations of technological and organizational power that have to be taken into account, and the learning processes for knowledge democratization that should be fostered. Hirschman advocated "trespassing" disciplinary boundaries in order to go "from economics to politics and beyond". Freeman advocated breaking isolated disciplinary kingdoms: "[N]either sociologists, nor economists, nor political scientists have satisfactory theories of social change and it is unlikely that they will develop them unless they overcome their fragmentation into separate jealously guarded kingdoms and learn to cooperated with each other and with natural scientists..." (Freeman 1977: 84). Nowadays, "thinking on development is pulling together, breaking out of disciplinary silos and drawing on ideas, concepts, and theories across the natural and social sciences" (Currie-Alder et al. 2014: 2).

On the basis of the NIS framework presented in this chapter, the propositional approach to Sustainable Human Development will be revisited. It was sketched in Chapter 2 with knowledge democratization as its foundation. In the next chapter, such an approach in terms of learning and innovation will be elaborated.

REFERENCES

Amsden, A. (1989). *Asia's Next Giant. South Korea and late Industrialization.* New York/Oxford: Oxford University Press.
Arocena, R., & Sutz, J. (2000). Looking at National Systems of Innovation from the South. *Industry and Innovation, 7*(1), 55–75.

Arocena, R., & Sutz, J. (2012). Research and Innovation Policies for Social Inclusion: An Opportunity for Developing Countries. *Innovation and Development, 2*(1), 147–158.

Bell, M., & Pavitt, K. (1997). Technological Accumulation and Industrial Growth: Contrasts Between Developed and Developing Countries. In D. Archibugi & J. Michie (Eds.), *Technology, Globalization and Economic Performance* (pp. 83–137). Cambridge: Cambridge University Press.

Block, F. L., & Keller, M. R. (Eds.). (2011). *State of Innovation: The U.S. Government's Role in Technology Development*. Boulder: Paradigm Publishers.

Castaldi, C., Cimoli, M., Correa, N., & Dosi, G. (2009). Technological Learning, Policy Regimes, and Growth: The Long-Term Patterns and Some Specificities of a 'Globalized' Economy. In M. Cimoli, G. Dossi, & J. Stiglitz (Eds.), *Industrial Policy and Development: The Political Economy of Capabilities Accumulation* (pp. 39–75). Oxford: Oxford University Press.

Chang, H.-J. (2011). Hamlet Without the Prince of Denmark: How Development Has Disappeared from Today's 'Development' Discourse. In S. Khan & J. Christiansen (Eds.), *Towards New Developmentalism: Market as Means rather than Master* (pp. 47–58). Abingdon: Routledge.

Chataway, J., Hanlin, B., & Kaplinsky, R. (2013). *Inclusive Innovation. An Architecture for Policy Development* (IKD Working Paper No. 65). Milton Keynes: The Open University.

Cipolla, C. (1967). *An Economic History of World Population*. Harmondsworth: Penguin.

Clark, B. (1995). *Places of Inquiry: Research and Advanced Education in Modern Universities*. Berkeley: The California University Press.

Couto, M. C., Scerri, M., & Marhajah, R. (2013). *Inequality and Development Challenges*. London: IDRC-Routledge.

Cozzens, S., & Sutz, J. (2014). Innovation in Informal Settings: Reflections and Proposals for a Research Agenda. *Innovation and Development, 4*(1), 5–31.

Cozzens, S., & Thakur, D. (2014). *Innovation and Inequality. Emerging Technologies in an Unequal World*. New York: Edward Elgar.

Crespi, G., & Dutrenit, G. (2014). *Science, Technology and Innovation Policies for Development: The Latin American Experience*. Dordrecht: Springer.

Currie-Alder, B., Kanbur, R., Malone, D., & Medhora, R. (2014). The State of Development Thought. In B. Currie-Alder, R. Kanbur, D. Malone, & R. Medhora (Eds.), *International Development. Ideas, Experience, and Prospects* (pp. 1–20). New York: Oxford University Press.

ECLAC (Economic Commission for Latin America and the Caribbean). (2016). *Horizons 2030: Equality at the Centre of Sustainable Development* (LC/G.2660(SES.36/3). Santiago de Chile: Economic Commission for Latin America and the Caribbean.

Fajnzylber, F. (1984). *La industrialización trunca de América Latina*. México D.F.: Centro Editor.

Freeman, C. (1977). Malthus with a Computer. In A. Teich (Ed.), *Technology and Man's Future* (pp. 82–98). New York: St. Martin's Press.

Freeman, C. (1987). *Technology Policy and Economic Performance – Lessons from Japan*. London: Pinter Publishers.

Freeman, C. (1996). Catching Up and Falling Behind: The Case of Asia and Latin America. In J. de la Mothe & G. Paquet (Eds.), *Evolutionary Economics and the New International Political Economy* (pp. 160–179). London: Pinter.

Freeman, C., & Lundvall, B.-A. (Eds.). (1988). *Small Countries Facing Technological Revolution*. London: Pinter.

Freeman, C., & Soete, L. (1997). *The Economics of Industrial Innovation* (3rd ed.). Cambridge, MA: The MIT Press.

Geels, F. W. (2014). From Sectoral Systems of Innovation to Socio-Technical Systems Insights About Dynamics and Change from Sociology and Institutional Theory. *Research Policy, 33*(6–7), 897–920.

Heeks, R. (2013). Conceptualizing Inclusive Innovation: Modifying Systems of Innovation Frameworks to Understand Diffusion of New Technology to Low-Income Countries. *European Journal of Development Research, 25*, 333–355.

Hess, D. (2007). *Alternative Pathways in Science and Industry. Activism, Innovation, and the Environment in an Era of Globalization*. Cambridge, MA: The MIT Press.

Hirschman, A. (1981). *Essays in Trespassing. Economics to Politics and Beyond*. Cambridge: Cambridge University Press.

Johnson, B., & Andersen, A. D. (2012). *Learning, Innovation and Inclusive Development*. Globelics Thematic Report No 1, Denmark. Available at: http:// vbn.aau.dk/files/70880770/Learning_Innovation_and_Inclusive_Development.pdf. Accessed 10 May 2017.

Judt, T. (2008). *Reappraisals. Reflections on the Forgotten Twentieth Century*. New York: The Penguin Press.

Khan, M., & Blankenburg, S. (2009). The Political Economy of Industrial Policy in Asia and Latin America. In G. Dosi, M. Cimoli, & J. E. Stiglitz (Eds.), *Industrial Policy and Development: The Political Economy of Capabilities Accumulation* (pp. 336–377). Oxford: Oxford University Press.

Kraemer-Mbula, E., & Wunsch-Vincent, S. (Eds.). (2016). *Informal Economy in Developing Nations. Hidden Engine of Innovation?* Cambridge, UK: Cambridge University Press.

Lorenz, E., & Valeyre, A. (2007). Organizational Forms and Innovative Performance: A Comparison of the EU-15. In E. Lorenz & B. A. Lundvalll (Eds.), *How Europe's Economies Learn. Coordinating Competing Models* (pp. 227, 248). Oxford: Oxford University Press.

Lundvall, B. Å. (1985). *Product Innovation and User-Producer Interaction* (Industrial Development Research Series No. 31). Aalborg: Aalborg University Press.

Lundvall, B. Å. (1988). Innovation as an Interactive Process: from User-Producer Interaction to the National System of Innovation. In G. Dosi, C. Freeman, R. Nelson, G. Silverberg, & L. Soete (Eds.), *Technical Change and Economic Theory* (pp. 349–369). London: Pinter.

Lundvall, B. Å. (Ed.). (1992). *National Systems of Innovation. Towards a Theory of Innovation and Interactive Learning.* London: Pinter.

Lundvall, B. Å. (2007). National Innovation Systems—Analytical Concept and Development Tool. *Industry and Innovation, 14*(1), 95–119.

Lundvall, B. Å. (2010). Postscript: Innovation System Research – Where It Comes from and Where It Might Go. In B. A. Lundvalll (Ed.), *National Systems of Innovation. Towards a Theory of Innovation and Interactive Learning* (pp. 317–366). London: Anthem Press.

Lundvall, B. Å. (2016). Innovation Systems and Development: History, Theory and Challenges. In E. Reinert, J. Ghosh, & R. Kattel (Eds.), *Handbook of Alternative Theories of Economic Development* (pp. 594–612). Cheltenham: Edward Elgar.

Lundvall, B. Å., & Borrás, S. (1997). *The Globalising Learning Economy: Implications for Innovation Policy.* Policy document of the Targeted Socio-Economic Research Program, European Commission, Bruxelles.

Lundvall, B. Å., Joseph, K. J., Chaminade, C., & Vang, J. (2011). *Handbook of Innovation Systems and Developing Countries: Building Domestic Capabilities in a Global Setting.* Northampton: Edward Elgar.

Mann, M. (1986). *The Sources of Social Power, Vol. I, A History of Power from the Beginning to AD 1760.* Cambridge: Cambridge University Press.

Mann, M. (1993). *The Sources of Social Power, Vol. II: The Rise of Classes and Nation-States, 1760–1914.* Cambridge: Cambridge University Press.

Mann, M. (2006). The Sources of Social Power Revisited: A Response to Criticism. In J. Hall & R. Schroeder (Eds.), *An Anatomy of Power. The Social Theory of Michael Mann* (pp. 343–396). Cambridge: Cambridge University Press.

Mann, M. (2012). *The Sources of Social Power, Vol. III (2012): Global Empires and Revolution, 1890–1945.* Cambridge: Cambridge University Press.

Mann, M. (2013a). *The Sources of Social Power. Vol. IV Globalizations, 1945–2011.* Cambridge: Cambridge University Press.

Martin, B. (2010). Inside the Public Scientific System: Changing Modes of Knowledge Production. In R. Smits, S. Kuhlmann, & P. Shapira (Eds.), *The Theory and Practice of Innovation Policy* (pp. 25–50). Cheltenham, UK: Edward Elgar.

Mazzoleni, R., & Nelson, R. (2009). The Roles of Research at Universities and Public Labs in Economic Catch-Up. In G. Dosi, M. Cimoli, & J. E. Stiglitz (Eds.), *Industrial Policy and Development. The Political Economy of Capabilities Accumulation* (pp. 378–408). Oxford: Oxford University Press.

Mokyr, J. (1990). *The Lever of Riches: Technological Creativity and Economic Progress.* New York: Oxford University Press.

Mokyr, J. (2005). The Intellectual Origins of Modern Economic Growth. *The Journal of Economic History, 65*(2), 285–351.

Muller, J. (2010). *Befit for Change: Social Construction of Endogenous Technology in the South.* FAU conference, Gjerrild.

Nelson, R. (1993). *National Innovation Systems.* Cary: Oxford University Press.

North, D. (2005). *Understanding the Process of Economic Change.* Princeton: Princeton University Press.

OECD. (2011). *Demand-Side Innovation Policies.* Paris: OECD Publishing.

Papaioannou, T. (2014). How Inclusive Can Innovation and Development Be in the Twenty-First Century? *Innovation and Development, 4*(2), 187–202.

Porter, M. (1990). *The Competitive Advantage of Nations.* New York: The Free Press.

RICYT. (2001). Red Iberoamericana de Indicadores de Ciencia y Tecnología. Standardisation of Indicators of Technological Innovation in Latin American and Caribbean Countries. BOGOTA MANUAL. Available at: http://www.ricyt.org/manuales/doc_view/149-bogota-manual. Accssed 10 May 2017.

Rodrik, D. (2007). *One Economics, Many Recipes: Globalization, Institutions, and Economic Growth.* Princeton: Princeton University Press.

Sabato, J. (Ed.). (1975). *El pensamiento latinoamericano en la problemática ciencia – tecnología – desarrollo – dependencia.* Buenos Aires: Editorial PAIDOS.

Sabato, J., & Botana, N. (1968). La ciencia y la tecnología en el desarrollo futuro de América Latina. *Revista de la Integración* 3 (Buenos Aires).

Schot, J., & Kanger, L. (2016). Deep Transitions: Emergence, Acceleration, Stabilization and Directionality. *SPRU Working Papers,* 2016–15.

Sen, A. (1999). *Development as Freedom.* New York: Anchor Books.

Singer, H., Cooper, C., Desai, R. C., Freeman, C., Gish, O., Hill, S., & Oldham, G. (1970). *The Sussex Manifesto: Science and Technology to Developing Countries During the Second Development Decade, IDS Reprints, 101.* Brighton: Institute of Development Studies.

Srinivas, S. (2014). Demand and Innovation. Path Towards Inclusive Development. In S. Ramani (Ed.), *Innovation in India: Combining Economic Growth with Inclusive Development* (pp. 78–106). India: Cambridge University Press.

Sutz, J. (2012). Measuring Innovation in Developing Countries: Some Suggestions to Achieve More Accurate and Useful Indicators. *International Journal of Technological Learning, Innovation and Development (IJTLID),* 5(1/2), 40–57.

von Hippel, E. (1998). *The Sources of Innovation.* New York: Oxford University Press.

Weiss, L. (2014). *America Inc.?: Innovation and Enterprise in the National Security State.* Ithaca/London: Cornell University Press.

Woolthuis, R., Lankhuizen, M., & Gilsing, V. (2005). A System Failure Framework for Innovationpolicy Design. *Technovation, 25,* 609–619.

CHAPTER 5

Inclusive Innovation Systems and Policies

Learning and innovation are social processes of interaction between different organizations and collective actors. Such more or less systemic interactions shape the strength and orientation of the production and use of knowledge. That is the context for innovation policies aiming at fostering social inclusion.

Specific strategies are needed to make knowledge and innovation able to contribute to social inclusion and to foster inclusive development. It is not only the issue of which questions are put forward and which problems are highlighted but also the issue of which heuristic is used to search for solutions.

The following questions, to be addressed in this chapter, stem from the previous assertions: What do we understand by inclusive innovation? How can different narratives be combined in ways that link knowledge, innovation, and social inclusion? What does it mean to conceive an innovation policy partly as a social policy? How can such an innovation policy be designed? What kind of interests and which "voices" may foster innovation policies as social policies?

The answers should contribute to the changes in development thinking and practices that were advocated in Chapter 2. Thus, it is useful to start by summarizing why changes are needed: "[T]he prevailing global economic and social trends are deepening the contradictions of a development pattern that has become unsustainable. These contradictions are undeniable, as evidenced by the unprecedented increase in global inequality in recent decades;

© The Author(s) 2018   93
R. Arocena et al., *Developmental Universities in Inclusive
Innovation Systems*, https://doi.org/10.1007/978-3-319-64152-2_5

the worsening environmental crisis, especially climate change; and the ambivalent role of the technological revolution that, while offering opportunities for sustainability, creates tensions in labour markets that are heightened as new technology becomes more widely used" (ECLAC 2016: 9).

FROM PREVAILING POLICIES TO DEMOCRATIC KNOWLEDGE POLICIES

Prevailing innovation policies, driven by commercial demand, mainly favor those countries and social groups that are already knowledge-strong, neglecting the problems and challenges hampering development for a vast part of the global population.

Something much stronger was said more than thirty years ago: "[I]t is on a global scale that the most extreme effects of worldwide inequality in incomes are apparent. The bias in the world research innovation system is so great as to constitute a danger to the future of human society" (Freeman 1982: 184).

This leads to a trend that we have already characterized as a "generalized Matthew effect": in terms of access to and use of knowledge, the knowledge-strong will become stronger and the knowledge-weak will become weaker. The more knowledge one builds and uses, the more one learns and thus one is more able to demand and get advanced knowledge.

Market-dominated innovation policies answer to commercial demand of knowledge, mainly stemming from countries and social groups that are already in the upper side of the learning divides. Thus, prevailing policies can be considered part of the problem of knowledge-based inequality: they increase the social differences that come from the main power resource in contemporary societies and thus they are not democratic. What can be done then to influence market-driven innovation policies toward democratization of knowledge production? Lundvall (2010) proposes that "[A]s a kind of countervailing power to the colonizing tendency emanating from market-oriented innovation policy we need to develop a wider field of politics—*knowledge politics*—that covers all aspects of knowledge production and takes into account that the production of knowledge has much wider scope than just contributing to economic growth" (Lundvall 2010: 346).

Thus, we may speak in general of knowledge policies, of which learning and innovation policies are fundamental chapters. Needed policies can be termed democratic knowledge policies. Such policies are directly related to fostering participation in a democratic polity: "an advanced democratic country would actively seek to reduce great inequalities in the capacities and opportunities for citizens to participate effectively in political life that are caused to an important degree by the distribution of economic resources, positions, and opportunities and by the distribution of knowledge, information and cognitive skills" (Dahl 1989: 324).

Democratic knowledge policies can be based on the fundamental assertion of the National Innovation System (NIS) conceptualization as previously presented, namely that actual innovations are shaped by the interactions of a plurality of actors in ways that are highly dependent on their specific interests and on their relative power.

The configuration of an NIS is not socially neutral, neither in its building nor in its effects. From the budget for research and development (R&D) and its main goals to the kind of regulations built around knowledge issues, the main social relations in which it is embedded, including external relations, mold the ensemble of facets of an NIS. On the other hand, the configuration of an NIS affects different groups differently, eventually favoring some and even threatening others. There is neither a "system of innovation determinism" over socio-economic evolution nor determinism in the other direction, even though there may be strong and lasting impacts of each aspect on the other. This means that it is always possible to build spaces—eventually at interstice level—where knowledge production and innovation are fostered following a normative inspiration with some impact on socio-economic features. If social inclusion is at stake, they may become building blocks of an "Inclusive Innovation System", a system that includes the explicit mandate of orienting the production and use of knowledge toward social inclusion.

Thus, the Innovation Systems framework suggests that innovation policies should pay more attention to usually neglected groups that can be seen as potential actors in innovation processes. We conjecture that by doing so it will be less difficult to foster social inclusion in the dominant knowledge-based and innovation-driven economy. Social inclusion requires a huge amount of cooperation. Thus, special attention should be given to the question posed by Heyer et al. (2002): "I[s] the market destroying cooperation?"

The Innovation Systems approach, with its emphasis on cooperation, converges with the fundamental notion of "coproduction". The latter gives a clue for democratic knowledge policies and is defined as follows: "[B]y coproduction, I mean the process through which inputs used to produce a good or service are contributed by individuals who are not 'in' the same organization. The 'regular' producer of education, health, or infrastructure services is most frequently a government agency. Whether the regular producer is the only producer of these goods and services depends both on the nature of the good or service itself and on the incentives that encourage the active participation of others. All public goods and services are potentially produced by those who are frequently referred to as the client. The term 'client' is a passive term. Clients are acted on. Coproduction implies that citizens can play an active role in producing public goods and services of consequence to them" (Ostrom 1996: 1073).

A big asymmetry exists between prevailing and alternative knowledge policies when their stakeholders are considered. For the former, stakeholders include strong networks of organized power that connect "really existing" actors like firms, academic teams, and public organisms. On the contrary, the stakeholders of democratic knowledge policies are frequently just potential networks that can be effectively organized only by means connecting and even promoting collective actors. Tasks related to this will be considered in the second part of this book—among those defining the notion of developmental universities. For the time being, let us recall that in this way no small challenge is posed to the prevailing mode of knowledge production and use as well as to the traditional academic approach to such issues: "…let me recommend that the bridging of the gulf between the analysis of private activities apart from those of government agencies needs to be high on the agenda of development theorists and activists. No market can survive without extensive public goods provided by governmental agencies. No government can be efficient and equitable without considerable input from citizens. Synergetic outcomes can be fostered to a much greater extent than our academic barriers have let us contemplate" (Ostrom 1996: 1083).

For fostering synergetic outcomes of learning and innovation policies that expand freedoms and capabilities, a main question is which actors and organized networks actually or potentially included in Innovation Systems can be interested in fostering democratic knowledge policies and, moreover, have enough power to do so. Concerning such a complex issue, a first step is to ask in what sense an innovation can be considered to be satisfactory.

INDIGENOUS KNOWLEDGE AND SATISFACTORY INNOVATION

Democratic knowledge policies obviously include the issue of knowledge production. For a long time, it was discussed whether overcoming the peripheral condition required fostering the indigenous production of knowledge or whether the best option was to learn how to use first-rate knowledge generated in other places, without "reinventing the wheel", perhaps a suboptimal version of it, and losing time and money in such attempts. In fact, it is usually accepted today that there is not a sharp divide between using advanced knowledge context-efficiently and being able to produce original knowledge. Moreover, even acknowledging that choosing and using first-rate knowledge generated in other places are part of the "knowledge-mix" any society needs to rely upon, this highlights rather than refutes the need for producing original knowledge (Nelson and Winter 1982; Freeman 1992). The latter does not ensure the former but is a necessary condition for it: efficient applications require problem-solving capabilities. That is, effective diffusion of new knowledge needs to be closely connected with research and innovation.

As previously recalled, "peripheral countries" are far from being homogeneous, both in a general sense as well as concerning their capabilities to produce and use knowledge. Some of them have quite consolidated research structures where often first-rate science is generated while, on the other end, many are still struggling to start building such structures. Nevertheless, a widely shared trait is the weak connection between the existing indigenous capabilities to produce knowledge and the capabilities to use all available knowledge to produce goods and services in ways that can be considered satisfactory. This weak connection is a fundamental trait of the "peripheral condition".

But, what is meant by a satisfactory production of goods and services? The normative characterization of development suggests that the answer should take into account three aspects: (1) in order to be compatible with the notion of Sustainable Human Development, the types of production should be harmful neither to people—particularly workers as direct producers—nor to the environment; (2) the goods and services produced should help people in general to live lives they have reasons to value, particularly by solving some of the main problems they face; and (3) the actual ways of producing should expand capabilities, which increasingly requires the incorporation to some extent of advanced knowledge.

There is a reciprocal relationship between producing satisfactory innovations and the satisfactory production of innovations. To analyze this issue, it is useful to start from the notion of "unsatisfactory innovations", proposed by Lundvall in 1985 in his first work on user-producer interactions. The general framework for this analysis may be put this way: "[I]nnovations might be regarded as 'invasions of unknown territories'. How should we possibly be able, ex ante, to deem if extensions in one direction is better than extensions in another? The optimal pattern of innovation is not a useful concept. But, this does not mean that any assessment of innovative performance is without meaning. It might be possible to locate situations where the actual rate and direction of innovations does deviate from the potential in a conspicuous way. A systematic analysis of technical opportunities and user needs can demonstrate that actual innovations do not exploit fully the opportunities present, or do not reflect user needs" (Lundvall 1985: 18).

The literature on innovation in highly industrialized countries is richly endowed with examples of innovations that do not properly fulfill user needs. The reasons are diverse, including producers of innovations that deliberately design them in ways that deter users from adapting them to their specific needs, including future uses (von Hippel 1988).

Lundvall's examples of "unsatisfactory innovations" in Denmark include cases of hyper-automation (in the dairy-processing industry). The reflections made on this case are easily recognizable in the landscapes of developing countries: "plants designed by the producers of equipment and systems were more capital intensive, more inflexible, and more highly automated, than what corresponded to cost-effective solutions and to the needs of the users. (...) The competence of users and producers was only partially overlapping and in certain key areas it was very unequally distributed. (...) In this relationship, a hierarchy had developed where the producers were able to impose their standards rather than adjusting to the needs of the users. But, why did producers develop technology which was not cost-effective at the user level? (...) It is difficult to substantiate, but we got the impression that non-economic factors were even more important (than economic ones). It seemed as the producers were following a technological trajectory in the direction of higher and higher levels of automation. It was (implicitly) assumed that a growing level of automation would imply an increasing degree of effectiveness" (Lundvall 1985: 19).

This comment refers to user-producer interactions in the same developed country. We can find examples of this type of difficulty in developing countries as well. An analysis of the Indian Council of Scientific and

Industrial Research's promotion of pro-poor innovation in rural agriculture uncovers similar patterns: "T[]he process of technology transfer is undertaken by *pushing the available solutions* without the technology adaptation effort required for fitting the technology to the conditions of the users. This is because the interactions of R&D workers with users are weak. There has been no attempt to understand the users as system and to manage technology transfer as an interactive process" (Abrol 2014: 362).

Given that one of the marks of underdevelopment is that the knowledge supply mainly connects the national productive structure with knowledge generation abroad, the unsatisfactory characteristics cannot but be aggravated. Lundvall's concluding remarks as early as 1985 resonate today when we are looking for democratic knowledge policies: "[T]his pattern (unequal distribution of technical competences between users and producers of technology) might inspire a technology policy which is more oriented towards strengthening the competence of users than the technology policy predominating today. An extension of such a new orientation that encompass the 'final users', workers and consumers, might have radical implications" (Op. cit.: 23–24). Those remarks point to a very complex-to-implement but nonetheless fundamental aspect of the production of "satisfactory innovations": the "satisfactory production" of innovations. One requirement for this is the active, engaged, and considered participation of users in the shaping of the problem, the evaluation process of the solutions, and the co-monitoring of changes until they become satisfactory. We can say in this regard that Lundvall's recommendation, directed to empower users, should be complemented with another, highlighted by Abrol's account on India and easily recognizable in any developing country, related to instilling respect for the users' perspectives from the innovation producer's side. This is no minor issue for universities: we shall come back to that.

When we look more closely at satisfactory/unsatisfactory innovations in developing countries, we arrive at new observations. Two starting points for this scrutiny are that (i) the overwhelming majority of innovations of some degree of complexity are imported and (ii) an important part of problems of all kinds cannot be addressed by means of these innovations. The first point is a well-known fact. The second point deserves some reflection. The most straightforward reflection relates to cost: in the public health realm, for instance, innovations related to pharmaceutical and medical equipment may be "unsatisfactory" just because they are unaffordable for the budget of a Ministry of Health. Another relates to infrastructure. Cold-chain for some types of vaccines or food, a reliable energy supply for the smooth functioning of artifacts of all sorts, and access to drinkable water all may be requisites to be able to use innovations. If they are not in place, such innovations become unsatisfactory in the plain sense of not solving the problem.

Besides innovations that may have proven satisfactory in some parts of the world but unsatisfactory in others, we have the issue of no-problems in some parts of the world that are problems in others. If the entire population of the developed countries has access to drinkable water through centralized distribution systems, the problem of how to access drinkable water when centralized systems are not in place and will not be in place for a long time is a no-problem there. Innovation radars in the developed world looking for problems to be solved will not detect this particular one. Innovation radars in prevailing innovation systems add to the no-problem issue from another standpoint: they are usually market-driven devices and so social demands without market appeal remain below their recognition threshold. Therefore, whole families of problems remain "under-innovated" and, even before that, under-researched, like the kind of illnesses affecting mainly the poor, baptized in the health literature as "neglected diseases" (Morel 2003).

We can visualize the above discussion by way of a four-quadrant matrix that illustrates different types of problems for which satisfactory solutions are available or not (Fig. 5.1). The two dimensions to be considered are

	Problems for which solutions have been found in developed countries	Problems for which solutions have not been searched in developed countries
Problems present in developing countries for which satisfactory solutions exist	*(I) Solutions provided through imports*	*(II) Solutions provided by indigenous innovation*
Problems present in developing countries for which satisfactory solutions do not exist	*(IV) No solutions available*	*(III) No solutions available*

Fig. 5.1 A matrix of solutions (satisfactory, un-satisfactory, and non-existent) from a Global South perspective
Source: Adapted from Srinivas and Sutz 2008

(i) problems for which solutions have been found in highly industrialized countries, or the North, and (ii) problems for which workable solutions exist (or not) in the Global South.

The cell containing solutions provided by imports (quadrant I) assuredly accounts for much of the technological innovation in developing countries, particularly when some degree of technical complexity is involved. We have two comments on this: (1) they may represent much of the solutions incorporated, but this does not mean that they tackle most of the problems at stake; (2) concomitantly, they leave many problems, small and large, resented by different actors, without solutions. Christopher Freeman warns against the illusion that everything can be bought ready-made from abroad, neglecting a serious effort to build indigenous capabilities—that is, acting as if this quadrant is in fact the whole matrix—and calls the consequences of such illusion "voluntary underdevelopment" (Freeman 1992: 48).

Following the already-mentioned distinction between "frivolous protection" and "protection for learning" made by Fajnzylber (1984), we may differentiate "frivolous imports" from "import and learn". To illustrate the point, we can take the example of telecommunications in Uruguay and in South Korea in the 1980s. Both countries were in urgent need of modernization of their telecommunication infrastructure, particularly the telephone system, which was extremely costly and outdated, and both countries relied on the same foreign provider, Eriksson, for the needed solutions. But there ended the similarities. Uruguay acquired the digital telephone system as a turnkey-project without any participation of local capabilities. South Korea put in place a complex system of interactions involving public and private actors to monitor and learn while the foreign technology was incorporated. In a dynamic process of successively strengthening the domestic technological level, "Korea has promoted exports of competitive products to pay for needed imports of technology which *at the time* could not have been manufactured domestically at about the same price or complexity level. Thus, Korea's telecom industry has been integrated in the international market by a selective and dynamic policy on technology imports and exports" (Göransson 1993: 182, emphasis in the original). From those early days, fostered by a public policy, comes the Samsung success saga in the telephone business (Mani 2005). Voluntary underdevelopment was avoided in one case and promoted in the other. "Import and learn" helps building indigenous capabilities able to address the problems that imports cannot solve; "frivolous imports" weaken the possibilities to do so.

The quadrant in Fig. 5.1 containing solutions provided by indigenous innovation for problems that were not addressed in the developed countries (quadrant II) reflects, as could be expected, a wide diversity. Often, such innovations remain invisible: unearthing them is not an easy task since they are performed by anonymous people, are not formalized, and often are not even communicated outside the realm in which they were developed. Their importance should not be understated, though. From these innovations, people find workable solutions for recurrent problems that may have lasting impacts on their lives. Anil Gupta recollected innovations "from below" of this type in India and made them widely known through the Honey-Bee Network (Abrol 2017). His motto is "people on the margin do not have minds on the margin".

A series of studies of socio-technological transformations at the popular level in Tanzania also show the economic and cultural importance of that type of innovative effort. Echoing Gupta, Muller asserts that "the majority of peasants and artisans in the South are reproducing their livelihood through innovative technological transformations and diversifications in response to their continually changing social, economic and environmental conditions of production. If they did not, they would not survive. They are *befit for change*, highly knowledgeable and skilled, certainly not ignorant as the public is commonly told. In other words, it is our contention that a significant social and productive potential is being disregarded and not seriously considered in conventional development research in general and by policy makers in particular" (Muller 2010: 3, emphasis in the original).

In the case of Brazil, an innovative way of accessing water in the semi-arid geography of Ceará (in the northeast), with related artifacts manufactured by small local firms, allowed poor farmers to diversify their subsistence agriculture incorporating horticulture and fruticulture (Amaral Filho 2006). In Uruguay, a more formally stated innovation project, also related to water, was developed. In this case, the problem consisted in providing drinkable water to isolated communities without access to central systems of water distribution. The devised solution was a portable plant, able to process non-chemically contaminated water, which can travel from village to village on a truck.

A main point in common among all of these examples is that the related problems are of no interest for the developed world: they simply do not exist there and no technology is available to purchase. When the solutions are worked out or led by the users, and those users belong to deprived sectors of the population, the resulting innovations have been denominated grassroots innovations. Recently, however, the idea of grassroots innovations has started to appear also in the North, with a search for innovations where the needs to be fulfilled are defined at the community level, and where communities themselves define the acceptable solutions, a trait that cannot be found in the market: "[I]n North and South, in cities and rural settings, networks of activists, development workers, community groups and neighbours have been working with people to generate bottom-up solutions for sustainable developments; solutions that respond to the local situation and the interests and values of the communities involved; and where those communities have control over the processes involved and the outcomes. Initiatives have flourished, and struggled, in sectors as diverse as water and sanitation, housing and habitats, food and agriculture, energy, mobility, manufacturing, health, education, communications, and many other spheres of activity. Whether born of material and economic necessity, or motivated by social issues marginalized by the conventional innovation systems of states and markets, networks of people promote and coordinate alternative activity attentive to these needs and issues. They develop discourse and mobilize supportive resources among wider publics. It is this activity that constitutes what we mean by grassroots innovation movements and gives us our working definition" (Smith et al. 2017: 3).

The first quadrant in Fig. 5.1, where satisfactory solutions for problems detected in developing countries are not available (quadrant III), is the one where such solutions were not searched for in developed countries. The problems included in this quadrant are mainly those affecting poor populations and stemming from poverty. They belong to the realm of "un-done science and innovations", extending the forceful expression of Hess (2007). The reasons why research agendas and innovation projects do not take these problems on board have already been mentioned: their market demand is weak. In health issues, there is an impressive amount of literature, including from the World Health Organization (WHO), denouncing the big pharmaceuticals' behavior in this regard. The WHO has been quoted as saying that, owing to pressures to maintain sales and generate profits, there is "an inherent conflict of interest between legitimate business goals of manufacturers and the social, medical and economic needs of providers and the public to select and use drugs in the most rational way" (Cassiolato and Couto 2015: 27).

The problems belonging to this quadrant are probably among the most complex to address. There is a long and complicated process that goes from recognizing a problem to transforming it into a voiced need and then into a concrete demand that can reach those embodying the different types of capabilities required to arrive at a satisfactory solution. This type of circuit is full of places where things may go wrong, leading to short circuits that halt the process (Alzugaray et al. 2012).

Smita Srinivas proposes that four types of needs/demands be considered: first, effective demand: "the consumer is willing and *able* to buy at every prize" (Srinivas 2014: 84, 86, emphasis in the original); second, a need that is not recognized as a need, related to the lack of agency to voice their needs on the part of those who have them; third, a need that is recognized as a need but does not appear as a demand because there is no effective demand; and, fourth, needs that are recognized but do not lead to a fulfilled demand, because even if the need is there, it has been recognized as such, it has been transformed into demand and a satisfactory solution may have been found, the fulfillment of the demand is nevertheless elusive because of mainly socio-organizational failures.

Problems in quadrant III of Fig. 5.1 can "migrate" to quadrant I if the problems hitherto neglected in the North begin to be tackled and if satisfactory solutions for the Global South are made available. They can migrate also to quadrant II. The persistence of the problems in this quadrant, which mostly originate in an extra-technological domain but which could be mitigated to some extent by technical innovation, like a vaccine against cholera or the Chagas disease, defies science and innovation policies alike.

Quadrant IV contains problems that have been solved in the North but whose solutions found are unsatisfactory for the Global South, and so, if nothing happens, such problems will remain unsolved there. Not only issues related to the vulnerable populations are at stake here but productive aspects as well. Most of the examples we can give relate to unaffordability, but in several of them the latter derives from specific conditions in the North that may be different in the South, resulting in unsatisfactory innovation. To give one example: the methods to avoid frost in fruticulture are different if the cold affects the seed or the fruit. If it is the former, the energy needed is higher than if it is the latter. The temperatures in the South are mild enough to avoid seed damage during frosts. Using the Northern systems in the South would lead to a significant waste of energy and money. But the systems available are directed to protect the seed, and that's it. This does not mean that there is no possible solution to protect fruticulture from frost in the South in a satisfactory way, but it does mean that such a solution will probably need to be developed in the South. This has been the case, and the innovation was achieved, in Uruguay (Guarga et al. 2000).

The problems in this quadrant are particularly tantalizing. When solutions exist, meaning that problems can be solved, the fact that their results are unsatisfactory or out of reach is frustrating, particularly when this may imply a continued situation of constitutive deprivation. Vaccines able to eliminate child morbidity and mortality that cannot be included in public health campaigns in Southern countries exemplify this case. On the other hand, the knowledge that a solution exists and has been widely implemented may lead to a "take it or leave it" sort of thinking that keeps from envisaging alternatives. Moreover, the assimilation of the existing solution with the "good ones"—even if they are affordable—directly leads the search for alternative solutions to a less desirable path, only to be followed if there is no other way.

Thinking differently, searching for alternative heuristics to problem-solving, and asking questions that nobody asked before to characterize a problem are some of the ingredients to find solutions to problems in this quadrant. Nothing too different from what is needed to innovate, *tout court*. But it is perhaps a bit more difficult to follow an alternative path knowing that there is a good one already opened. In the next section, we will turn to the main traits of the specific heuristics that have led to solutions in this quadrant as well as in quadrant II.

NEW HEURISTICS FOR INCLUSIVE AND FRUGAL INNOVATION

What are the main differences that a solution designer in the North and one in the Global South face? The first striking difference that comes to mind is the rich endowment of what is needed for design in one place and its scarcity in the other. The items to be included in an account of the differences are long and quite diverse: money to develop projects, access to up-to-date facilities, necessary inputs at hand and well adjusted to fine requirements, well-trained support staff, well-behaving infrastructures of several kinds, institutional arrangements that favor innovation, and would-be users able to pay the resulting costs. When working in an environment where these things are present, the designer can take for granted that what is necessary for the implementation of what she has in mind will be in place. This gives great freedom to the design process. We can call the heuristics developed around this type of design processes "the capacity to innovate in conditions of abundance".

When one works in an environment where some of these items are missing, or are difficult to access, the design process changes substantially. The design is constrained by what you have at hand. If you know that the users of the solution need a combination of good quality and low production cost or low price—after all, a great deal of unsatisfactory innovations are such because they are unaffordable—this constrains your options even further. We can call the heuristics developed to achieve success in this type of design processes "the capacity to innovate in scarcity conditions" (Srinivas and Sutz 2008).

The capacity to innovate in scarcity conditions implies the ability to solve problems, some of them never addressed before, some of them addressed in environments of abundance, making use of a restricted mix of resources and considering specific operational conditions in such a way that the solutions found are satisfactory for the users. This capacity is behind the solutions found in quadrant II of Fig. 5.1. It, moreover, provides hope of finding satisfactory solutions in the third and fourth quadrants. The link of this heuristic with inequality is obvious: problems affecting vulnerable populations may be addressed with better tools.

The issue of the problem-solving heuristics or "common sense" of designers is widely present in innovation studies. Carlota Pérez, for instance, associates the transformation of that common sense to the emergence of a techno-economic paradigm shift (Pérez 1985). Vincenti, in his thorough analysis of engineering design practices, describes how "ambiance" factors are added to calculable factors in the design processes, something that goes further than the well-known differentiation between explicit and tacit knowledge: "[T]heoretical tools and quantitative data are, by definition, precise and codifiable; they come mostly from deliberate research. They are not, however, by themselves sufficient. Designers also need for their work an array of less sharply defined considerations derived from experience in practice, considerations that frequently do not lend themselves to theorizing tabulations (…) Such considerations are mostly learned on the job rather than in school or from books; they tend to be carried around, sometimes more or less unconsciously, in designer's minds. (…) The practice from which they derive necessarily includes not only design but production and operation as well, though such practice may not be – typically it is not – by the designers themselves" (Vincenti 1990: 217).

The considerations that designers carry around, derived from a practice that includes their own experience along with inputs coming from other parts involved in the problem setting, configure the environment in which innovative proposals to problem-solving arise. Such considerations evolve toward a "common sense" or heuristics that incorporates influential traits found in practice. Scarcity is one of them in the Global South. Scarcity has been incorporated into the design culture because people have learnt how to cope creatively with it. The capacity to innovate in scarcity conditions is not a way of producing second-bests, but a truly new way of considering problems and problem-solving. It is widely diverse. It can be found in low-tech practices and in science-based solutions. It is a cultural strength, not usually recognized or used as a lever for development or as a tool against inequality. We may think that the capacity to innovate in scarcity conditions represents negligible resources for development. However, as Hirschman (1958: 5) puts it, "[D]evelopment depends not so much on finding optimal combinations of productive factors and resources as on using resources that are hidden, scattered or badly utilized". This under-recognized strength may start to be seen with new eyes, as we will argue in the following.

Doing better with less is no small task when the socio-technical imaginary of a society is "what economists call the pig principle: if something is good, more is better" (Weizenbaum 1976: 27). The antithesis of the pig principle seems to be frugality. "Frugal innovation" is a buzzword. It was coined in India, with a clear Ghandian background; *The Economist* praises it. It has a dedicated academic journal. Several management books have been published in the last five years with "frugal innovation" in the title, some of them becoming best-sellers. The European Commission has made frugal innovation part of the issues to be studied in the Horizon 2020 program (2014–2020). Specifically, a tender was opened under the label "Study on frugal innovation and reengineering of traditional techniques". The fuzziness of the definition used in the tender is an example of the Babel-like proliferation of meanings of a term in high fashion: "[F]rugal (also known as inclusive or grassroots) Innovation is the process of reducing the complexity and cost of a good by removing non-essential features" (European Commission 2015: 11). The interim report of the study that won the tender makes a review of the literature that suggests that "frugal innovation" has become a term with different meanings and implications depending on the interests of its users (European Commission 2016).

In the characterizations of frugal innovation, there is an important differentiation among those considering only "frugal products" and those that include its processes of production (Brem and Wolfram 2014), the latter being more akin to the concept of "capacities to innovate in scarcity conditions". The following characterization gives a flavor of both aspects: "[F]rugal innovation responds to limitations in resources, whether financial, material or institutional, and using a range of methods, turns these constraints into an advantage. Through minimising the use of resources in development, production and delivery, or by leveraging them in new ways, frugal innovation results in dramatically lower–cost products and services. Successful frugal innovations are not only low cost, but outperform the alternative, and can be made available at large scale" (Bound and Thornton 2012: 6).

Besides interest-related definitions, opposing multinationals seeking the "millions at the bottom of the pyramid" and grassroots activities and movements, frugal innovation, in principle, implies a prudent vision of the use of resources, akin to the revitalized concern on sustainability. It also implies attention to underserved populations. However, caution is needed. Advancing consumerism of affordable "good enough" things in a sort of down-sized and partial "American way of life" for everyone may not be conducive either to sustainability or to fighting inequality and social exclusion.

It is worth coming back to quadrant IV in Fig. 5.1 and giving an example of solutions to important problems implemented in developed countries that are unsatisfactory in developing countries, leaving the problem untouched, almost as orphaned as the problems that have not been even considered. The following is a statement of the problem: "*[H]aemophilus influenzae* type b (Hib) is a pathogen that, before the introduction of Hib conjugate vaccines in 1988, was the leading cause of bacterial meningitis in children in the United States of America. These vaccines, which contain capsular polysaccharide isolated from the pathogen, have reduced the incidence of bacterial meningitis and pneumonia in the developed world by more than 95%. However, introduction of the vaccine in developing countries has been slow owing to its high cost and limited availability. The World Health Organization estimates that, in the developing world, Hib is currently responsible for approximately three million serious illnesses and an estimated 386,000 deaths per year, almost all of which are children under the age of 5 years old" (Astronomo and Burton 2010: 316).

In some developing countries, the conjugate vaccine was imported, despite its cost. This was the case, for instance, of Uruguay and Chile in the mid-1990s as an answer to an epidemic upsurge of meningitis in the Latin American Southern Cone. Even if the Pan American Health Organization then estimated that by the end of the 1990s almost all countries in Latin America and the Caribbean would have introduced the Hib vaccination in their public health schemes, the cost of the vaccine prevented the fulfilment of this forecast (Landaverde et al. 1999).

The effectiveness of the vaccine against the bacteria producing Hib was tantalizing for countries unable to pay for it. We are talking of a pathogen responsible for illnesses that produce death or severe sequelae mainly among children less than five years old. The biological character of the vaccine was at the root of its high cost of production; as an additional inconvenience, a cold-chain was required during storage and distribution. Here, the power of the idea of changing heuristics through the capacity to innovate in scarcity conditions is shown at its best. In conditions of abundance, the cumbersome and expensive biological procedure (the vaccine is made from smaller pieces of the whole Hib bacterium) is not a serious problem; in a different context, it becomes an inexpugnable barrier. A different procedure, looking for synthetic antigens, could be the answer but was never attempted: the chemistry involved is very complex, and given that biological vaccines worked well, this path was not envisaged. It started to be researched in Cuba right after the development of the first vaccine. In the words of the Cuban researcher who led the project, "[F]irst of all, conjugated vaccines are complex; they are produced using complex and costly technology. So even though *Haemophilus influenzae* type b (Hib) is important for the world, recommended even in the Extended Immunization Program (EIP), the cost is what largely prevents this vaccine from reaching all children. In this case, where we know the vaccine works, but expensive technology keeps it from reaching the whole world, we have two possible avenues for development. One is to try to simplify that same technology to reduce costs. Work has been done on this for years and there has been some progress. The other is to look for alternatives; one of those alternatives is to make a synthetic antigen" (Vérez-Bencomo 2007).

The project, which lasted 14 years and involved 17 clinical trials, ended with an innovative solution and a 99.7% success rate in children and was incorporated in 2004 in Cuba's national vaccination program (Astronomo and Burton 2010: 316). It was recognized as an important scientific achievement: "[C]hemical synthesis of the Hib saccharide antigen was a breakthrough in conjugated vaccines" (Zarei et al. 2016).

Given the definition of frugal innovation, the synthetic vaccine against bacteria Hib is indeed frugal: through minimizing the use of resources in development, production, and delivery, the innovative vaccine, made available on a large scale, resulted in a dramatically lower-cost product with outstanding therapeutics results. Frugal innovation does not necessarily lead to social inclusion or to diminishing inequality in some dimension, but it can be asserted that many innovations aiming at this will need to be frugal, to be built by means of new heuristics, and to profit from the capacities to innovate in scarcity conditions. Making room for them implies swimming against the current in terms of policy design, both at the supply side—science, technology, and innovation policy—and at the demand side, involving the whole gamut of public policies. To this we will return at the end of this chapter.

BEYOND HIGH-TECH ALONE

Innovation policies often concentrate on the so-called high-tech sectors because they are considered to be essentially the only "engines of growth". In such cases, it is explicitly or implicitly assumed that primary production and typically low-tech activities are doomed to remain at low levels of knowledge and qualifications. This is a very important factual issue. If such assumptions were corroborated, the possibilities for democratizing knowledge policies would be meager, especially in the Global South, where so many countries are highly dependent on primary production or "light" industry or both. Consequently, these issues deserve careful consideration.

During the initial years of the twenty-first century, the high prices of commodities led to an expanding production and, when the commodity boom seems to be over, many primary producing countries once again are caught in low-knowledge and low-productivity activities. The emphasis on high tech appears to be corroborated and can be considered as sound as it was some decades ago with its emphasis on industry as the carrier of technical progress.

Nevertheless, a longer view casts some doubts: "[E]xporting primary products is not a road to underdevelopment. Most of the richest developed countries have been exporters of primary products" (Bairoch 1993: 173). It is asserted that productivity in industry grew quicker than productivity in agriculture up to the early 1950s but that for some decades after a reversal could be observed: "[T]he total increase in the Western world's agricultural productivity over the last 40 years has been greater than during the preceding 900 years" (Idem: 151). This increase in productivity was fostered by knowledge-based technologies, underlining, as the examples below show, that it is not the type of production per se that may stick countries in low knowledge and low productivity, but the way it is performed.

When the price of oil abruptly fell, the situation for many oil-exporting countries could deservedly be considered as the confirmation that being rich in oil is more a curse than a blessing. But some cases point in another direction. In Brazil, the expansion of deep-water oil production in the ocean was combined with a significant knowledge push. The case of Norway seems particularly telling: "[T]he size, importance and technical complexity of the Norwegian oil and gas system is reflected in the data on people with Higher Education. As of 2003, the largest share of people with Higher Education in the labour force was found within oil, gas and mining, where 16 per cent of all employees had a Higher Education, as compared to less than 5 per cent in manufacturing. It is also within oil, gas and mining that we find the highest share of people educated within technology and natural sciences" (Gronning et al. 2008: 295).

In some countries, natural resources-based production has been the cradle of flourishing, sophisticated, technologically based industries in their own terms. As Freeman (1988) points out, "[T]he original specialization of particular small countries was influenced by resource endowment but more often by accumulative patterns of technology and skill accumulation over long periods. Examples of resource-based industries are forest products and paper in the Scandinavian countries, iron ore in Sweden, PVC and aluminium based on hydro-electric power in Norway, petro-chemicals based on natural gas in the Netherlands. But in every case the original resource endowment was reinforced by a strong process of technological development, leading often to improved processes and in many cases to the development of successful specialized plants, equipment and machine-building activities, that is depended on 'learning by interacting'" (Freeman 1988: 80).

Even if an "impenetrable web of obsolescence" may obscure its origins, the Finish Nokia was founded in 1856 as a forest company (Dalum et al. 1988: 132). This natural-resources background has provided a base for skill accumulation and technological development for the company and for Finland. Lemola and Lovio (1988: 148) find that "[I]t is not by chance that Finland, being a traditional country of forest industry, is one of the leading countries also in electronics applied to the forest industry". Another case in point is Denmark, where "[E]ven when advanced Danish technology apparently is directed towards non-agro activities (…) the technological competence can often be traced back to learning experiences made in the agro-industrial area…" (Andersen and Lundvall 1988: 11).

A wrong-directed emphasis on high tech per se has often ended in a misguided dichotomy: either you have a high-tech economy, particularly a high-tech–led export structure, or you should concentrate on your static comparative advantages, mainly your resource-based strengths, without caring for advanced knowledge. This leads to the conclusion that if your biotech industry does not export it is not worth considering it as an economic asset, even if your agricultural exports depend to a high degree on its knowledge-based products. Policies are not always so misguided, though. When in the 1980s the Basque Country decided to put a great effort into revitalizing its traditional industries, heavily hurt by economic crisis and technological obsolescence, it turned to the small and incipient electronic industry by supporting it in a massive effort of "digital alphabetization" of small firms and the population in general and by promoting and subsidizing user-producer interactions among Basque professional electronic industries and the whole productive structure (Plaza 2000). Finland followed a similar path: "[I]n a small country such as Finland the question is rather of renewing the old production structure and production processes with the aid of electronics than replacing them with electronics. The indirect importance of the electronic industry may be even greater than its direct importance" (Lemola and Lovio 1988: 154).

This is not the only direction to be considered in order to widen the scope of knowledge policies beyond the usual realm of high-tech activities per se, which by the way should keep their high priority, particularly when related to the learning process stemming from the knowledge accumulation in any sector of the economy. It is crucial to remember that all the activities of "symbolic analysts"—in the sense of Reich (1992)—include advanced learning and systematic innovation. For example, "[A] supplementary explanation of the overall performance of the Danish NIS could be that innovations flourish in industries not usually regarded as traditional engines of growth, the so-called 'creative industries'. These include, for example, the music industry, the film industry, leisure, sports and arts" (Christensen et al. 2008: 408).

Innovation in creative industries has seldom been a target for market-dominated innovation policies. The rationale for that has been the perception by policy makers that it has an almost negligible effect on competitiveness and employment. Nevertheless, the Swedish music industry shows that this type of innovation offers substantial commercial and other socio-economic benefits. At its peak, that industry was the largest exporter of pop music per capita in the world; in absolute numbers, it trailed only the USA and Great Britain (*The Atlantic* 2017). Many believe that the public policy supporting local and egalitarian music education was paramount for a grassroots-led development directly connected with the phenomenal success of the Swedish music industry.

In general, it should be remembered that it is necessary but not sufficient to invest in science and high tech: "heavy investment in science in systems where organizational learning within and between firms is weakly developed, and where there is a weak focus on user needs, has only a limited positive impact upon innovation and economic growth. One important challenge for innovation system research is to develop the analysis of innovation systems so that it takes into account experience- based learning and interaction with users" (Lundvall 2016: 603).

In all of the examples given, the building of more productive activities by introducing high-tech—in oil, agro-industry, forestry, or traditional industry—was done in a bottom-up way with intense user-producer interactions, taking into account experiences that allowed further processes of experience-based learning. More often than not, high-tech tailor-made solutions were the first attempt to solve a user problem in new ways. These solutions were not always scaled-up, giving rise to a full-fledged high-tech industry on its own or to a dramatic shift of the productive structure. But the limited positive impact on innovation and economic growth warned by Lundvall was avoided precisely because heavy investment in science was accompanied by policies with a strong focus on users' needs and where experience-based learning was highly valued.

SOCIAL DEMAND OF KNOWLEDGE

As has been stressed above, the dynamism of learning processes is a main indicator of development prospects. Societies where such dynamism is weak—due mainly to a productive structure in which (market) demand for highly skilled people and knowledge is also weak—face great difficulties to foster development. However, market demand for knowledge is not the only starting point for a virtuous circle of demand for knowledge: achieving good results, which lead to a strengthening of the knowledge base, which in turn lead to renewed good results and so on. Social demand for knowledge and innovation may, under specific circumstances, play that role, helping to build the knowledge base for development. This can be a fundamental clue for alternative policies.

Social demand for knowledge is strong everywhere. This is a fundamental link between the factual approach and the propositional approach. To elaborate this link, the NIS approach is a great help, particularly in the Aalborg school version discussed above, in which not only the systemic aspects of innovation processes but also their socially distributed character is stressed. This means that actual innovation is shaped by the interactions between a broader set of actors than those usually taken into account by public knowledge policies.

Examples of what we are saying are the emphasis in user-producer interactions and in social cohesion as main characteristic of the Danish Innovation System in the descriptions offered by the Aalborg school (Lundvall 1985, 2002; Christensen et al. 2008).

A similar conclusion comes from a different source: "one feature that invariably characterizes successful innovation is ongoing communication between the producers and users of knowledge" (Sarewitz and Pielke 2007: 7). One of the first systematic analyses of "success and failure in industrial innovation" was a homonymous study conducted in 1972 at the Science Policy Research Unit. Its conclusions are quite strong: both for the user of the innovation and for the innovative firm, the major determinant of innovative success was understanding users' needs (Rothwell et al. 1974).

Even if these findings and considerations relate mainly to innovations mediated by the market, they can be extended to situations where the market is not the main institution inducing innovations or diffusing them. This leads us to consider the demand of knowledge that could come from social groups without purchasing power, the interactions between many actors that could be promoted by taking into account such demand, and the increasing cooperation it could favor in ways that go against knowledge-based inequality. In other words, the theoretical aspects of the NIS framework referred to above integrate the fundamental role of the users, including the relevance of seeing frequently neglected groups as potential actors of innovation processes in ways that foster social inclusion in the knowledge-based and innovation-driven economy.

Related to the impacts in the North on the financial crisis of the first decade of the twenty-first century, the need for a direct relation between "innovation" and "the social" was revamped. The Organisation for Economic Co-operation and Development (OECD), for instance, launched a series of workshops, case studies, and texts addressing the concept of "social innovation", a term that has acquired an important policy standing as well as an arborescent set of definitions and meanings (Brundenius 2017; Pisano et al. 2015). The OECD expresses clearly why the new concept is considered necessary and what it encompasses: "[T]here is a wide consensus that the disconnection between economic growth and well-being is increasing. At the same time research and innovation have become one of the main engines of growth. However, these two overarching trends have not yet been reconciled: there is a clear lack of exploitation of innovative solutions to address (...) social challenges. Failing to mobilise innovation to address some of the issues that affect populations at the global and local level has very high opportunity costs. Social innovation can be a way to reconcile these two forces, bringing growth and social value at the same time" (OECD 2011: 7, 8).

At the European Commission, arguments go in a similar direction, with the social challenges and growth going hand in hand and with a special emphasis on inclusiveness in terms of outcomes and of processes to achieve them: "the well-held belief that economic growth creates employment and wealth to alleviate poverty has been disproved by recent events, and the time has now come to try new ways of bringing people out of poverty and promoting growth and well-being not only *for*, but also *with*, citizens" (Hubert 2010: 6, emphasis in the original). "Social innovation" is markedly less technological than "frugal innovation"; the examples usually given—except for some Information and Communication Technology (ICT) applications—are not technological at all: "[A]s many examples of social innovation have shown, it should (...) be underlined that many of those did not depend on new technological developments but rather on a better use of existing technologies" (Op. cit.: 75). This conceptualization does not systematically link the answers to social demands to new scientific and technological efforts, either in terms of the problems tackled or in terms of the heuristics employed to find solutions. Perhaps that it is not the case even in the North. Be that as it may, as we have tried to show, the solution to many social problems in the Global South needs new scientific, technological, and innovation agendas.

It cannot be taken for granted that whatever knowledge is produced contributes to Sustainable Human Development or that development efforts cannot influence the production of knowledge. Not being aware of the former contributes to not being aware of the latter, which leads to treating science, technology, and innovation as unmodifiable facts that eventually need to be fought against reactively but not re-directed proactively.

A sort of blending of the technological heuristics of frugal innovation with the insistence of engagement of people in the design of solutions of social innovations may be a good approach to the kind of innovation needed to fight the hard problems of inequality and unsustainability that are so pressing today worldwide. We will elaborate on this in the following section.

Even though inequality and unsustainability are currently affecting all societies, the specific conditions of underdevelopment—particularly the weak knowledge market demand and the historical neglect of efforts to overcome the learning divide—recommend that we keep looking for specific ways of addressing them. In this sense, the elementary but highly non-trivial remark that social demand of knowledge is potentially high in the Global South suggests a democratic strategy toward a "non-peripheral" specialization: detecting and promoting social demand of knowledge can help both to expand advanced knowledge capabilities and to solve relevant collective problems.

Effective policies for managing structural change foster the incorporation of the whole range of goods and services production using first-rate knowledge and highly qualified people. They can be termed democratic policies if such incorporation aims at solving the most pressing collective problems and seeing people as agents. A first step in that direction is to detect and promote the social demand of related knowledge; a second step is to foster the expansion of advanced capabilities to solve those problems. It may be assumed that, if that is done in a systematic way, the social legitimacy of investing in expanding the knowledge supply will be enhanced. A virtuous circle combining supply and demand of advanced learning and first-rate science and technology may result and expand to a widening set of productive activities. Such a combination of supply and demand oriented by social aims can be seen as a clue for a democratic strategy toward structural change.

DEMOCRATIZING ACCESS TO INFORMATION

As discussed in detail above, learning and innovation are social processes of interaction between different organizations and collective actors. These systemic interactions shape what kind of knowledge is produced and how and where it is put to use. A crucial component in this process—as indeed for the ongoing transition toward knowledge-based societies in the North—is the ubiquitousness of ICTs. Innovation policies aimed at fostering social inclusion must take into consideration the persistent unequal global distribution of ICTs that effectively shuts out large groups from participating in the process of shaping innovations. The lack of access is particularly acute in the Global South where the proliferation of ICTs lags behind that of the North but at least carries with it the potential for inclusive and knowledge-sharing systems. Because ICTs are both a result of and a driving force for innovation, they are indispensable elements in an inclusive and democratizing innovation system with a free flow of information and knowledge-sharing opportunities.

In order to make knowledge and innovation able to contribute to social inclusion and to foster inclusive development, specific strategies are needed. Notwithstanding the uneven distribution of access to ICTs, new and innovative models for their effective and low-cost use have emerged in the Global South, employing ICTs as a means to democratize knowledge through intellectual commons, open source, wiki-initiatives, telecenter movements, and so on. ICTs vastly change the ways in which problem-solving as well as production and application of knowledge can take place in an organization (Collison and Parcell 2001) and in social processes. In ICT-poor regions, there are different ways of organizing such interactions between knowledge systems as well as between collective actors.

One much preferred way in the early phases of ICT proliferation was through community telecenters or knowledge centers, providing affordable access to information-deprived areas. Fuchs (1998: 8) asserts that "[T]he most important reason for telecenter establishment, and their most enduring legacy, is the 'diffusion effect' which telecenter services and the people who run them have on the communities and the regions which they serve. In every place where successful telecenters have been established there is a visible and identifiable change in the skills and capacities of the people and institutions". Moreover, "[S]uccessful telecentres alter this paradigm [the trickle-down theory of innovation and diffusion]. They bring 'state of the market' technologies and skills to 'back of the market' communities. This transforms the human, organizational and commercial capabilities of marginal communities and peripheral areas to participate in the Information Society" (Fuchs 1998: 8).

Thus, access to ICT can also facilitate learning and innovation processes in peripheral areas, areas that are peripheral in the world or peripheral in a country. In addition to its facilitating function, ICT can be the innovation itself. In a study on innovation and scaling of ICT, Foster and Heeks (2013) point to the particular relevance of ICT for bottom-of-the-pyramid markets through its flexibility that allows it to be quickly adapted for users by actors in the local innovation system.

Bringing ICT to deprived areas can also foster links between local and traditional knowledge systems. Typically, traditional knowledge systems existing in developing countries evolve slowly over time and are locally bounded (Balaji 2005). With adequate access to ICT, a community can—irrespective of its geographical location—tap into a knowledge system immensely larger than the existing traditional knowledge system. The merging of knowledge systems is an idea that is catching on in many countries. Bolivia is a leading country in a global movement to regard traditional or ancestral knowledge as an integral part of the development strategy of the country and an important component to promote in the innovation system. Tapping into traditional knowledge is, from this perspective, seen as "…a way to rediscover more efficient techniques of production and management of the land. Thus, there is a development vision based on the belief that a dialogue between local and traditional knowledge, academy and enterprises, is possible. Such an approach is termed 'dialogue between knowledges'" (Aguirre-Bastos et al. 2016: 91). In this dialogue, ICT enables as well as promotes innovation activities that are more inclusive and socially distributed.

We still do not know much about what specifically happens when traditional and indigenous knowledge systems are extended to reach the academy and enterprises in local knowledge systems or global knowledge systems, but evidence suggests an important potential for inclusive development (Davison et al. 2005). Furthermore, it seems reasonable to assume that democratizing access to information and providing opportunities for deprived areas to partake in social processes of interaction between different organizations and collective actors will result in a more inclusive innovation system.

Technological, institutional, or social innovations are the results of a combination of organized knowledge and interactions involving a diverse set of individuals and institutions. Such interactions take place not only among scientific disciplines but also among various types of practical experience and traditional or local knowledge. New technology in the form of ICT has radically improved opportunities for knowledge accumulation and interaction between individuals and institutions previously unable to interact with each other. Under appropriate conditions, marginalized groups previously excluded from global or local knowledge flows can tap into resources for innovative and capacity-building purposes through the appropriate use of ICT. Thus, policies for promoting access to ICT for disenfranchised groups would contribute to knowledge democratization and a more inclusive and knowledge-sharing Innovation System. However, such an inclusive development model would require that appropriate framework conditions be in place and, above all, that policies identifying and promoting social demand of knowledge be implemented.

INNOVATION POLICIES AS SOCIAL POLICIES
(AND THE OTHER WAY ROUND)

Now is a good time to address the question put forwards at the beginning of this chapter: what do we understand by inclusive innovation? As with the case of frugal and social innovation, the proliferation of meanings had led to elaborate taxonomies of the term: who uses it in what sense and with what definition (Heeks et al. 2014; Iizuka and Sadre Ghazi 2012). We do not want to add a new definition. What we need is a notion of inclusive innovation that serves to devise science, technology, and innovation policies to foster Sustainable Human Development.

The notion we are searching for will answer the following five questions:

(i) Who are the beneficiaries of inclusive innovations? Answer: lower-income and excluded groups.

(ii) What are the goals of knowledge production and innovation aimed at social inclusion understood in the broadest sense of the term as Sen recommends? Answer: to produce workable solutions for problems hampering some dimensions of social inclusion for lower-income and excluded groups.

(iii) What is the main heuristic of problem-solving? Answer: building upon the capacity to innovate in scarcity conditions to find solutions that share with the definition of frugal innovation the attributes of using dramatically less resources of all types and of delivering high-performing solutions.

(iv) What are the social relations involved? Answer: non-hierarchical knowledge relations, prone to facilitate and to promote multiple actors expressing their opinions on what the problems to be solved are and what type of solving strategies should be attempted, with special attention to the voices of lower-income and excluded groups; attention to fostering agency is a main concern, sharing in this sense the emphasis that social innovation conceptualization puts on "innovation with" and not only "innovation for".

(v) Which is the most important issue related to inclusive innovation? Answer: the systemic character of the efforts required to make inclusive innovation successful.

In a nutshell, inclusive innovations are those that contribute to Sustainable Human Development of lower-income and excluded groups; inclusive innovation policies are those that foster inclusive innovations; Inclusive Innovation Systems are those that provide the systemic behavior necessary for the achievement, diffusion, and impact of inclusive innovations.

The relevance of knowledge, coupled with the need for a systemic behavior to achieve successful inclusive innovations, suggests, as a main part of knowledge democratization, the promotion of innovation policies conceived partly as social policies. Such a connection is unusual but highly necessary: "[T]he reduction of inequality should be a priority for everyone. Within government, it is a matter for the minister responsible for science as well as for the minister responsible for social protection" (Atkinson 2015: 3).

For an innovation policy to be partly conceived as a social policy means that it shares aims and accountabilities by which it will be assessed with social policies. It is common to praise or to criticize knowledge policies in terms of their contribution to economic growth, while social policies are judged by how well they solve problems related to health, education, sanitation, nutrition, or housing, particularly those of the poor and vulnerable. So an innovation policy partly conceived as a social policy will need to focus on the contribution it can make to the solution of such problems. But it will not be able to do that in isolation, on its own. If social policies, for instance, are conceived mainly as cash transfers with which individuals solve—as well as they can—their problems through the market, there is little room for innovation policies to participate. If, on the other hand, a social policy seeks innovative solutions to provide better public goods to more people, then innovation policies can be central in achieving that aim. However, even if the latter is the case, it may not convey indigenous efforts: developing countries are full of examples of social policies implemented through imports of innovative solutions that are expensive and not adequately adapted to local conditions. The case would be different if social policies were conceived in harmony with innovation policies, relying as much as possible on the indigenous capacities to solve problems when pressing social situations need to be addressed.

We stated earlier that the great structural change of today is driven by the incorporation of advanced knowledge and highly qualified people to a permanently widening set of productive activities. This great structural change has taken place—and continues to take place—in highly industrialized countries, where the dynamics of their innovation systems fosters a reinforcing system-like behavior that, in terms of Nathan Rosenberg, allows for rapid technological convergences and upward spirals of well-solved technological disequilibria (Rosenberg 1976).

This is hardly the case in the Global South, a fact sketched out by the "ex ante" characterizations of their NIS. A relevant question is, then, from where may the demand come for knowledge and the opportunities to learn by addressing it. Social policies can be a source of such demand; successful inclusive innovations may provide solutions well beyond the society in which they were developed; scaling up this type of solutions may lead to wholly new productive activities, organized in a variety of ways, from almost self-production at a community level to formal industries with regional or international scope. Structural change has been hailed as the key to (economic) development for a long time; the recommended way to foster it was to try to catch up with highly industrialized countries; it has failed. But structural change in terms of a more intensive utilization of all types of knowledge, including state-of-the-art knowledge, part of which will come from today's "un-done" science that will eventually be done, is indeed fundamental. The social demand for knowledge, satisfied through inclusive innovation, has been a neglected piece in the structural change puzzle. The world of today, particularly the rise of inequality and the threat to the sustainability of life on Earth, may open a window of opportunity to take it seriously into account, opening the road to inclusive systems of innovation.

The Innovation Systems approach shows that inclusive innovations must be fostered by means of interactive processes where different actors play effective roles. Related policies must include relevant actors from deprived sectors with pressing problems—actors who must participate in the whole process, from the detection of such problems to the implementation of solutions. It must be taken into account, as already stressed, that inclusive innovations usually need to be designed in a framework of different types of scarcities, which means that the usual heuristic to search for solutions may not be appropriate.

Emerging innovation policies considered as part of social policies actually mobilize embryonic networks consisting of academics, policy makers, and non-governmental organizations. A fundamental question which must be asked is whether these policies are ideologically related to significant "popular actors", parties, and social movements; an affirmative response appears to require feedback between these policies and a more general ideological outlook concerning the democratization of knowledge.

Hess (2007: 19) considers "alternative pathways and their relationship to industrial innovation, empirically grounding the overall argument that social movements and activists have played and are playing a significant role not only in scientific but also industrial innovation, at least in [some] environmentally oriented cases".

A closer connection between innovation and inclusion may give new forces to the welfare state and political democracy. Both are being weakened by globalization, thus posing great dangers for common people and for living together with some degree of peace and cooperation. In the words of Judt (2008), "the need for representative democracy—which makes it possible for a large number of people to live together in some measure of agreement while retaining a degree of control over their collective fate— is also the best argument for the traditional state. [...] It is because the free flow of capital threatens the sovereign authority of democratic states that we need to strengthen these, not surrender them to the siren song of international markets, global society, or transnational communities" (Judt 2008: 424). And "[J]ust as political democracy is all that stands between individuals and an over mighty government, so the regulatory, providential state is all that stands between its citizens and the unpredictable forces of economic change" (Judt 2008: 425).

Socially oriented innovation policies have been fostered recently in Brazil in the context of a general orientation that gives priority to social inclusion: "[S]ocial policy and tackling inequality have become the core of government policy, and the social dimension of innovation has gradually become inserted in the STI agenda. The Ministry of Science, Technology and Innovation and its agencies have devised policy programmes to address social demand for innovation" (Cassiolato et al. 2014: 75).

In 2015, that policy was seen as a fundamental change in the making: "Brazilian innovation policy has not traditionally put social inclusion center stage. However, there is a growing effort to address social issues, especially in areas where innovation policy overlaps with other policies. Technological diffusion and the development of technologies adapted to the needs of economically disadvantaged people have been very relevant in the context of local productive arrangement policies (APLs) and regional development policies. The development of new technologies for infrastructure and housing connect to the program for expanding popular housing (Minha casa, Minha vida—'My home, my life')" (Mazzucato and Penna 2015: 54).

Local productive arrangements (APLs is the abbreviation in Portuguese) have been influential concerning not only commonly neglected social groups but also commonly neglected productive structures and regions: "[I]n most cases, those productive structures that have been left out of major structural and sectoral programs are targeted through the APLs policy. Often these are traditional sectors activities, which tend to be more dispersed throughout the national territory, including less dynamic regions. This underlines the complementary and often compensatory character of the APLs policy. It also constitutes an interesting starting point for promoting the decentralization of production. A main heading of the national development program is 'regionalization'. In this context, APLs are a channel for the mobilization of local and regional potential and for promoting productive activities associated with major infrastructure projects" (Mazzucato and Penna 2015: 55).

APLs are outstanding examples of inclusive innovation policies, fostered by an academic network, RedeSist, that at the same time elaborated theory and connected it with practice. "RedeSist was formally set up in 1997, aimed at investigating and understanding local processes of learning and capability creation and accumulation, as well as putting forward proposals for their promotion" (Cassiolato et al. 2014: 88). The notion of APLs was elaborated in such a way that it became the guiding notion of concrete policies implemented in several Brazilian regions, containing innovative features: "[A]lthough representing de facto support for local development and small and medium-sized enterprises, its novelty lies in the fact that policies target not only enterprises, but also the development of the territory, with the idea that knowledge and local innovation should be of paramount importance. It is also the first policy in Brazil to recognise the systemic character of innovation and development" (Cassiolato et al. 2014: 74).

The articulating role of the state in innovation policies in general is surely even more important concerning innovation policies seen as social policies, particularly because a wider diversity of actors needs to be connected. Thus, the possibilities of those policies are highly dependent on the prevailing attitudes of different sectors of the state that could potentially help in articulating actors as well as in connecting innovation and social dimensions of specific policies. The last assertion is based on the assumption that the state cannot always be considered a "unitary actor". This is well known; nevertheless, "[P]rescriptive innovation policy studies continue, in the welfare economics tradition, to treat policy as if it were the product of a unitary 'policy maker'" (Flanagan et al. 2011: 705).

We see fostering inclusive innovation in the Global South not only as a promising way of cooperating in the fight against social exclusion but also as a strategy for expanding advanced indigenous capabilities for Sustainable Human Development. If such a task is left to market demand, the dominant trend does not allow much hope. As already stated, the starting point of a propositional approach is to consider not only market demand but socially justified demand of knowledge in general. The next step is to elaborate a wide gamut of learning and innovation policies as part of social policies that see people not as patients but as agents. This is the main clue stemming from the normative approach to development and a most necessary condition to relate "popular actors" to knowledge policies. If this succeeds at least partially, then such policies will have more stakeholders. Consequently, indigenous knowledge production and use will expand and so will indigenous capabilities, thus fostering the upgrading of productive activities in general and also basic research. Concerning the last point, relying on market demand has not, generally speaking, given impressive results in the Global South, while the emphasis on the supply of knowledge has been limited time and again by the restriction of public funding and the weakness of private demand. Thus, giving high priority to connections of indigenous capabilities with the solution of pressing social problems can be seen as a fundamental component of a strategy for structural change that fosters the inclusive aspect as well as the strength—research included—of Innovation Systems.

Such a strategy includes prioritizing some goals for science and technology, and in a sense this is close to the first of fifteen proposals formulated by Atkinson: "[T]he direction of technological change should be an explicit concern of policy-makers, encouraging innovation in a form that increases the employability of workers and emphasises the human dimension of service provision" (Atkinson 2015: 118).

Now, concerning innovation policies seen as social policies, it seems that up to now only almost marginal or "interstitial" examples can really be detected. Who are their potential stakeholders? Potentially at least, deprived populations, related social movements, politicians and officials interested in social policies, technicians and academics worried about the social use of knowledge. Coordination problems are big while actual incentives for coping with such problems look rather limited.

Nevertheless, it deserves to be stressed that the NIS framework is particularly fruitful concerning inclusive innovation. Related possibilities and policies should be considered in such a framework that highlights social processes of learning. In order to have real impact, inclusive innovation needs to be especially distributed, interactive, and systemic. Participation must go beyond the usually considered actors of Innovation Systems. For example, deprived groups and environmentally damaged communities cannot be absent. Their effective participation is highly dependent on their possibilities to learn, both technologically and organizationally. What is being said entails that, in Inclusive Innovation Systems, interactions should be wider than usual, that more distributed and systemic initiatives are needed, and consequently that coordination tasks will be more demanding. Quite different actors must combine their specific types of knowledge if inequality is to be diminished and sustainability fostered. In other words, interactive learning processes and agency in general become more complicated and more necessary than usual.

WHO ARE THE STAKEHOLDERS OF INCLUSIVE INNOVATION SYSTEMS?

Besides prompt and targeted novel solutions directed to, or built by, specific less-privileged actors, the whole idea of an Inclusive Innovation System is that of a well-oiled social dynamic where the problems that hamper the fulfillment of "development as freedom" for diverse parts of the population gain center stage in knowledge and innovation agendas. The systemic features here are even more necessary than in "common" Innovation Systems. The interrelatedness of the factors at stake to tackle inequality, deprivation, destitution, and marginalization requires that innovation efforts dialog with a complex and not always well-coordinated web of diverse social undertakings and social actors. Such a dialogue is a precondition for inclusive innovation: without it, the problems to be tackled cannot even start to be identified and characterized. But if the systemic features of an Inclusive Innovation System need to be particularly strong, the difficulties of achieving that are formidable. To the well-known coordination obstacles derived from silo-like public policies, we have in addition the distance between the type of problems tackled by knowledge and innovation policies mainly directed to the supply side and those tackled by social policies, mirroring the gulf that separates advanced knowledge producers and users and less-privileged groups.

The transformations needed to reach Inclusive Innovation Systems are deep and difficult; one feature in particular of the characterization of "deep transitions" proposed by Schot and Kanger seems valid here: "the emergence of qualitatively new solutions (the emergence of new 'species', rather than the optimization of the existing ones)" (Schot and Kanger 2016: 29). Qualitatively new solutions include those emerging from heuristics geared by scarcity instead of abundance; a fruitful alliance between fostering inclusive innovation and advancing sustainability may be built around them. But the more qualitatively new the innovations are, particularly if they are not "absolutely" new but deeply different from an already known way of solving a problem, the more difficult it is to overcome the obstacles of not being recognized and valued. So the ability of the stakeholders in Inclusive Innovation Systems to face these difficulties is important indeed.

Another way to refer to the need of a deep shift is the following: "[I]n a structuralist view, two macro-agendas and discourses currently struggle for the future of the 21st century: (1) neo-liberalism and globalization (with associated notions such as international competitiveness, economic growth, limited regulation, market based processes, privatization, individual responsibilities), and (2) sustainable development and social transformation (ecological modernization, risk society, stronger government roles, corporate social responsibility, public participation, democratization). While the first macro-agenda has dominated since the 1980s, sustainability transitions may require a shift towards the second agenda" (Geels 2010: 499).

Powerful interests foster such "first macro-agenda", while environmental and social risks may push toward the alternative agenda, akin to Sustainable Human Development, but the shift will require no small amount of agency. Now, who can have agency? According to Long (2001: 182), "central to the notion of social actor is the concept of human agency, which attributes to the actor (individual or social group) the capacity to process social experience and to devise ways of coping with problematic situations. [...] It requires organisation". Moreover, "*[S]ocial actors* are all those social entities that can be said to have agency [...]: individual persons, informal groups or interpersonal networks, organisations, collective groupings and what are sometimes called 'macro' actors (e.g., a particular national government, church or international organisation)" (Op. cit.: 241).

The connection between agency and actors suggests that Sustainable Human Development needs to be based on convergences or coalitions of several actors: "[T]he success of policies to implement the 2030 Agenda for Sustainable Development and to achieve the Sustainable Development Goals will hinge on a new development pattern: a progressive structural change centred on equality and environmental sustainability and based on social coalitions and compacts for governance at the global, regional and national levels" (ECLAC 2016: 169).

Stakeholders in a progressive structural change that has as a central aim to redress facets of inequality by means of knowledge production and use are diverse. The normative importance given to agency and the recognition that users play a vital role in innovation—they possess unique knowledge about the "border conditions" that a satisfactory solution needs to fulfill—signals the importance of two types of stakeholders in inclusive innovation: those for which technology has been mainly an imposition and those whose situation and needs have hardly conveyed innovation at all. The former are workers in industry, agriculture, or services; the latter are the less-privileged people in general and the poor in particular.

In the preceding, we have presented examples that show that the innovative agency of organized workers can be a source of technically successful innovations that at the same time are inclusive, in process and outcomes. However, the establishment of a sort of long-term alliance between workers and technological designers—present in the examples given and logically necessary to tap into the power of knowledge—has proven difficult. An example of an attempt to build an alliance of this type is the establishment of the Amsterdam Science Shop in 1977. This was done on the belief that "our society was going through a period of change in power relations caused mainly by the rise of science and technology as sources of production, power and legitimation and therefore *access* to science and technology might be a crucial resource. The Science Shop was intended as a specific instrument to give access to groups underprivileged in this respect" (Leydesdorff and Van Den Besselaar 1987: 137, emphasis in the original). The analysis of the difficulties faced by this initiative is sobering. The core of the difficulty for a social actor aiming at developing "technologies that are needed from a social perspective" is said to be the lack of abilities "to generate the precise mixture of cognition and organizational power which seems necessary to act upon the S&T system" (Op. cit.: 156). This problem is even more acute in relation to innovation and when the social actors involved are deprived sectors of the population.

Having access to science, technology, and innovation— at least in the sense of being able to intervene in the setting of its working agendas—is a crucial resource to foster democracy, build more equal societies, and promote sustainability. For this to happen, underprivileged groups need to become stakeholders in the process; it seems clear that they will not be able to become stakeholders on their own. This leads us to pay attention to advanced-knowledge holders and to ask where their loyalties are. We need to ask, moreover, how such loyalties can be transformed from the probable allegiance to their employers in the private case and to the prestige system in the academic case to a commitment to build knowledge needed from a social perspective. Important institutional changes are required for this to happen in the knowledge system; in science, technology, and innovation policies and in the university system; and in the interface between them.

This, again, is far from simple. Forging coalitions or compacts fostered by the agency of different groups poses well-known problems: "[A]ctors may play multiple roles. The roles they elect to play may be in tension with or even in contradiction with the expectations or demands of other actors or the constraints of institutions. Individual human actors are members of organisations, research groups, disciplinary communities and policy networks which, as collectives, can all have agency and which may play different and contradictory roles from those played by the individuals that make them up" (Flanagan et al. 2011: 706).

In the academic realm, these tensions are well known: "[I]ncentives for researchers (e.g. publication rules) may be at odds with societal problem agendas, meaning that research does not contribute to solving the problems" (Geels 2014: 914).

Consequently, attention must be paid to the question of who are the actual or potential stakeholders of a shift from the globalizing neoliberal "macro agenda" to the Sustainable Human Development "macro agenda" that needs inclusive innovation as one of its pillars.

The prospective approach sketched in Chapter 2 suggests that, quite probably, knowledge-based inequality and environmental degradation will keep worsening. Both are connected because, generally speaking, deprived people are more exposed than the rest to damages stemming from environmental and climatic changes. Wealth is no minor asset for obtaining better living conditions. It helps particularly to pay for research and innovation related to environment protection and repairing, improving transportation, shifting to clean energies and the like. Thus, knowledge-based inequality can be detected in such issues.

So it can be assumed, first, that everybody is interested in avoiding climatic damages and, second, that non-privileged human groups are especially interested in opposing the combination of knowledge-based inequality and environmental degradation. But even if such interests are strong, their translation into action does not look easy. Concerning the interest of humankind as such in preventing climatic risks, it has been remarked that "[N]ew environmental problems, such as climate change, biodiversity and resource depletion, have gained prominence on the political agenda in the 1990s and early 2000s. These pervasive problems differ in scale and complexity from the environmental problems of the 1970s and 1980s, such as water pollution, acid rain, local air pollution and waste problems. While the latter problems have been addressed fairly well with incremental clean technologies, responses to the new environmental problems require more substantive 'transitions' in the coming decades, i.e. major changes in energy, transport, and agri-food systems [...]. These system changes are labelled 'socio-technical' because they not only entail new technologies, but also changes in markets, user practices, policy and cultural meanings" (Geels 2010: 495).

It could be added that the above-mentioned "environmental problems of the 1970s and 1980s" were such—in several cases at least—that proposals for solving them directly benefited concrete sectors and so related policies could have quite strong stakeholders. That is not usually the case in issues related to climate change, where specific proposals are often costly for concrete groups while their benefits are not easy to see and are highly dependent on what is done in other contexts.

Concerning the interests of less-privileged people, let us recall something happening in the world of underdevelopment where knowledge-based inequality is apparent. Transference of polluting manufacturing and extractive activities to underdeveloped countries has been happening for several decades already. Multinational corporations are relevant protagonists of such transference. In turn, underdeveloped countries often do not have the technical expertise or the economic and political power that are needed to enforce environmental regulations. Related asymmetries are easily seen when regulations are infringed by multinational corporations.

Perhaps no less consequential is that underdeveloped countries frequently have few opportunities for creating jobs in non-polluting activities. More generally, opportunities for working in acceptable conditions are often scarce. That stems directly from the specialization in productive activities with low value added of knowledge and qualifications. Thus, some poor people in underdeveloped countries frequently have to choose between unemployment and working in polluting activities. The last option in turn may open conflicts with other deprived sectors (for example, those living in places that are especially damaged by such activities). Employment and related living conditions may be affected if environmental regulations are thoroughly enforced while, if they are not enforced, global and also local environmental problems are aggravated. That can be seen in many places of the Global South. It is a major obstacle for fostering collective action with shared general purposes that may contribute to Sustainable Human Development.

This type of obstacle deserves closer attention. When a prospective approach was sketched, a fundamental contradiction was stressed: the contradiction between increasing production and environmental protection.

It is especially acute for poor and powerless sectors, particularly those located in underdeveloped countries: social relations being what they are, it is very difficult to diminish poverty without expanding production, while such sectors are usually the first victims of environmental degradation generated by prevailing techno-productive forms. Their weakness concerning knowledge and social power hampers their possibilities for promoting or backing changes that diminish inequality and environmental damage. If the two problems are closely connected, something similar happens with possible solutions: "human development should be seen as a major contribution to the achievement of sustainability" (Anand and Sen 2000: 2038). This assertion can be read as saying that overcoming the great contradiction between production and environment requires expanding capabilities, in the first place of non-privileged sectors. In this way, the problem of agency leads to the very difficult political problem of connecting advanced knowledge and collective actors related to non-dominant social sectors, which can be called popular actors. This is a watershed and so it deserves further comments that can be seen as a reappraisal of some main topics discussed in the first part of this book which comes to its end in this section.

Factual and prospective approaches sketched in Chapter 2 suggest that power stemming from advanced knowledge will keep increasing. From such a perspective, knowledge democratization was presented as the core of a propositional approach to Sustainable Human Development. Its significance is stressed by the role of knowledge in rising inequality, the specific issue of Chapter 3. Any acceptable characterization of knowledge democratization surely includes expanding the beneficial consequences from knowledge to non-dominant social sectors. If these sectors are estranged from advanced learning, knowledge generation, and innovation, in the best of circumstances they will be benefited only as patients, not as agents. That is not what the normative approach to Sustainable Human Development recommends. Agency is valued for ethical reasons and also for practical reasons. The last point means that, as history shows, passive reception of benefits is at best limited.

The above can be formulated in terms of the NIS framework briefly presented in Chapter 4. It can be asserted that, when popular actors are estranged from advanced knowledge, they really do not belong to the Innovation System. At most, they play a marginal role in the interactions that shape the system and its consequences for different social groups. When knowledge becomes the main basis of collective power, its distribution will probably be weakly influenced by collective actors divorced from learning and innovation processes. Counteracting knowledge-based inequality demands knowledge-related popular agency. Nevertheless, this issue receives scant attention, perhaps even less now than some decades ago. The following remark concerning agriculture in India could be extended to other sectors and large regions in the Global South, notably Latin America: "[B]ecause the politics of knowledge production is no more on the priority of the socio-political forces active among the people, there is no viable political force to take up the political battle of pro-poor innovation making in the Indian agricultural system of innovation" (Abrol 2014: 354).

Since the first years of this century, relevant collective actors have backed strong redistribution policies in Latin America. Their implementation was supported by political changes and moreover by increased external incomes stemming from high prices of exported commodities. As a consequence, poverty diminished significantly and even inequality came down, not a small feat in a region usually considered to be the most unequal of the planet. Now, alternative learning and innovation policies in Latin America still have quite weak stakeholders. The problem has received scant attention from political parties and social movements. When the commodity boom seems to be over, the transformation of productive structures appears to have been comparatively small (ECLAC 2016). The peripheral condition still dominates the landscape, fettering further economic growth. After the bonanza, redistribution becomes harder and the social progress of recent years is under threat.

From a different but not unrelated point of view, the political problems posed by fostering (economic) development in so-called "middle income countries" have been described as the obstacles for organizing "upgrading coalitions" (Doner and Schneider 2016). Obstacles stem from high inequality and from fragmentation of social groups. It is argued that the last point has special relevance in the case of business and labor that should be the core constituencies of an upgrading coalition. Such a coalition is needed for improving education, expanding research, and backing policies oriented to overcome the "middle income trap" described in Chapter 3 while dealing with the learning divides. Overcoming this situation requires long-term political and economic investments, but owing to their inherently short-term perspective in order to stay in office, governments in more or less democratic settings may not be encouraged to foster such costly investments.

In the framework presented in this book, it could be said that those "semi peripheral" countries face great difficulties to climb the ladder of catching up with central countries. Upgrading production activities in order to become knowledge-based and innovation-driven economies is inherently difficult. Central countries often try to kick away the ladder (Chang 2002). Prevailing ways for upgrading—that is, climbing the ladder—pose increasing environmental and social obstacles. Economic growth has become a very important requisite for the continuity of incumbent governments, perhaps not only in more or less democratic settings, so "short termism" is a general political problem. Surely, inequality and fragmentation hamper the building of "upgrading coalitions". But the problem seems to be even deeper. Prevailing ways of "upgrading" suffer from diminishing returns in economic terms and increasing costs in terms of sustainability. Differently oriented upgrading coalitions are needed for shifting the development agenda to inclusive innovation and, more generally, to knowledge democratization. Such coalitions look scarcely feasible if popular actors are not agents of change. That condition is surely not sufficient, but it is argued that it is absolutely necessary, so attention is especially paid to it in the following.

In order to conclude this Chapter 5—and with it the first part of the book—some remarks concerning academic work are perhaps of some value. On the one hand, without strong academic commitment to knowledge democratization, such a process does not look feasible. On the other hand, policy and more general proposals stemming from academic studies can only be seen as a modest input for practical work aimed at fostering agency for democratization. For that, quite different though not necessarily contradictory interests have to be articulated. That is the role of politics. In the words of Mann (2013: 414), "[T]he challenge in the twenty-first century is for electorates and political elites to devise policies to counter the tendency toward an included/excluded divide, to restrain mass consumerism, and to accept more global international coordination".

In any case, the global damages and risks entailed by prevailing trends have been fostering countervailing policies, with different degrees of support. It may be expected that present global challenges will promote interactions of ideological power and technological power that can protect life and fight inequality. The ideology of consumerism must be checked; science and technology must be oriented in ways that help to produce better rather than more goods and services, and in sustainable ways. Both types of changes look difficult, but perhaps social and environmental threats may open some spaces for them. That in turn could intertwine positively with the problem of stakeholders and agency: if knowledge democratization fosters first-rate inclusive innovation, its social support may expand, in the South as well as in the North.

REFERENCES

Abrol, D. (2014). Pro-Poor Innovation Making, Knowledge Production, and Technology Implementation for Rural Areas: Lessons from the Indian Experience. In S. V. Ramani (Ed.), *Innovation in India. Combining Economic Growth with Inclusive Development* (pp. 337–378). Delhi: Cambridge University Press.

Abrol, D. (2017). The Honey Bee Network. In A. Smith, M. Fressoli, D. Abrol, E. Around, & A. Ely (Eds.), *Grassroots Innovation Movements* (pp. 145–164). New York: Routledge.

Aguirre-Bastos, C., Aliaga Lordeman, J., Garrón Védia, I., & Rubín de Célis Cedro, R. (2016). National Innovation System in Bolivia: Making Research and Innovation Matter. In B. Göransson, C. Brundenius, & C. Aguirre (Eds.), *Innovation Systems for Development: Making Research and Innovation in Developing Countries Matter*. Northampton: Edward Elgar Publishing.

Alzugaray, S., Mederos, L., & Sutz, J. (2012). Building Bridges. Social Inclusion Problems as Research and Innovation Issues. *Review of Policy Research, 29*(6), 776–796.

Amaral Filho, J. (2006). Pingo D'água: un arranjo innovativo no semi-árido do ceará. In H. Lastres & J. Cassiolato (org.), *Estratégias para o desenvolvimento: um enfoque sobre arranjos produtivos locais do Norte, Nordeste e Centro-Oeste Brasileiros* (pp. 49–66), e-papers, Río de Janeiro.

Anand, S., & Sen, A. (2000). Human Development and Economic Sustainability. *World Development, 2812*, 2029–2049.

Andersen, E. S., & Lundvall, B.-Å. (1988). Small National Innovation Systems Facing Technological Revolutions: An Analytical Framework. In C. Freeman & B.-Å. Lundvall (Eds.), *Small Countries Facing the Technological Revolution*. London: Pinter Publishers.

Astronomo, R., & Burton, D. (2010). Carbohydrate Vaccines: Developing Sweet Solutions to Sticky Situations? *Nature Reviews, 9*, 308–324.

Atkinson, A. B. (2015). *Inequality: What Can Be Done?* Cambridge, USA: Harvard University Press.

Bairoch, P. (1993). *Economics and World History. Myths and Paradoxes.* Chicago: The University of Chicago Press.

Balaji, V. (2005). Sustainability Issues in Rural Asian Telecenters. In R. Davison, R. Harris, S. Qureshi, D. Vogel, & G.-J. de Vreede (Eds.), *Information Systems in Developing Countries. Theory and Practice.* Hong Kong: City University of Hong Kong Press.

Bound, K., & Thornton, I. (2012). *Our Frugal Future: Lessons from India's Innovation System.* Available at: https://www.nesta.org.uk/sites/default/files/our_frugal_future.pdf. Accessed 11 May 2017.

Brem, A., & Wolfram, P. (2014). Research and Development from the Bottom Up – Introduction of Terminologies for New Product Development in Emerging Markets. *Journal of Innovation and Entrepreneurship, 3*, 9.

Available at: http://innovation-entrepreneurship.springeropen.com/articles/ 10.1186/2192-5372-3-9. Accessed 10 May 2017.

Brundenius, C. (2017). Challenges of Rising Inequalities and the Quest for Inclusive and Sustainable Development. In C. Brundenius, B. Göransson, & J. M. Carvalho de Mello (Eds.), *Universities, Inclusive Development and Social Innovation. An International Perspective* (pp. 9–48). Ottawa: Springer.

Cassiolato, J., & Couto, M. C. (Eds.). (2015). *Health Innovation Systems, Equity and Development*, e-papers, Río de Janeiro.

Cassiolato, J. E., Lastres, H., & Couto, M. C. (2014). The Brazilian National System of Innovation: Challenges to Sustainability and Inclusive Development. In G. Dutrénit & J. Sutz (Eds.), *National Innovation Systems, Social Inclusion and Development: The Latin American Experience* (pp. 68–101). Cheltenham: Edward Elgar.

Chang, H.-J. (2002). *Kicking away the Ladder: Development Strategy in Historical Perspective*. London: Anthem Press.

Christensen, J. L., Gregersen, B., Johnson, B., Lundvall, B.-A., & Tomlinson, M. (2008). An NSI in Transition? Denmark. In C. Edquist & L. Hommen (Eds.), *Small Country Innovation Systems Globalization, Change and Policy in Asia and Europe* (pp. 403–441). Cheltenham: Edward Elgar.

Collison, C., & Parcell, G. (2001). *Learning to Fly – Practical Lessons from One of the World's Leading Knowledge Companies*. Oxford: Capstone.

Dahl, R. A. (1989). *Democracy and Its Critics*. New Haven: Yale University Press.

Dalum, B., Fagerberg, J., & Jorgensen, U. (1988). Small Open Economies in the World Market for Electronics: the Case of the Nordic Countries. In C. Freeman & B.-A. Lundvall (Eds.), *Small Countries Facing Technological Revolution* (pp. 113–138). London: Pinter.

Davison, R., Harris, R., Qureshi, S., Vogel, D., & de Vreede, G.-J. (Eds.). (2005). *Information Systems in Developing Countries. Theory and Practice*. Hong Kong: City University of Hong Kong Press.

Doner, R., & Schneider, B. R. (2016). The Middle-Income Trap: More Politics than Economics. *World Politics, 4*, 608–644.

ECLAC (Economic Commission for Latin America and the Caribbean). (2016). *Horizons 2030: Equality at the Centre of Sustainable Development* (LC/G.2660(SES.36/3). Santiago de Chile: Economic Commission for Latin America and the Caribbean.

European Commission. (2015). *Call for Tenders: 'Study on Frugal Innovation and Reengineering of Traditional Techniques'*. Available at: https://infoeuropa. eurocid.pt/files/database/000065001-000066000/000065237_2.pdf. Accessed 10 May 2017.

European Commission. (2016). *A Conceptual Analysis of Foundations, Trends and Relevant Potentials in the Field of Frugal Innovation (for Europe)*. Interim Report for the Project "Study on frugal innovation and reengineering of traditional techniques" Commissioned to Fraunhofer ISI and Nesta.

Fajnzylber, F. (1984). *La industrialización trunca de América Latina*. México D.F.: Centro Editor.

Flanagan, K., Uyarra, E., & Laranja, M. (2011). Reconceptualising the 'Policymix' for Innovation. *Research Policy, 40*(5), 702–713.

Foster, C., & Heeks, R. (2013). Innovation and Scaling of ICT for the Bottom-of-the-Pyramid. *Journal of Information Technology, 28*(4), 296–315.

Freeman, C. (1982). *The Economics of Industrial Innovation* (2nd ed.). London: Pinter.

Freeman, C. (1988). Technology Gaps, International Trade and the Problems of Smaller and Less Developed Countries. In C. Freeman & B.-A. Lundvall (Eds.), *Small Countries Facing Technological Revolution* (pp. 37–66). London: Pinter.

Freeman, C. (1992). Science and Economy at the National Level. In C. Freeman (Ed.), *The Economics of Hope* (pp. 31–49). London: Pinter Publishers.

Fuchs, R. (1998, June). *"Little Engines that Did": Case Histories from the Global Telecentre Movement, IDRC.* Available at: https://idl-bnc-idrc.dspacedirect. org/bitstream/handle/10625/12989/108350.pdf?sequence=1. Accessed 15 May 2017.

Geels, F. W. (2010). Ontologies, Socio-Technical Transitions (to Sustainability), and the Multi-Level Perspective. *Research Policy, 39*(4), 495–510.

Geels, F. W. (2014). From Sectoral Systems of Innovation to Socio-Technical Systems Insights About Dynamics and Change from Sociology and Institutional Theory. *Research Policy, 33*(6–7), 897–920.

Göransson, B. (1993). *Catching Up in Technology—Case Studies from the Telecommunications Equipment Industry*. London: Taylor Graham.

Gronning, T., Moen, S. E., & Sutherland, D. (2008). Low Innovation Intensity, High Growth and Specialized Trajectories. In C. Edquist & L. Hommen (Eds.), *Small Country Innovation Systems Globalization, Change and Policy in Asia and Europe* (pp. 281–318). Cheltenham: Edward Elgar.

Guarga, R., Mastrangelo, P., Scaglione, G., & Supino, E. (2000). Evaluation of the SIS, a New Frost Protection Method Applied in a Citrus Orchard. In *Proceedings of the 9th Congress of the International Society of Citriculture* (p. 583), Orlando, USA.

Heeks, R., Foster, C., & Nugroho, Y. (2014). New Models of Inclusive Innovation for Development. *Innovation and Development, 4*(2), 175–183.

Hess, D. (2007). *Alternative Pathways in Science and Industry. Activism, Innovation, and the Environment in an Era of Globalization*. Cambridge, MA: The MIT Press.

Heyer, J., Stewart, F., & Thorp, R. (2002). *Group Behaviour and Development. Is the Market Destroying Cooperation?* Oxford: Oxford University Press.

Hirschman, A. (1958). *The Strategy of Economic Development*. New Haven: Yale University Press.

Hubert, A. (2010). *Empowering People, Driving Change: Social Innovation in the European Union*. Report to the European Commission, BEPA, Luxembourg.

Iizuka, M., & Sadre Ghazi, S. (2012). *Understanding Dynamics of Pro-poor Innovation: Mapping the Disputed Areas*. Paper presented at the Dynamics of Institution and Markets in Europe (DIME) Final Conference, 6–8 April 2011, Maastricht.

Judt, T. (2008). *Reappraisals. Reflections on the Forgotten Twentieth Century*. New York: The Penguin Press.

Landaverde, M., Di Fabio, J. L., Ruocco, G., Leal, I., y de Quadros, C. (1999). Introducción de la vacuna conjugada contra Hib en Chile y Uruguay. *Rev Panam Salud Publica, 5*(3), Washington. Available at: http://www.scielosp. org/pdf/rpsp/v5n3/top200.pdf. Accessed 10 May 2017.

Lemola, T., & Lovio, R. (1988). Possibilities for a Small Country in High-Technology Production: The Case of Finland. In C. Freeman & B.-A. Lundvall (Eds.), *Small Countries Facing Technological Revolution* (pp. 139–155). London: Pinter.

Leydesdorff, L., & Van Den Besselaar, P. (1987). What We Have Learned from the Amsterdam Science Shop. In S. Blume, J. Bunders, L. Leydesdroff, & R. Whitley (Eds.), *The Social Direction of the Public Sciences* (pp. 135–162). Dordrecht: D. Reidel Publishing Co.

Long, N. (2001). *Development Sociology. Actor Perspectives*. London: Routledge.

Lundvall, B. Å. (1985). *Product Innovation and User-Producer Interaction* (Industrial Development Research Series No. 31). Aalborg: Aalborg University Press.

Lundvall, B. Å. (1988). Innovation as an Interactive Process: from User-Producer Interaction to the National System of Innovation. In G. Dosi, C. Freeman, R. Nelson, G. Silverberg, & L. Soete (Eds.), *Technical Change and Economic Theory* (pp. 349–369). London: Pinter.

Lundvall, B. Å. (2002). *Innovation, Growth and Social Cohesion. The Danish Model*. Cheltenham, UK: Elgar.

Lundvall, B. Å. (2010). Postscript: Innovation System Research – Where It Comes from and Where It Might Go. In B. A. Lundvalll (Ed.), *National Systems of Innovation. Towards a Theory of Innovation and Interactive Learning* (pp. 317–366). London: Anthem Press.

Lundvall, B. Å. (2016). Innovation Systems and Development: History, Theory and Challenges. In E. Reinert, J. Ghosh, & R. Kattel (Eds.), *Handbook of Alternative Theories of Economic Development* (pp. 594–612). Cheltenham: Edward Elgar.

Mani, S. (2005). *Keeping Pace with Globalization. Innovation Capability in Korea's Telecommunications Equipment Industry, Working Paper 370*. Maastricht: UNU-INTECH.

Mann, M. (2013). *The Sources of Social Power. Vol. IV Globalizations, 1945–2011*. Cambridge: Cambridge University Press.

Mazzucato, M., & Penna, C. (2015). *The Brazilian Innovation System: A Mission-Oriented Policy Proposal*. Brasília, DF: Centro de Gestão e Estudos Estratégicos.

Morel, C. (2003). Neglected Diseases: Under-Funded Research and Inadequate Health Interventions, EMBO Reports, Special issue. Available at: https://www. ncbi.nlm.nih.gov/pmc/articles/PMC1326440/. Accessed 10 May 2017.

Muller, J. (2010). *Befit for Change: Social Construction of Endogenous Technology in the South.* FAU conference, Gjerrild.

Nelson, R., & Winter, S. (1982). *An Evolutionary Theory of Economic Change.* Cambridge: The Belknap Press of Harvard University Press.

OECD. (2011). *Demand-Side Innovation Policies.* Paris: OECD Publishing.

Ostrom, E. (1996). Crossing the Great Divide: Coproduction, Synergy, and Development. *World Development, 24*(6), 1073–1087.

Pérez, C. (1985). Microelectronics, Long Waves and World Structural Change: New Perspectives for Developing Countries. *World Development, 13*(3), 441–463.

Pisano, U., Lange, L., & Berger, G. (2015). *Social Innovation in Europe. An Overview of the Concept of Social Innovation in the Context of European Initiatives and Practices.* ESDN Quarterly Report, 36.

Plaza, B. (2000). Política Industrial de la Comunidad Autónoma del País Vasco 1981–2001. *Economía Industrial, 235*(236), 299–314.

Reich, R. (1992). *The Work of Nations.* New York: Alfred A Knopf.

Rosenberg, N. (1976). Technological Change in the Machine Tool Industry, 1840–1910. In N. Rosenberg (Ed.), *Perspectives on Technology* (pp. 9–31). Cambridge: Cambridge University Press.

Rothwell, R., Freeman, C., Horlsey, A., Jervis, V., Robertson, A., & Towsend, J. (1974). SAPPHO Updated. Project Sappho Phase II. *Research Policy, 3,* 258–291.

Sarewitz, D., & Pielke, R. A. (2007). The Neglected Heart of Science: Reconciling Supply and Demand for Science. *Environmental Science and Policy, 10,* 5–16.

Schot, J., & Kanger, L. (2016). Deep Transitions: Emergence, Acceleration, Stabilization and Directionality. *SPRU Working Papers,* 2016–15.

Smith, A., Fressoli, M., Abrol, D., Around, E., & Ely, A. (2017). *Grassroots Innovation Movements.* New York: Routledge.

Srinivas, S. (2014). Demand and Innovation. Path Towards Inclusive Development. In S. Ramani (Ed.), *Innovation in India: Combining Economic Growth with Inclusive Development* (pp. 78–106). India: Cambridge University Press.

Srinivas, S., & Sutz, J. (2008). Developing Countries and Innovation. Searching for a New Analytical Approach. *Technology in Society, 30*(2), 129–140.

The Atlantic. (2017). *Why Is Sweden so Good at Pop Music?* Available at: https://www.theatlantic.com/entertainment/archive/2013/10/why-is-sweden-so-good-at-pop-music/280945/. Accessed 10 May 2017.

Vérez-Bencomo, V. (2007). Interview. *MEDICC Review, 9*(1), 14–15.

Vincenti, W. (1990). *What Engineers Know and How They Know It. Analytical Studies from Aeronautical History.* Baltimore: John Hopkins University Press.

von Hippel, E. (1988). *The Sources of Innovation.* Nueva York: Oxford University Press.

Weizenbaum, J. (1976). *Computer Power and Human Reason. From Judgement to Calculation.* San Francisco: Freeman, and Co.

Zarei, A. E., Almehdar, H., & Redwan, E. M. (2016). Hib Vaccines: Past, Present, and Future Perspectives. *Journal of Immunology Research.* Available at: https://www.hindawi.com/journals/jir/2016/7203587/. Accessed 10 May 2017.

PART II

The Idea of the Developmental University

CHAPTER 6

Challenged Universities

Universities that embrace the task of democratizing knowledge as a contribution to Sustainable Human Development may be considered developmental universities. This is the idea to be elaborated in this and the following chapters. Universities fulfill such a task largely by furthering general access to advanced education, by providing effective incentives to include in their research agendas the kind of problems whose solutions can lead to an enhancement of social inclusion, and by cooperating with other actors in the socially valuable use of knowledge.

Universities are facing a series of tensions that force them to re-think and reshape their missions, including teaching, research, and the "third mission" in its many meanings. Everywhere, universities are fundamental actors in knowledge production. The orientation of their research agendas is influenced by different actors with uneven power resources. A more socially inclusive orientation of knowledge production in universities needs to be backed through a strong-enough expression of interests as to be able to open spaces to new types of research agendas.

Such assumptions lead to the following questions to be addressed in this chapter: Which types of issues shape the evolution of universities? Which are the main differences among current proposals for the third mission of universities? How are the demands for social responsiveness of universities expressed and by whom? How do universities react and answer to such demands?

© The Author(s) 2018
R. Arocena et al., *Developmental Universities in Inclusive Innovation Systems*, https://doi.org/10.1007/978-3-319-64152-2_6

LOOKING BACK

From the twelfth century to the nineteenth century, the evolution of universities in Europe was intertwined with the whole history of the continent with such relevant consequences that it has been asserted that "the university is a European institution; indeed, it is the European institution *par excellence*" (Rüegg 1992: xix).

Müller (1996) presents the history of Western universities in four periods, each characterized by a dominant type that can be seen as an ideal type in the sense of Weber. He calls them the university of faith, the university of reason, the university of discovery, and the university of calculation.

The university of faith was the original medieval university that emerged when the political and commercial importance of cities started rising in Europe during the twelfth century. That institution was the heir of medieval cathedral schools and monastic schools. Already from the beginning, universities were closely connected to the leading strata of society, particularly those ruling and financing their operation. The university of faith offered education for the elite of the clergy, the ideologically dominant strata of the period that commanded the church and also provided the intellectual bureaucracy of the state. The Faculty of Theology was its core. That university also answered the demands for applying existing knowledge in the realms of health and jurisprudence. Thus, the Faculties of Medicine and Law had quite a relevant place and were emblematic for some universities. "It may be said that this initial model dominated the history of universities at least up to the 18th century. Teaching was its defining function. Its main emphasis was not on the creation of new knowledge but on reproducing and commenting what was already accepted as true knowledge. Its source was the authority of the church and of some classic scholars, not research based on independent reason and experiment. Nevertheless, in such a setting knowledge was not only preserved in general but also expanded in some realms. But the institutional mission was not to foster change in any sense but essentially to preserve the ideological as well as the political status quo. They were seen as such to the extent that the French Revolution, in 1793, first nationalized the universities' endowments, considered ecclesiastical, and some months later suppressed the institutions for good" (Howard 2006: 1).

The university of faith was the somewhat unlikely precursor and, in some sense, was in strong opposition to the next step in the evolution of the university. Structurally, the most important and profound change in the history of universities was started when the "university of faith transformed itself in the university of reason" (Müller 1996: 15). That transformation is called the First Academic Revolution. Although its roots and first steps are much older, that Revolution is usually associated with the foundation of the University of Berlin in 1810. "University-based intellectual networks have existed before, but never with such autonomy for researchers to define their own path and such power to take over every sphere of intellectual life" (Collins 2002: 618). The project for it was elaborated by Wilhelm von Humboldt. The fundamental idea was that research should be as important and legitimate a function for the university as teaching and, moreover, that the joint performance of both functions would benefit each of them. Thus, the "Humboldtian project" can be represented by the joint practice of teaching and research (Clark 1995, 1997). It has been accompanied by the explosion of disciplinary paths: "[S]tructurally, the academic revolution divided the old all-purpose intellectual role of the philosopher into a multitude of academic specialties. The process of specialization, not yet ended today, has affected the content of intellectual life in several ways. Most obvious is the crystallization of the subject matters in the new disciplines, ranging from psychology, sociology, and the other social sciences, to the natural sciences, humanities, and literature, now incorporated as academic subjects" (Ibid: 619). The Academic Revolution was a decisive contribution to such important processes as the institutionalization of research and the emergence of the professional scientist (Ben-David 1984).

The German "idea of University" based on the Humboldtian project prescribed teachers to also be researchers in order to instill *Bildung*—or personal development—in shaping the student's character and worldview. Thus, the notions of research and *Bildung* became closely linked (Anderson 2004). That project included academic freedom as a guarantee for researchers to choose their working topics based only on their own interpretation of cultural priorities and to be free from external conditions or pressures. Such freedom would be guaranteed by the directing role of academics themselves in university governance. It was assumed that the best condition for the emergence of new scientific knowledge was a peer-guided process within the academic community itself, a process that would indirectly provide relevant benefits to society.

The Humboldtian project aimed at an "institutional decoupling of science by four major separations": of cognition and property, of ideas and interest, of theory and practice, of science and state (Schmoch 2011: 270). "These separations were introduced to permit independent research activities by universities without the government or private enterprises exerting influence. This concept induced a distinct orientation of universities toward the generation of pure knowledge and thus toward basic research. Humboldt's concept was revolutionary in the context of that time which was characterized by a strong central government which tried to control nearly everything" (Ibid: 270).

In fact, with the rise of the nation-state in Europe, Higher Education in most countries became increasingly located in the area of influence of the state. Modern governance structures of universities were shaped, in one way or another, by such process. Academic freedom and autonomy of universities were always limited by the influence of the state and of other powerful economic and ideological actors.

Other influences were also important. It is worthwhile recalling that public concern in Victorian England about poverty and its causes promoted academic research in the relations between economic growth and social justice. Those who fostered such inquiry included Beatrice and Sydney Webb, co-founders of what today is a well-known academic institution, the London School of Economics and Political Sciences.

The Humboldtian model was imported and creatively adapted in the United States, where its most famous Higher Education institutions were to become the best-known examples of what today is called the research university: "[T]he combination of research and teaching in Higher Education has been carried much further in the United States than elsewhere" (Mowery and Rosenberg 1998: 36). Concerning the institution that would become the main reference worldwide, it is asserted that "[T]he modern American university emerged between the Civil War and World War I as a bifurcated hybrid of the tradition from England of one-track, broad, general education to prepare the elite to be leaders and the tradition from Germany of preparing for specialization in a field of work and carrying on research" (Roper and Hirth 2005: 7).

The Humboldtian model was elaborated during a time when another way of organizing Higher Education and research was the most influential. We are referring to the "French model" that assigned the first task to professional schools or faculties and the second one to specialized and separated institutes. That was the model that oriented Latin American countries when they became independent during the first decades of the nineteenth century and tried to build new institutions for cultivating advanced knowledge. It was also the preferred model for the Soviet Union and other socialist countries during and up to the end of the twentieth century.

However, the Humboldtian model was successful in the long run. Why did this model of university become dominant? The Humboldtian project was put into practice by German universities that were able to carry out a great deal of basic research directly connected with the education of potential new researchers and appliers of science. Its influence was spread by important ties with industry and complemented by application-oriented polytechnic institutes. Thus, it may be conjectured that it contributed better to the "wedding of science and technology" discussed in Chapter 4.

The adaptation of this model in the USA favored the approaching of science and technology. It was better for cultivating links between different disciplines than the French model of separated professional schools. Germany and the USA forged ahead, displacing England in the industrialization race precisely during the "Second Economic Revolution" of the late nineteenth century. Around 1900, German universities were leaders of scientific progress. The Humboldtian project seemed the best option for institutionalizing teaching and research. During the following decades, its contribution to the expansion of knowledge became evident: "[D]uring the course of the twentieth century the university became the key knowledge-production institution, at any rate in large parts of northern and western Europe and in North America" (Nowotny et al. 2001: 79).

In the United States, a quite different model also emerged. In that country, legislation during the nineteenth century fostered some changes in a system previously characterized by offering religious and liberal education for elites. Access was expanded, attention was given to practical arts, and the service role to the surrounding society made its appearance. But the last point lost relevance by comparison with the dominance of research in the following century (Roper and Hirth 2005).

In particular, the so-called land-grant colleges were created in the United States during the second half of the nineteenth century to complement the liberal arts education then prevailing with practical knowledge for promoting economic growth and fighting poverty in rural areas. That was quite an innovation concerning technological teaching. It so happened that their "research centers became a second component" of such colleges and that in "the early 1900s, state extension activities became another component of the land-grant colleges" (Rogers 1995: 358). Cooperating with regional economic development thus appeared as a new function for Higher Education institutions.

Extension has also been seen as a function of Latin American universities, but not with exactly the same meaning. It appeared at the beginning of the twentieth century, essentially in public universities, understood as cultural diffusion and technical assistance oriented to deprived groups, with the aim of not only improving the living conditions but also fighting together with these groups against those benefiting from social injustice. Extension was a third mission, to be carried out conjointly with teaching and research. Fostering such a mission was a key issue in the program of the Latin American University Reform Movement. Its birth is usually dated in June 1918, when the students of the University of Cordoba in Argentina went on a strike against the authorities of that university and issued their famous "Manifesto". A wide wave of student mobilization during the following years extended to almost every country in Latin America. Participation of students in the government of universities was demanded as a way of democratizing such institutions. In turn, such an internal process would commit universities to democratizing society at large. A socially committed university would contribute to the transformation of a region that was and still is the most unequal one in the world. As a consequence, at least up to the 1980s, programs and changes in Latin American public universities were closely connected with the search for alternative ways for development. Thus, a specific Latin American "idea of university" was forged.

In each region of the Global South, modern universities emerged as combinations of European influences and internal processes. National universities created in African countries when they became independent were mandated to confront poverty and underdevelopment. But for a long time, such universities did not reach the population beyond small elites and had only marginal effects on development (Mosha 1986). African universities face severe difficulties to cope with its basic duties, let alone to work on a development-directed agenda. Among such difficulties, extreme budgetary constraints, heavy brain-drain, and scarce academic freedom rank high; the inheritance of colonial times, with its tight control over the number of students and the subjects to be addressed, is under the assault of a rapid expansion of a secondary educated population willing to study a diversity of subjects that the university is ill equipped to provide (Teferra and Altbach 2004).

Several countries in the Third World followed the Soviet model of separating education and research institutions. That does not seem to have favored the contributions of universities to development. In China and Vietnam, integrating education and research and combining them to address economic and developmental problems have been relatively late processes. In spite of rapid progress, both countries still struggle with inadequate linkages between the academic research environment and the users of research and innovation results. A major concern in China is the conversion of scientific and technological research results into products (Haiyan and Yuan 2011). However, the rise of the Chinese budgetary effort on research and development is remarkable. The sheer numbers of annual PhDs awarded by Chinese universities is reputed to be as high as those of the United States (National Science Board 2010). In Vietnam, low quality of university research and weak linkages between teaching and research continue to afflict the efforts of universities to effectively contribute to the developmental efforts (Tran Ngoc Ca 2016).

With decolonization after World War II, national higher educational systems were seen as fundamental for redressing educational backwardness in general as well as for nation-building. In that context, Coleman (1986) wrote his paper entitled "The idea of the developmental university". There he described what he saw as the prevailing concept in the Third World and tried to explain why that had ensued. It was a quite sympathetic but not optimistic description that ended as follows: "[I]n their own self-interest universities in the Third World (and elsewhere as well) might critically examine and continuously monitor what functional load they can realistically and responsibly assume and ensure that their performance of whatever mix and magnitude of traditional and developmental functions they select to take on is both manageable and creditable" (Coleman 1986: 493).

By then, as Coleman documents, hopes of the developmental role of universities and of development itself were rapidly diminishing. Equating development with giving priority to economic growth in order to quickly catch up with rich countries has not been an overall success. It remains to be seen whether universities can make a better contribution to revised and more recent ways of understanding development. For that, the last quotation from Coleman should not be forgotten. Nevertheless, we shall try to go beyond the notion he discussed by proposing an idea of a Developmental University where "traditional and developmental functions" are not differentiated. Rather, "traditional functions" will be reformulated with the aim of showing that improving performance and cooperating with development can be one and the same thing.

RECENT CHANGES

The increased role of advanced knowledge in society puts the university at the forefront of several ongoing changes, discussions, and conflicts. Historically, access to Higher Education has been a privilege reserved for a tiny minority of the population. It is still a privilege but the situation is changing. University enrollment became massive in the North during the second half of the twentieth century, and the phenomenon has been reaching other regions. In China, enrollment grew from 3.4 million students in 1998, a very low figure for such a populous country, to more than 21 million in 2010 (China Statistical Yearbook), a sixfold increase in twelve years. In the first years of this century, there were more than 150 million tertiary students in the world, but "despite greater inclusion, the privileged classes have retained their relative advantage in nearly all nations" (Altbach et al. 2009: vi, vii).

Higher Education has been experiencing not only massification but also stratification and differentiation: "[D]ifferentiation certainly seems to be an important way by which Higher Education can pull off the trick of simultaneously achieving both elite and mass functions. Where once entry to Higher Education was the passport to power and privilege, today it may only be entry to a relatively small number of institutions that can provide equivalent opportunities. But this should not hide the fact that entry to any form of Higher Education is likely to maintain or improve a person's life chances and that this is especially the case for people from disadvantaged social groups" (Brennan and Naidoo 2008: 291).

The last sentence of the preceding quote should be kept in mind when considering proposals for transforming Higher Education. If stratification is a worrying trend, increased access to Higher Education is an overall positive evolution.

Now, particularly in the countries where universities became institutions of mass education with an increasing public funding, demands for greater contributions of universities to society have been growing. The relevance assigned to universities in invention and innovation was fostered during the second half of the twentieth century by momentous advances in scientific knowledge with surprising impacts in practical activities, as evidenced by computer and life sciences. A third stage in the history of the university was identified: the "mission of the university began to be described in such terms as expanding the frontiers of knowledge and penetrating the hitherto unknown". In such a context, the "university of discovery" flowered in the second half of the twentieth century (Müller 1996: 16–17).

Two decades ago, it was remarked that many universities had become direct producers of goods and services for final users (Sutz 1997). Perceptions about their incidence in society shifted, particularly among governments. Many discussions about the tasks of universities became focused on its third mission or third role, beyond teaching and research. Thus, potential or actual contributions of universities to upgrading productive activities are considered a priority, and particular attention is usually dedicated to university-industry relations.

It is said that in the United States the third mission of the university reemerged during the 1980s as a "pathway to economic renewal and accountability". The passage of the Bayh-Dole Act in 1980 was "something of a milestone in partnerships between Higher Education and business" (Roper and Hirth 2005: 10).

What has been remarked in the previous two paragraphs is partly a consequence of the way that new knowledge impacts production; generally speaking, it takes less time since knowledge is generated at the moment it is productively used, while an ever-expanding gamut of new products reflects the findings of recent research. So universities are demanded to educate more people, to offer students a more relevant education and better prospects for finding jobs when they graduate, to provide the wide array of specialists that industry needs, to put more knowledge to work for economic growth, and to address pressing social and health problems. It is said that the university is an institution in crisis because it cannot cope with all that society demands of it (Clark 1998).

New questions and concepts arose as the last century was ending. Is it better that university research agendas and priorities should be shaped first of all by the academy, as claimed by the supporters of the Humboldtian model, or should they be negotiated with external actors? The latter alternative has been highlighted—and recommended—by those who posit that the main mode of knowledge production has shifted to work centered on problems with significance for actors outside academia and demanding the cooperation of several disciplines and of non-academic actors, rather than strict disciplinary cooperation between specialists. In the terminology of Gibbons et al. (1994: 1), "[B]y contrast with traditional knowledge, which we will call Mode 1, generated within a disciplinary, primarily cognitive, context, Mode 2 knowledge is created in broader, transdisciplinary social and economic contexts". Given that many other players besides academic institutions are involved in the new mode of knowledge production, the importance of the latter, particularly of universities, has been seen as diminishing. However, it is precisely their role as Mode 1 knowledge producers that make universities especially valued by innovation managers in big business enterprises. This is the somehow surprising result presented in a widely cited article by Richard Nelson and Nathan Rosenberg (1994), who through a survey to innovation managers of American firms found that such managers generally valued the advancement of knowledge in disciplinary terms more than the involvement of faculty in the solution to concrete problems of industry. They interpret this sort of counterintuitive result by positing that for industry the most valuable assets coming from universities are creative graduates and that this can be achieved only if their learning process takes place in a research-intensive environment. This notwithstanding, universities more and more need to engage in Mode 2 knowledge production, not only because this is the way of getting resources but also because it is a way of legitimization in the face of governments.

That transformation in knowledge production can be seen as being parallel to a profound sea change in the ethics of research. The ideal of academic research was classically formulated by Merton (1973, first published in 1942) in terms of five rules that should be followed when pursuing the advance of knowledge: Communalism, Universalism, Disinterestedness, Originality, and (organized) Skepticism. They are frequently mentioned by its acronym CUDOS. It is worth noting that CUDOS expresses "what should be": the norms were proposed at a time when the incidence of arbitrariness of power over science resulted in Nazi "Arian science" or terribly consequential frauds like Lysenko-ism. CUDOS is not a good descriptor of collective scientific behavior. And this is so because knowledge production today has specific social traits that complicate the fulfilling of such norms. As posited by Broad and Wade (1982: 19), "[M]odern science is a career. Its stepping-stones are articles published in the scientific literature. To be successful a researcher must get as many published articles as possible, secure governmental grants, build up a laboratory and the resources to hire graduate students, increase the production of published papers…". This endless striving for recognition, blended with the particular reward system of science, where priority in discovery or in proposing concepts and explanations is paramount, can be at odds with following the behavior proposed by the Mertonian rules. Such rules have been considered a main guidance. But even if they continue to be vindicated by some part of the scientific community, mainly researchers in basic sciences, they have turned out to be less appealing to the whole research enterprise. As knowledge became a more important and more direct productive force in societies deeply shaped by private property, it can come as no surprise that a powerful trend toward knowledge privatization emerged. Production of knowledge for private ends is at odds with Mertonian ideal rules, particularly with Communalism and Disinterestedness. The ensuing change of the research ethos has been described as a move to post-academic science (Ziman 1996). Such change deserves a closer look.

The relevance of knowledge grew in parallel with the costs of producing it, and so academic survival strategies had to give priority to accessing external funding. Thus, the Communalism stressed by Merton receded and proprietary knowledge expanded (Ziman 1994), while leaders of research groups tended to become "quasi-managers" (Etzkowitz 1990). The old motto that oriented research, "to publish or to perish", is still with us and—as we will explore in a later chapter—has become even more imperative, but now it is accompanied by a new one, "to apply or to die" (Ziman 1994).

While universities in general were pressed to get closer with firms in order to cooperate with economic growth, some argued that short-term economic imperatives could endanger the long-term contributions of academic work carried out in a Humboldtian spirit (Dasgupta and David 1994). The factual basis of such a claim has been discussed by studies suggesting that high rates of publishing and collaborating with firms may reinforce each other instead of diminishing scientific productivity (D'Este and Perkmann 2007). Be that as it may, the growing relevance of the relations between universities and firms seems to be a fact acknowledged by different normative evaluations of such a trend. More than twenty years ago, a descriptive and normative approach to the changes discussed above was summarized as the recent emergence of a fourth stage in the history of universities. It was called the "university of calculation", seen as "a huge, expensive institution, highly functional in terms of training and continuing innovation in science and technology, no longer committed to learning per se not to character development, and representing a convenient aggregation of talents more like a marketplace of research and training than an intellectual community. A further implication of such an institutional evolution is that participants in its activities would not necessarily share any common set of values beyond the economic imperative of producing well enough to be compensated, and vice versa. If this forecast is justified then the university of calculation would play no institutional role based on its own set of values in the public affairs of society" (Müller 1996: 21).

In this forecast, the idea of the university seems to vanish. Both the medieval university and the Humboldtian university included such an "idea" that, if different from reality as always happens with ideals and models, was a powerful factor among those shaping academic interests, struggles, and efforts.

Surely massification, stratification, and differentiation of Higher Education point in that direction. That stems from an analysis centered on the Latin American landscape, where a strong "idea of university" has played an important role, as previously recalled, in connection with the Latin American Movement of University Reform: "[A]s a corollary of this variety of weakly-structured situations, the idea of the university itself, which had in the past been generally agreed upon and endowed with a clearly valorative connotation, has in common use come to be seen as an imprecise conceptual reference, not always accepted, and frequently confused. In this sense, one can declare unequivocally that in the recent past the novelty in the fashioning of systems of Higher Education has been the adoption of marked forms of stratification" (Landinelli 2008: 152).

Brunner (2015) asserts that the traditional university—that pre-capitalist institution of mandarins and inheritors—has disappeared with the expanded role of knowledge in capitalist dynamics. Unstoppable trends toward massification and new modes of producing knowledge aggravate financial problems and foster privatization processes.

If the "university of calculation" as described by Müller is a fair description of some prevailing aspects of contemporary Higher Education, new alternatives are urgently needed. Thus, "Higher Education's contribution to the achievement of equity and social justice may well require both cultural change within the academic profession and new forms of relationship between institutions of Higher Education and the societies of which they form a part" (Brennan and Naidoo 2008: 298).

THE NEW DOMINANT MODEL

The term "academic capitalism" was coined to describe a trend first visible in the USA system of universities and Higher Education in general (Slaughter and Leslie 1999; Slaughter and Rhoades 2004). The essence of academic capitalism is that universities and academic institutions systematically develop a market-like behavior. Even if relationships with firms and the state to sell universities' services are far from new, academic capitalism refers to a much deeper phenomenon, driven by the shrinking public budgets assigned to universities plus the increasing cost of performing high-level research and teaching. Organizational changes accompany the shift toward academic capitalism, with a visible increase in a more managerial style of decision-making at academic institutions, from research agendas to teaching proposals.

In this context, a new dominant model has emerged: "[T]he Humboldtian research university became a global model in the nineteenth century, spreading from Europe to USA (and further, through colonialism, to Latin America and Asia); in recent years, a reverse policy transfer has taken place where the North American 'entrepreneurial' university has become the beacon of university reformers worldwide" (Benner 2011: 13). It is a natural birth place: the "mechanisms for integrating the research system with the market are [...] exceptionally well developed in USA [...] the universities are often based on an entrepreneurial tradition and are accustomed to operating according to market or quasi-market conditions [...] academic have historically been subject to many incentives to combine traditional academic tasks with entrepreneurial activity [...] the infrastructure for science-based entrepreneurship is highly developed, with a rich flora of venture capitalists, organizational brokers, university patenting, and licensing organizations surrounding the academic centers" (Benner 2011: 15).

As previously stated, that shift to a new dominant model has taken place in the context of a broad discussion about the "third role" of universities, mainly seen as a more relevant contribution to economic growth when knowledge becomes a fundamental productive resource that has to be implemented by direct collaboration with firms.

The "entrepreneurial university", as characterized by Etzkowitz (1990, 1997, 2003), is defined by the incorporation of a new mission, capitalization of knowledge, besides teaching and research. In this view, the "entrepreneurial university" has factual, prospective, and prescriptive aspects. On the basis of detailed studies, it is asserted that such a notion is a description of what is actually happening, that its consolidation may be prognosticated, and also that it should be pursued as a leading goal for Higher Education policies.

Several motives can be given in order to back the assertion that the "entrepreneurial university" has become the dominant model. Ideologically, such a conception of the university is fully compatible with prevailing affinities to market individualism. Factually, several universities around the world show important resemblances to defining traits of that model; that can be seen especially in a number of the most influential universities located in the North. From a prospective viewpoint, the expansion of the entrepreneurial role of universities looks like a strong trend, fostered by the fundamental dynamics of the capitalist knowledge society. Concerning policies, although many governments seem simply to be devoid of an articulated project for universities, some are fostering rather global changes that are explicitly or implicitly oriented by the model under consideration, while at this level no other model seems to be a more or less strong competitor.

So it should not be a surprise that "[A]t the turn of the twentieth century the US model of entrepreneurial universities and of university engagement with the corporate world and the marketplace has become a dominant policy model of Higher Education, just as the German Humboldtian model was at the turn of the last century" (Rhoades et al. 2004: 316). Nevertheless, even in the country where it appeared, this model is not the only game in town. Since the 1990s, engagement links between academy and community have been promoted in new ways to cope with quickly changing realities. Engagement appeared as a new conception of the third mission, substituting one-way transference with the two-way street of interactions, encouraging "the new trilogy of *learning*, *discovery*, and *engagement* rather than the older teaching, research, and service" (Roper and Hirth 2005: 12). Nevertheless, the "entrepreneurial university" prevails as the main reference for discussing and promoting changes in Higher Education, in the US and beyond.

Teaching and research have become, to some extent, a joint endeavor in most universities; such institutions can thus be seen as novelty producers. Research is done in the pursuit of answers to yet-unanswered questions, or of better answers to questions already addressed. In this sense, universities are, broadly speaking, innovation-in-knowledge producers. The entrepreneurial university may be seen as the model for the prevailing definition of innovation in economic parlance, where novelties are considered innovations if they have been traded at the market. The privatization of knowledge through the assurance of proprietary rights is a necessary step to making it tradable; this is a constitutive part of the entrepreneurial university. Recently, it seems that innovation has become a less clear concept. Clarifications as well as the signaling of normative aims are searched for by adding adjectives: frugal, inclusive, grassroots, pro-poor, co-produced, responsible. The characterization of such innovations is complex because they go beyond newness and tradability. Like innovations in current parlance, they are not necessarily based on new knowledge, but when this is the case, such knowledge will not be produced under market logic.

This new dominant model collides with the normative approaches both of the traditional academic Humboldtian university and of a diversity of service-oriented proposals and experiences. Nevertheless, the trends we highlighted in the prospective approach to development issues—not only the increasing role of knowledge in every sphere of practice but also the push it gives to benefits for elites and to inequalities—suggest that this model is naturally connected with "really existing" globalization:

"[U]niversities have become the most important instrument for securing a position in the globalized knowledge-based economy—by securing scientific visibility and by fostering networks of innovators and innovating sectors around them. [...] Universities are being highlighted as engines of economic development, and research policy is empowering a small number of elite institutions" (Benner 2011: 20).

What is happening in universities in the North is an aspect of the expanding influence of market relations: "[S]ince the 1980s, there has been a general shift in the public service philosophy toward more and more marketization [...] This tendency has also made its entry into the academic institutions and its relations to other actors in the innovation system [...] it is reflected in the increased policy focus on the production of so-called useful knowledge primarily defined as knowledge with a direct economic benefit for the private sector" (Gregersen and Rasmussen 2011: 303). This policy implies that "issues related to technology transfer and the relation with the productive sector are high on the agenda in the university debate [... in several countries] perhaps a reflection of policy measures aimed at distilling an entrepreneurial spirit among the university researchers" (Brundenius and Göransson 2011: 347).

The dominant policy is quite clear but actual results are open to discussion: "stronger university-industry cooperation is not a panacea for all the weakness of the industry. There are still no conclusive studies, other than anecdotal illustrations, that the university-industry cooperation or the measures to encourage such cooperation as the establishment of science parks have led to significant economic benefits either regionally or nationally" (Reddy 2011: 46). On this issue, many different opinions can be found. In any case, it is not easy to be sure that commercialization of knowledge by universities is the main avenue to upgrading industry everywhere, assuming that one size fits all. The results of innovation surveys back Reddy's assertion: North and South, business firms list universities as the least important source of information for innovation; universities are key actors for innovation, but, at least in firms' opinion, for different reasons than the direct cooperation with them.

An evaluation of the potential role of the entrepreneurial university in development depends directly on the normative characterization of development as well as on the specific socio-economic contexts and its dominant trends. The dominant model is usually proposed for reforming universities in ways that are able to contribute to the processes of catching up with the North. Our conjecture, to be elaborated in the following chapter, is twofold: (1) the entrepreneurial university fosters inequality, North and South, with worse consequences in the second case, and (2) the defining traits of underdevelopment imply that, in the Global South, that model will have few possibilities of achieving its promise of making universities main actors of economic development.

REFERENCES

Altbach, P., Reisberg, L., & Rumbley, L. (2009). *Trends in Global Higher Education: Tracking an Academic Revolution*. París: UNESCO.

Anderson, R. D. (2004). *European Universities from the Enlightenment to 1914*. Oxford: Oxford University press.

Ben-David, J. (1984). *The Scientist's Role in Society*. Chicago: The University of Chicago Press.

Benner, M. (2011). In Search of Excellence? An International Perspective on Governance of University Research. In B. Göransson & C. Brundenius (Eds.), *Universities in Transition. The Changing Role and Challenges for Academic Institutions* (pp. 11–24). Ottawa: Springer.

Brennan, J., & Naidoo, R. (2008). Higher Education and the Achievement (and/ or Prevention) of Equity and Social Justice. *Higher Education, 56*(3), 287–302.

Broad, W., & Wade, N. (1982). *The Betrayers of the Truth*. New York: Simon and Schuster.

Brundenius, C., & Göransson, B. (2011). The Three Missions of Universities: A Synthesis of UniDev Project Findings. In B. Göransson & C. Brundenius (Eds.), *Universities in Transition. The Changing Role and Challenges for Academic Institutions* (pp. 329–352). Ottawa: Springer.

Brunner, J. J. (2015). Transformaciones del espíritu comunitario de la universidad: base de la responsabilidad social de la academia. In E. Aponte Hernández (Ed.), *La responsabilidad social de las universidades: Implicaciones para América Latina, IESALC-UNESCO* (pp. 97–114). San Juan: IESALC-UNESCO.

Clark, B. (1995). *Places of Inquiry: Research and Advanced Education in Modern Universities*. Berkeley: The California University Press.

Clark, B. (1997). The Modern Integration of Research Activities with Teaching and Learning. *The Journal of Higher Education, 68*(3), 241–255.

Clark, B. (1998). *Creating Entrepreneurial Universities: Organizational Pathways of Transformation*. New York: Pergamon Press.

Coleman, J. S. (1986). The Idea of the Developmental University. *Minerva, 24*(4), 476–494.

Collins, R. (2002). *A Global Theory of Intellectual Change*. Cambridge, MA: Harvard University Press.

D'Este, P., & Perkmann, M. (2007). *Why Do Academics Work with Industry? A Study of the Relationships Between Collaboration Rationales and Channels of*

Interaction. Paper presented at the Druid Summer Conference on Appropriability, Proximity, Routines and Innovation, Denmark.

Dasgupta, P., & David, P. (1994). Toward a New Economics of Science. *Research Policy, 23*(3), 487–521.

Etzkowitz, H. (1990). The Second Academic Revolution: The Role of the Research University in Economic Development. In S. E. Cozzens, P. Healey, A. Rip, & J. Ziman (Eds.), *The Research System in Transition* (pp. 109–124). Dordrecht: Kluwer Academic Publishers.

Etzkowitz, H. (1997). The Entrepreneurial University and the Emergence of Democratic Corporatism. In L. Leydesdorff & H. Etzkowitz (Eds.), *Universities and the Global Knowledge Economy* (pp. 141–152). London: Pinter.

Etzkowitz, H. (2003). Research Groups as 'Quasi-Firms': The Invention of the Entrepreneurial University. *Research Policy, 32*(1), 109–121.

Gibbons, M., Limoges, C., Nowotny, H., Schwartzman, S., Scott, P., & Trow, M. (1994). *The New Production of Knowledge.* London: SAGE Publications.

Gregersen, B., & Rasmussen, G. (2011). Developing Universities: The Evolving Role of Academic Institutions in Denmark. In B. Göransson & C. Brundenius (Eds.), *Universities in Transition. The Changing Role and Challenges for Academic Institutions* (pp. 283–306). Ottawa: Springer.

Haiyan, W., & Yuan, Z. (2011). China: Challenges for Higher Education in a High Growth Economy. In B. Göransson & C. Brundenius (Eds.), *Universities in Transition. The Changing Role and Challenges for Academic Institutions* (pp. 143–170). Ottawa: Springer.

Howard, T. A. (2006). *Protestant Theology and the Making of the Modern German University.* Oxford/New York: Oxford University Press.

Landinelli, J. (2008). Scenarios of Diversification, Differentiation, and Segmentation of Higher Education in Latin America and the Caribbean. In A. L. Gazzolla & A. Didriksson (Eds.), *Trends in Higher Education in Latin America and the Caribbean.* Caracas: IESALC-UNESCO.

Merton, R. (1973). The Normative Structure of Science. In R. Merton (Ed.), *The Sociology of Science: Theoretical and Empirical Investigations* (pp. 267–280). Chicago: The University of Chicago Press.

Mosha, H. J. (1986). The Role of African Universities in National Development: A Critical Analysis. *Comparative Education, 22*(2), 93–109.

Mowery, D., & Rosenberg, N. (1998). *Paths of Innovation. Technological Change in 20th-Century America.* New York: Cambridge University Press.

Müller, S. (1996). The Advent of the University of Calculation. In J. Müller (Ed.), *Universities in the Twenty-First Century* (pp. 15–23). Oxford: Berghahn Books.

National Science Board. (2010). Global Higher Education and Work-Force Trends. In *Science and Engineering Indicators 2010.* Washington, DC: National Science Board.

Nelson, R., & Rosenberg, N. (1994). American Universities and Technical Advance in Industry. *Policy Research, 3*, 323–348.

Nowotny, H., Scott, P., & Gibbons, M. (2001). *Re-thinking Science. Knowledge and the Public in an Age of Uncertainty.* Cambridge, UK: Polity Press.

Reddy, P. (2011). The Evolving Role of Universities in Economic Development. In B. Göransson & C. Brundenius (Eds.), *Universities in Transition. The Changing Role and Challenges for Academic Institutions* (pp. 25–49). Ottawa: Springer.

Rhoades, G., Maldonado, A., Ordorika, I., & Velázques, M. (2004). Imagining Alternatives to Global, Corporate, New Economy Academic Capitalism. *Policy Futures in Education, 2*(2), 316–329.

Rogers, E. M. (1995). *Diffusion of Innovations* (4th ed.). New York: Free Press.

Roper, C. D., & Hirth, M. A. (2005). A History of Change in the Third Mission of Higher Education: The Evolution of One-Way Service to Interactive Engagement. *Journal of Higher Education Outreach and Engagement, 10*(3), 3–21.

Rüegg, W. (1992). Foreword. In H. d. Ridder-Symoens (Ed.), *A History of the University in Europe, Volume 1: Universities in the Middle Ages.* Cambridge: Cambridge University Press.

Schmoch, U. (2011). Germany: The Role of Universities in the Learning Economy. In B. Göransson & C. Brundenius (Eds.), *Universities in Transition. The Changing Role and Challenges for Academic Institutions* (pp. 261–282). Ottawa: Springer.

Slaughter, S., & Leslie, L. (1999). *Academic Capitalism. Politics, Policies and the Entrepreneurial University.* Baltimore/London: Johns Hopkins University Press.

Slaughter, S., & Rhoades, G. (2004). *Academic Capitalism and the New Economy: Markets, State, and Higher Education.* Baltimore/London: Johns Hopkins University Press.

Sutz, J. (1997). The Third Role of the University. In H. Etzkowitz & L. Leydesdorff (Eds.), *Universities and the Global Knowledge Economy* (pp. 11–20). London: Cassell.

Teferra, D., & Altbach, P. (2004). African Higher Education: Challenges for the 21st Century. *Higher Education, 47*(1), 21–50.

Tran Ngoc Ca. (2016). The National Innovation System in Vietnam and Its Relevance for Development. In B. Göransson, C. Brundenius, & C. Aguirre-Bastos (Eds.), *Innovation Systems for Development—Making Research and Innovation Matter in Developing Countries* (pp. 138–183). Cheltenham: Edward Elgar.

Ziman, J. (1994). *Prometheus Bound: Science in a Dynamic 'Steady State'.* Cambridge: Cambridge University Press.

Ziman, J. (1996). 'Postacademic Science': Constructing Knowledge with Networks and Norms. *Science Studies, 9*(1), 67–80.

CHAPTER 7

Universities and Underdevelopment

The starting point of this chapter is that universities are important everywhere, but in underdevelopment, given its specific conditions of knowledge production and use, universities are potential "system builders". This building capacity faces two intertwined obstacles: (i) the low proportion of young people who reach Higher Education and (ii) the scarcity of spaces where university graduates may find jobs in which to apply the knowledge they have acquired creatively, and in that way keep on learning. Fostering developmental universities and Inclusive Innovation Systems are strategies to fight such obstacles.

Concerning such issues, the following questions are addressed in the chapter: How can the situation of universities in underdevelopment be characterized? Why are they potentially such important actors in the incipient National Innovation Systems of the Global South? Which are the main indicators of the developmental role of the universities?

ACADEMIC INSTITUTIONS IN THE GLOBAL SOUTH

Above we characterized underdevelopment as a combination of the peripheral condition—that is, the specialization of activities with relatively little knowledge content—with foreign subordination. Underdeveloped countries therefore experience an interconnected set of major obstacles for (i) overcoming external disadvantages regarding living conditions and (ii) improving the internal situation of the most disadvantaged people. Underdevelopment

© The Author(s) 2018
R. Arocena et al., *Developmental Universities in Inclusive Innovation Systems*, https://doi.org/10.1007/978-3-319-64152-2_7

is therefore an objective phenomenon which at the same time constitutes a principal obstacle for the creation of capabilities and an environment ill suited for the expansion of freedoms. The tasks of universities are more difficult but also more relevant in underdevelopment than in other contexts.

In the Global South, much less knowledge is produced than in the North, but frequently universities are, in relative terms, more important producers of knowledge. In the Global South, Innovation Systems are often more virtual than real and, in any case, are much weaker and less "systemic" than in the North; but frequently universities are the most connected actors in Southern (proto) Innovation Systems, so their contributions to productive and social policies "build system".

Another relevant factual difference between North and South, directly connected with the previously recalled one, is that "the business sector [...] is by far the largest contributor to R&D in the developed countries, while it is the government sector that supplies most of the financing in developing countries" (Brundenius and Göransson 2011: 341).

Even in countries with a long and outstanding scientific tradition, like Russia, advances in research and innovation are compromised when the main driver of the economy is the exploitation of natural resources rather than advanced knowledge: "[T]he Russian NIS (National System of Innovation) has substantial potential for development, but nowadays the national economy is oriented toward natural resources, instead of innovation. Lack of demand for innovation will keep the NIS frozen until the drop of world prices on natural resources or until the NIS looses its potential irreversibly" (Gokhberg et al. 2011: 258).

Marketization is increasing in the academy of the South as in the North. Below, we shall discuss its role concerning economic development. Here, we point out that it fosters knowledge-based inequality, even more so in the South than in the North.

One connection between those issues is given by the problem of financing Higher Education. Free or nearly free access has been reverted in several cases, including countries as diverse as China, Vietnam, the United Kingdom, and Austria.

That issue is one of the hottest discussions related to universities in every country studied by the UniDev project (Göransson and Brundenius 2011). For example, in Vietnam, the "introduction of tuition fees for Higher Education has also brought substantial extra resources for the universities" (Tran Ngoc Ca and Nguyen Vo Hung 2011: 130). Cost sharing was introduced in Tanzania, where education was free of charge up to the late 1980s;

as a consequence, "complaints from the public started emanating that it is only the children from the richer families that can have access to the university education, which is unfair not only for the children from poor families, but also for the country, as there is a possibility of leaving behind the best brains" (Mwamila and Diyamett 2011: 187). So "the issue of financing Higher Education in Tanzania is not only a big problem but also a crisis!" (Ibid: 188).

Crisis is a word that surely corresponds to what happened in Chile during the first years of this decade. In that country, Higher Education has expanded in a very stratified way, including many institutions of low quality, but in a very expensive way for poor students and their families, leading to high indebtedness. Even public universities introduced considerable fees. In 2011 and 2012, one of the most massive student mobilizations in the whole world during recent times erupted. With remarkable approval in citizenship at large, it demanded free and unrestricted access to public Higher Education. Such events changed the political agenda, the prevailing views, and even party alliances. Free public Higher Education was endorsed by the government that took office in 2014. There, as in quite different places—South Africa and the United States, for example— "unequal access to Higher Education [...] is one of the most important problems that social states everywhere must face in the twenty-first century" (Piketty 2014: 485).

That seems to happen also in China, where in "May 2006, the State Council restricted enrollment to control the rapid growth of students, in order to increase their teaching quality. [...] Parents of would-be applicants still believe increased growth in enrollment could provide better chances for their children, while undergraduates are concerned that the expansion would exert more pressure on the employment market" (Haiyan and Yuan 2011: 162).

As previously described, some main trends shape the evolution of universities worldwide: "[T]he central realities of Higher Education in the 21st century—massification, accountability, privatization, and marketization— shape universities everywhere, and those who work at them, to differing degrees" (Altbach 2003: 2). Nevertheless, the consequences are quite different in different regions. In the Global South, the peripheral condition of the academy is apparent more often than not.

According to Altbach (2003), the academic community in the Global South cannot expect to compete with their counterparts in the North in terms of wealth, resources, and position. The lack of resources does not permit them to challenge the academic leadership of the well-established and well-connected academic communities centered on the North. This unequal footing means that, to a high degree, researchers in the peripheral South are shut out from academic power structures defining the direction and norms of the knowledge-producing system. Moreover, they are dependent on the center for international academic recognition as well as for funding opportunities for global research collaboration. This does not mean that researchers in the South are in any way irrelevant to their communities or less creative than their counterparts in the North. It does mean, however, "that they will seldom be at the frontiers of world science and will not share in the control over the main levers of academic power worldwide" (Altbach 2003: 4).

Several corollaries follow from Altbach's global view of the academic landscape in the Third World. First, it is shaped by "the unequal world of centers and peripheries". That global division emerged with the global expansion of the industrialized West during the nineteenth century and subordinated most of the Rest. Centers and peripheries have changed but not disappeared with the emergence of the global knowledge-based and innovation-driven economy, which increased the role of the academy in society; the actual pattern of such division is apparent in the world of the academy. Second, we characterized underdevelopment by the combination of the peripheral condition in the knowledge economy with external subordination (that is, dependency). That characterization is reflected in the academy: "[R]elated to peripherality is dependency" (Altbach 2003: 4). Third, dependency has very concrete manifestations in the realm of power: concerning academic work, decisions are based mainly in the North and reflect a "vast inequality".

Such inequality seems to be reproducing itself. When advanced capabilities and knowledge become key power resources, it is of increasing importance where highly educated people work and for whom. Several Northern governments are well aware of that: "[M]any developed countries, hoping that international graduates will not return home, increasingly work to adjust immigration laws and other incentives so that they will remain after degree completion. This concentration of talent in the developed world contributes to international academic inequality" (Altbach et al. 2009: 8).

Academic migration has been seen as "brain circulation", a process that benefits everybody. Now, "underdeveloped countries have seen a trend whereby a substantial brain drain effectively dismantles academic institutions, as seen in the departure of researchers from emerging countries to work in the university and business centers of highly developed countries, as well as the way in which the latter set absorbs the best graduate students once they conclude their studies" (Didriksson and de la Fuente 2015: 39). The last opinion is held not only in the South: "[T]he academic labor market has increasingly globalized [...] the largest flow is South-North [...] patterns of academic migration continue to work to the disadvantage of developing countries" (Altbach et al. 2009: xv). Fostering academic migration—not only brain circulation—has been an explicit target for policy makers in some highly industrialized countries. During her 2007 presidential campaign, Hillary Clinton has been reported receiving from some hundred CEOs of Silicon Valley firms "a round of applause when she said she supports increasing the current cap on H1B visas. She advocated relaxing green card restrictions of engineers 'so they don't go home'" (*The Mercury News* 2007).

As stressed when a prospective approach was sketched, globalization in general seems to foster both production and inequality. The same happens in the world of the academy: "[I]f current trends of internationalization continue, the distribution of world's wealth and talent will be further skewed" (Altbach et al. 2009: x).

UNIVERSITIES AND KNOWLEDGE DEMAND

The university research agendas are partly shaped by the prevailing knowledge demand. Some main differences between the North and the Global South are related to differences in a specific type of knowledge demand: the commercial one. However, social knowledge demand, even if directed to different types of problems, is very important everywhere. Fostering such demand is a key for the democratization of knowledge.

Concerning such issues in this section and in some of the following ones, we address the following questions: why and how does knowledge-demand shape universities' research agendas and university organization? Which differences between North and the Global South can be derived from the latter? What strategies may strengthen the influence of social demand over universities' research agendas? If this happens, can it be asserted that the democratization of knowledge has been enhanced?

In the Global South, as a dominant phenomenon with many exceptions, we can speak of the "loneliness of the university actor" (Arocena and Sutz 2001). It means that very often universities, while systematically pursuing cooperation with productive sectors, do not find actors with the means and the will to cooperate with them.

In spite of that, it is necessary to keep on trying to strengthen the relations between the academy and production, perhaps by different policies. In any case (for example, in Latin America, where public universities generate most of the advanced knowledge), such cooperation is a necessary condition for upgrading production to more complex activities, which in turn is necessary for rising from economic growth to economic development. In an already-quoted path-breaking paper (Sabato and Botana 1968), written in Spanish, the urgency of fostering cooperation between government, the academy, and production was strongly and eloquently stated.

Now, the lasting weakness of such cooperation, in Latin America and in other places—major counterexamples notwithstanding—is not a consequence of ignorance or bad luck, but of the peripheral condition in itself. When economies are not knowledge-based and innovation-driven, entrepreneurial profits are seldom related to investment on the generation of advanced knowledge. A weak commercial knowledge-demand follows; moreover, such demand is often not addressed to endogenous generators of knowledge, local universities in particular. More generally, knowledge is a comparatively minor issue in productive strategies.

Brazil is a telling example of such a situation. Its R&D system is the strongest in Latin America and is remarkable also from a global perspective. Until recently, Brazilian economic growth was quite impressive. In quantitative terms, the total number of Brazilian R&D personnel grew from 133.002 in 2000 to 266.709 in 2010. The bulk of this increase took place at universities and colleges: from 68.331 to 195.614. In industry, the total was 55.436 in 2000 and 55.436 in 2010, exactly the same number (Cassiolato et al. 2014: Table 3.1, 77). That happened in spite of one the most important policies that was "put into practice in the 2000s (that) was the concession of subsidies to firms for the employment of university graduates to work in R&D labs. In a certain way, this is connected with the regressive specialisation of the Brazilian economy in the 2000s [...]. Such re-specialisation implied a decreasing economic importance of activities containing a higher technological content" (Cassiolato et al. 2014: 78).

The loneliness of the university actor implies that, as a rule, it cannot be assumed that there is a strong market where an entrepreneurial university in the Global South can commercialize the knowledge it generates. Let us repeat that such a general statement, which we believe to be correct, does not mean that it is difficult to find several examples both of commercial demand of knowledge and of university-industry cooperation in the Global South.

Where the economy is knowledge-based and innovation-driven, strong market demand is addressed to knowledge producers, especially universities. In such cases, universities tend to forge strong ties to industry by emphasizing natural sciences and technology, by co-publications with industry partners, and by setting up offices for technology transfer to industry. A main mediator among university-industry relations in knowledge-based and innovation-driven economies has been the demand from the State, particularly strong in military issues but also associated with the provision of various public goods like health, infrastructure, and the environment. After World War II, in the United States, "a greater and greater proportion of spending on science and technology was carried by the Federal Government (reaching some $17 billion by the end of the 1960s); however, rather than adopt the strategy of establishing Federal laboratories and a scientific civil service, as in Europe, in the U.S. the policy was towards contract research in the universities and industry. By the mid-1960s, by far the greatest proportion of university science was being done on federal contract, often for the Department of Defense, and the linkage was most powerful in the elite, high science, ivy-league colleges" (Rose and Rose 1972: 119). Regarding health research, the web page of the US National Institutes of Health states that "[M]ore than 80% of the NIH's funding is awarded through almost 50,000 competitive grants to more than 300,000 researchers at more than 2,500 universities, medical schools, and other research institutions in every state and around the world" (NIH 2017).

In the absence of stakeholders able to raise a voice for other types of social commitments for universities, the current combination of a normative bias toward a stronger relationship of universities with businesses and the trend toward tighter measurements and assessments in terms of publications as a main measure of individual achievement seems to favor mainly combinations or "mixtures" of the new entrepreneurial university and the old Humboldtian university.

It is quite difficult to believe that such "mixed universities" have a relevant social role where there is neither a strong knowledge-demand stemming from private actors nor demand stemming from the State and addressing indigenous producers of knowledge. But in the Global South and in the North, social demand of advanced knowledge and innovation is actually or potentially large. That remark leads to the idea of the Developmental University seen as an institution that is perceptive to demands of society as a whole, not only from segments of the population that can articulate and pay for the knowledge they want but also from other segments, particularly marginalized groups with weak or non-articulated demand for innovation.

Policies are needed to detect and foster such social demand, to connect it with teaching and research of the highest quality available, and to transform research results in effective innovations that contribute to solve the original problems. When successful, such socially oriented or inclusive innovations are ways of democratizing knowledge.

A NOTION OF THE DEVELOPMENTAL UNIVERSITY

As elaborated in Chapter 5, the core of the propositional approach we present in this book is to explore the possibilities of knowledge democratization as a main strategy for Human Sustainable Development.

It is commonly accepted that "the best way to increase wages and reduce wage inequalities in the long run is to invest in education and skills" (Piketty 2014: 313). More generally, "[O]ver a long period of time, the main force in favor of greater equality has been the diffusion of knowledge and skill". But "the principal force for convergence—the diffusion of knowledge—is only partly natural and spontaneous. It also depends in large part on educational policies, access to training and to the acquisition of appropriate skills, and associated institutions" (Piketty 2014: 22). That is the starting point for elaborating knowledge policies that contribute to the expansion of freedoms and capabilities. The notion we consider in the following can be seen as an attempt to foster universities' contribution to knowledge democratization.

That notion was first presented in Sutz (2005) in relation to "the so-called third mission, that is, what do universities do in order to be relevant to society?" (Brundenius and Göransson 2011: 329). We now recall two ways of understanding this question that are akin to the notion of the Developmental University.

The first example comes from the South. In Brazil, we can see a renewal of a fundamental tradition of public Latin American universities: the "extension services were taken to a new level, by force of the Constitution of 1988. The extension services were raised to the level of teaching and research activities and all three are considered to be inseparable missions. [...] Extension activities are traditionally understood to mean services provided for disadvantaged social groups. They are supposed to represent the commitment of the university to overcoming situations of inequality and social exclusion. Today [some of the Deans responsible for these activities] seek to integrate those actions with areas of knowledge (communication, culture, human rights, education, environment, health, technology, and work) in the form of offers for training or economic opportunities. [...]

The importance of the services rendered to the citizenry is worthwhile recording: [in 2004] 180 million patients were treated in academic health units and 350.000 cases were provided by academic judicial units. A novelty concerns the emergence of incubators for popular cooperatives [...]. In 2005, 34 universities already had incubators of popular cooperatives" (de Mello et al. 2011: 74).

The second example is a Scandinavian one: "[I]n 1997, Swedish universities were given a third mission in the Higher Education Act, besides education and research, to support economic and social development and play a greater role in expanding academia to the broader public" (Brundenius et al. 2011: 316).

From the "third mission" point of view, the Developmental University could be "characterized, in a neo-Humboldtian perspective, by the joint practice of three missions: teaching, research and cooperation for development with other institutions and collective actors. That means that developmental universities can only exist as active partners in Innovation Systems" (Arocena and Sutz 2011: 93). The idea was to stress its commitment to social inclusion through knowledge democratization. That implies that "developmental universities can only exist in active partnerships with external stakeholders. It also implies that the developmental role of universities demands more and better teaching and research, not less" (Arocena et al. 2014: 591). Thus, the developmental role of universities should be seen not in one but in the three missions of universities, considering them inseparable, as stated in the Brazilian Constitution.

The teaching mission appears as a central contribution to Human Sustainable Development, first of all, as a major clue for the expansion of capabilities and freedoms. From this perspective, knowledge-based inclusive development requires generalizing access to Higher Education. We are talking about active teaching, focused on the students and on learning how to keep on learning at every stage of life. That, in a neo-Humboldtian approach, means connecting teaching with creation and innovation. The relation between learning processes in general and problem-solving, that characterizes the Innovation Systems approach, appears here as a main orientation for teaching at the tertiary level. Problem-based learning (Gregersen 2017) is thus a fundamental dimension of teaching in developmentally oriented universities. It contributes to connect teaching with research and extension— understood as when the Brazilian experience was mentioned—even at the undergraduate level. That suggests that extension activities are included in the curricula. By connecting teaching with innovation that addresses social exclusion, both the ethical and the technical dimensions of teaching can be taken into account.

University research can be a main component of innovation policies as social policies and, more generally, of policies oriented to incorporate advanced knowledge as well as highly qualified people to every socially valuable activity. From an Innovation Systems perspective, such an aim requires positive interactions between several different actors, including productive actors, governmental departments, non-governmental organizations, academic teams, other entities and—last but not least—social groups with pressing problems but without market potential to foster innovations that may solve them, who should be considered not as patients but as agents. In such a cooperation, universities should contribute with their highest-quality research. That means that related issues should be given high priority in the research agenda and in academic evaluation. Contributions can come from the humanities and arts, social sciences, health, technologies, and natural sciences as well as from their interdisciplinary combinations. The developmental character of a university can be strongly based on its research mission in the whole landscape of knowledge and culture.

We have been saying that the developmental role of universities includes cooperating with external actors in teaching and research. Such cooperation is thus not restricted to third-mission activities. But in the idea of university we are sketching, its contribution to development is not restricted to teaching and research. That seems to happen in some more or less updated versions of the Humboldtian model that acknowledge the need for an academic contribution to development. The third mission of Developmental Universities should be seen as updating extension and service-type activities to the factual reality of the power of knowledge and to its democratization as a leading aspect of a propositional approach for development in the twenty-first century.

Such an approach is not the same as giving priority to technology transfer, often seen as the main content of the third mission of universities, as has already been indicated. When technology transfer is characterized in a strict sense, as a one-way process going from sellers or donors of technologies to receivers, its limitations stem from the experience of development. In summary, it can be efficient only with standardized technologies and even then only if no significant tacit knowledge is involved. Providing more or less routine procedures is not an efficient way of using university resources. Instead, they should contribute to innovation (that is, to solve problems in new ways, using advanced knowledge as a main basis).

Let us recall that relevant innovation processes are interactive learning processes. In such processes, both producers and users of innovations have knowledge that needs to be utilized in order to effectively and satisfactorily innovate; when this happens, both types of actors learn.

In some cases, particularly in Latin American universities, it is more or less usual to understand that extension is the core of the "third mission". Now, speaking of extension may suggest, as when technology transfer is mentioned, a unilateral transfer of knowledge from those who know to those who do not now. The elaboration of the notion of extension resulted, on the contrary, in giving a defining character to the combination of the different types of knowledge of different actors. The unilateral notions of the third role, especially concerning services offered by universities to deprived sectors, mean seeing people not as agents but as patients. This is alien to Human Sustainable Development.

We can consider the way in which extension is understood here as akin to the notion of "technologies of humility", proposed by Sheila Jasanoff: "[T]hese are methods, or better yet institutionalized habits of thought, that try to come to grips with the ragged fringes of human understanding (...) They require not only the formal mechanisms of participation but also an intellectual environment in which citizens are encouraged to bring their knowledge and skills to bear on the resolution of common problems" (Jasanoff 2003: 227).

Thus, promoting the "third role"—extension services and cooperation with external actors for problem-solving in general—of Developmental Universities has a fundamental component in fostering interactive learning processes oriented to innovation. At least two clues should guide the academic actors that participate in such processes: first, they must pay attention to what other actors know and try to learn from them; second, they should contribute—with the highest level of scientific and technological knowledge that they are able to provide—to the joint task of problem-solving. The last point is necessary for a "university that connects local interests with global research dynamics", as Benner (2011) briefly describes the developmental university.

The preceding discussion leads to the following redefinition of the notion we are considering.

The Developmental University is characterized by its commitment to Human Sustainable Development by means of the interconnected practice of three missions: (i) teaching, (ii) research, and (iii) fostering the socially valuable use of knowledge. Such commitment means that developmental universities must contribute to building inclusive Learning and Innovation Systems by cooperating with other institutions and collective actors:

(i)   The teaching mission aims at generalizing access to Higher Education, seen as lifelong advanced learning of increasing quality and increasingly connected with work, citizen activities, cultural expansion, and, in general, freedoms and capabilities for living lives that people value and have reason to value.

(ii) The research mission aims at expanding endogenous capabilities for generating knowledge—at local, regional, and national levels—in all disciplines and in interdisciplinary activities, with international quality and social vocation.

(iii) The mission of fostering the socially valuable use of knowledge aims above all to cooperate with a wide variety of actors in interactive learning processes that upgrade the capabilities for producing goods and services as well as for solving problems, with priority given to the needs of the most deprived sectors.

The definition could be given in a nutshell by saying that the Developmental University is characterized by its commitment to the democratization of knowledge.

ANTECEDENTS AND RELATED CONCEPTS OF A PUBLIC GOOD

Fostering the developmental role of universities means engaging universities in the fight against underdevelopment in the context of prevailing global knowledge-based power structures. Now, the aims of Human Sustainable Development make sense not only in the Global South but also in the North. So perhaps the notion of the Developmental University is also of some interest to the North. It is akin to the "engaged university" (Roper and Hirth 2005; Weerts and Sandmann 2008; Benneworth 2013). We have already made a reference to engagement as a renewed conception of the third mission of universities. That notion includes making a meaningful contribution to excluded communities as "a core activity for the university" (Benneworth 2013: 22). Other similarities between developmental and engaged universities will become apparent in following sections.

A related notion is the "public research university", which, according to Newfield (2008), has been submitted to a process of "unmaking" in the US: "[A]merican Higher Education is highly stratified: the wealthiest private universities can spend ten times as much per student as can a four-year public university. I discuss this inequality in some detail, but in the context of a distinctive type of public university that tried to overcome this stratification within the limits of the American social system. That type has been the public research university. In spite of its frequent ambivalence about inclusion, it sought to combine nearly universal access with the highest quality in teaching and research, and saw access and quality as not only compatible but, in a profound way, as mutually reinforcing" (Newfield 2008: 3).

The last sentence gives a fundamental clue: access and quality need to be mutually reinforcing if knowledge is to be democratized. Socially committed universities must pursue "the highest quality in teaching and research" because, if not, only privileged sectors will be educated in the best contexts and because contributing to the solution of collective problems requires the best knowledge available. In this sense, the university is potentially a public good as this concept is defined: non-excludability, meaning that everyone has the right to access a public good, and non-rivalry, meaning that the use of a public good by someone does not diminish the ability of other people to use it as well. This does not necessarily mean that the social value of Higher Education is evenly distributed among all members of society. In examining this issue, Brennan and Naidoo (2008: 295) find that "[T]his leads us beyond questions of Higher Education as a measure of individual achievement or as the appropriation of a private good to the question of Higher Education's wider contribution to society. This wider function of Higher Education is often encapsulated in the notion of Higher Education as a public good and is also closely related to concerns over who pays for Higher Education. Contemporary discussions on these issues are also frequently linked to debates in Higher Education about the role of market forces, new systems of management and accountability, and the perceived erosion of academic autonomy".

The last quote is eloquently illustrated by the British transformation of Higher Education, following the Brenner Report of 2010, which "...recommended a Higher Education system directed by market forces and the replacement of direct funding of undergraduate courses by student fees" (Holmwood 2011: 1). The cut in public spending in Higher Education by following the proposed strategy was estimated to be 80% (Ibid). Moreover, "[W]hat is distinctive at the present time, (...) is the development of the idea that education is not something external to the market, upon which the latter's fair and proper functioning might depend, but something that may itself be subject to the market" (Ibid: 4). Almost fifty years ago, as

Holmwood reminds us, another British report on Higher Education, the Robbins Report of 1963, pointed in a totally different direction: "[E]ducation was seen as a public good in its own terms, valuable both for the student and the wider society. University education, according to Robbins, served to cultivate the mind, and was concerned with the development and transmission of knowledge and culture, as well as serving democratic citizenship by improving debate and the capacities of citizens (Robbins Report 1963: paras 25–8)" (Holmwood 2011: 7). At present, however, Higher Education is recommended to be seen "as a source of private profit rather than public good" (Reay 2011: 115).

The Latin American "idea of university" is arguably a conception of Higher Education as a public good. But such a conception has been much eroded in reality: "in the face of contemporary trends of Higher Education reforms, Latin American universities have lost much of their traditional identity. Universities have been forced by structural conditions—reduced public funding and privatization among others—to adopt policies and strategies that have been deemed successful by international experts and agencies in the establishment of entrepreneurial institutions. The identities, meaning, and purposes of Higher Education institutions in most Latin American countries are in the process of being lost in attempts to imitate policies and practices of internationally acclaimed research universities" (Rhoades et al. 2004: 325).

Nevertheless, the ideals of the Latin American University Reform Movement started in Cordoba in June 1918 have not vanished. They were stressed in the UNESCO Regional Conference on Higher Education in Latin America and the Caribbean, held in June 2008 in Cartagena de Indias, Colombia. Its Declaration starts by asserting that "[H]igher education is a social public good, a universal human right, and a responsibility of States. This is the conviction and the basis for the strategic role that it should play in the processes of sustainable development of the countries of the region" (IESALC 2008: 47).

The Conference took place "90 years after the Cordoba Reform, the principles of which are today fundamental guidelines in terms of university autonomy, co-government, universal access, and social commitment" (IESALC 2008: 48).

These principles are related to the conception of Higher Education as a social public good in several ways. First, access to it is considered "a true right of all citizens" (IESALC 2008: 50).

Second, university autonomy, co-government, and social commitment should not be separated: "[A]utonomy is a right and a necessary condition for unfettered academic work, while also being an enormous responsibility in the fulfilling of its mission with quality, pertinence, efficiency and transparency in the face of society's challenges. This also includes social accountability. Autonomy involves social commitment, and both must go hand in hand. The involvement of academic communities in their own management, and particularly, student participation, are indispensable" (IESALC 2008: 51).

It can be argued that a notion of socially committed autonomy emerges from the previous quote. To elaborate such a notion, the following fragment is useful. Agency of universities is not mentioned, neither is social inclusion. But both concepts are unmistakably there: "[I]nstitutions of Higher Education must move forward in establishing a more active relationship with their different environments. Quality is linked to both pertinence, and responsibility toward sustainable development. This means fostering an academic model marked by the examination of problems within their contexts; the production and transfer of the social value of knowledge; joint work with communities; scientific, technological, humanistic, and artistic research based on an explicit definition of the problems being addressed, of fundamental interest for national or regional development, and the well-being of the population; an active dissemination effort aimed at educating for citizenship, rooted in respect for human rights and cultural diversity; extension activities that enrich education, helping to detect problems for the agenda of research, and that create areas for joint action involving diverse segments of society, especially the most neglected" (IESALC 2008: 51).

The concept of "public good" in relation to Higher Education can be easily manipulated, pointing in quite different directions. We can have claims identifying public good with serving the interests of the people, a rhetoric used to fight against the extreme ivory-towerism of some academic aristocracies. From the other ideological end, academics respond to claims for responsibility to taxpayers by delivering public goods identified as results that are tradable and producing monetary value. On the other hand, we have those who, in a rather self-serving rhetoric, claim that public good means just quality knowledge put in the public domain, in the name of all the good that sooner or later comes from it. These claims tend to be side-minded; straw-men are usually built to gain argumentative strength. Higher Education considered as a public good cannot be identified with one direction to the exclusion of others; the institutional challenge is precisely to open room for the cross-fertilization of directions while fostering the conditions for each of them to develop. In particular, when university autonomy is demanded just as a right of its internal bodies to govern the institution, with scant attention to the problems of its environment, with weak commitment to development, and with minor efforts for expanding access, Higher Education cannot be considered a public good. Prevailing trends do not help. But a fundamental issue is at stake: "[T]he role of Higher Education as a public good continues to be fundamentally important and must be supported. We emphasize this in the trend report because this aspect of Higher Education is easily neglected in the rush for income and prestige" (Altbach et al. 2009: xxi).

Such a role will continue to be strongly attacked in the years to come. It is alien to the dominating model of the university. More important, it is antagonized by the configuration of powers that be. But it is a necessary condition for democratizing knowledge in this age. Higher Education as a public good was not really a relevant trait of the old dominant models of the university. Trying to go back to them is neither feasible nor desirable. New orienting models and specific proposals are needed to foster the engagement of universities as a public good with Sustainable Human Development in close cooperation with the main actors of Inclusive Innovation Systems.

STAKEHOLDERS AND ALTERNATIVE MODELS

Who are the potential stakeholders of alternative models for committing universities to knowledge democratization? This question is a particular case of the one considered in Chapter 5: who are the stakeholders of Inclusive Innovation Systems? In that section, it was remarked that, given the global reach of the problems related to environmental damage and climatic change, potentially everybody has a stake in fostering a turn to frugal innovation. Also, given the depth of prevailing inequality, in no small measure related to the expansion of knowledge, the material and ideal interests of many people can be connected with a turn to inclusive innovation and knowledge democratization more generally. But the difficulties of agency in such issues were recalled too. It was argued in that chapter that when popular actors are estranged from advanced learning, knowledge generation, and innovation, they really do not belong to the Innovation System, which in turn cannot be inclusive. In such a context, we present some brief remarks specifically concerning Higher Education.

Universities in general are interacting with a widening set of external communities and stakeholders. Thus, universities become increasingly integrated in society. Often that overburdens them with external stakeholders' demands while internal fragmentation is aggravated, and so effective cooperation with society comes under threat (Jongbloed et al. 2008: 304, 308). This notwithstanding, the developmental role of universities cannot be expanded without working jointly with several external actors. Before we address that problem more concretely, some remarks concerning internal stakeholders may be useful. In fact, without commitment to development from within, it is difficult to expect that the alternative models under consideration can be something more than good intentions.

Concerning internal stakeholders, a starting assumption should be the following: "[T]he community of scholars may be seen as an important internal stakeholder category. The academic community represents the nucleus of scientific production. It is the basic internal constituency without which the university cannot function properly" (Jongbloed et al. 2008: 311).

That does not mean that the university is the first concern of its academic body: "[R]esearchers first and foremost see themselves as belonging to a disciplinary community and often seek alliances, recognition and support in their disciplinary field—that is, among their peers. Strategic partnerships between university departments therefore are not confined to a university's immediate region, but increasingly extend even beyond national borders" (Jongbloed et al. 2008: 311). Moreover, "...scholars view themselves as being more committed to their disciplinary invisible college, and thus to their profession, that to the employing organization" (Weiherl and Frost 2016: 174).

This assertion suggests reasons for doubting the possibilities of universities to be in some sense unitary actors (that is, to have agency as such). Generally speaking, the university is both an actor and an arena. But it may be assumed that in general the latter prevails, particularly because of the central role of the academic communities and the nature of its identities and interests: "[I]t is the academic professionals who act in the university as an arena, rather than the university itself as an organizational actor" (Enders et al. 2013: 4). Thus, incentives for (different types of) academic work are main factors shaping the landscape of universities and their interactions with external actors, as we will see in the following chapter on academic evaluation.

Students are of course also fundamental internal stakeholders. Their agency shows a much wider range of variability than that of teachers.

Often, they behave mainly as individual customers but sometimes become very influential collective actors. It is good to remember that "[I]t is not only through lecturers, professors, or other efforts of universities that students are educated, but also through the contributions of fellow students. Students are partly educated through their peers and the quality of peers co-determines the outcome of learning. When it comes to engagement with external communities, students drive a lot of the activities here" (Jongbloed et al. 2008: 311).

The occasional activation of the student movement can be a lever for internal change and for external engagement. This is certainly not sufficient for promoting the developmental role of universities, but in some contexts it may be absolutely necessary. That does not mean that student activism always points in that direction, but it does mean that such activism always deserves close attention, at least in the South.

Politicization of universities is common in developing countries. Altbach (2003: 15) finds that this "has directly affected the academic profession. In developing countries, universities are important political institutions—not only do they train elites but they also play a direct political role as a forum for student political activism, dissident perspectives, and even mobilization of opposition activities. Especially in societies with unstable governments, universities often serve an oppositional political function".

Such politicization is usually centered on the distribution of (comparatively small amounts of) power in the internal sphere of universities. Sometimes, it is a factor of academic change. Occasionally, it goes well beyond the academy, such as when student movements become fundamental actors in fighting authoritarian governments, often involving their universities in the struggle. Can that democratizing action in the realm of state politics be expanded to "dissident perspectives" in the realm of knowledge? Positive answers can be very specific, context-dependent, and made possible only by creative individual and collective agency. In any case, a sober appreciation of the potential of universities for cooperating with social change has to be kept in mind. More often than not, universities, academic bodies, and graduates are on the side of the establishment rather than against it.

Generally speaking, only some elementary recommendations seem to be possible. For example, internal efforts to stress the developmental role of universities should always be related to external actors who have concrete interests in the proposed changes, in order to foster systemic and interactive spaces of collaboration and learning about cooperation. Such interactive learning spaces can be, at the same time, places where potential stakeholders discover each other and "cells" of the tissue of Inclusive Innovation Systems. This remark can be a guiding thread when paying attention to the indicators of the developmental role of universities, the topic of Chapter 9. But first we will take a closer look at the prospects of fostering Developmental Universities in the presence of challenged academic autonomy and academic evaluation systems that impede the ability of universities to pursue effective policies for Sustainable Human Development.

REFERENCES

Altbach, P. (Ed.). (2003). *The Decline of the Guru. The Academic Profession in the Third World*. New York: Palgrave Macmillan.

Altbach, P., Reisberg, L., & Rumbley, L. (2009). *Trends in Global Higher Education: Tracking an Academic Revolution*. París: UNESCO.

Arocena, R., & Sutz, J. (2001). Changing Knowledge Production and Latin American Universities. *Research Policy, 30*(8), 1221–1234.

Arocena, R., & Sutz, J. (2011). Uruguay: Higher Education, National System of Innovation and Economic Development in a Small Peripheral Country. In B. Göransson & C. Brundenius (Eds.), *Universities in Transition. The Changing Role and Challenges for Academic Institutions* (pp. 77–96). Ottawa: Springer.

Arocena, R., Göransson, B., & Sutz, J. (2014). Universities and Higher Education in Development. In B. Currie-Alder, S. M. R. Kanbur, D. Malone, & R. Medhora (Eds.), *International Development: Ideas, Experience, and Prospects*. Oxford: Oxford University Press.

Benner, M. (2011). In Search of Excellence? An International Perspective on Governance of University Research. In B. Göransson & C. Brundenius (Eds.), *Universities in Transition. The Changing Role and Challenges for Academic Institutions* (pp. 11–24). Ottawa: Springer.

Benneworth, P. (2013). University Engagement with Socially Excluded Communities. Towards the Idea of 'the Engaged University'. In P. Benneworth (Ed.), *University Engagement with Socially Excluded Communities* (pp. 3–31). Netherlands: Springer.

Brennan, J., & Naidoo, R. (2008). Higher Education and the Achievement (and/or Prevention) of Equity and Social Justice. *Higher Education, 56*(3), 287–302.

Brundenius, C., & Göransson, B. (2011). The Three Missions of Universities: A Synthesis of UniDev Project Findings. In B. Göransson & C. Brundenius (Eds.), *Universities in Transition. The Changing Role and Challenges for Academic Institutions* (pp. 329–352). Ottawa: Springer.

Brundenius, C., Göransson, B., & Ågren, J. (2011). The Role of Academic Institutions in the National System of Innovation and the Debate in Sweden. In

B. Göransson & C. Brundenius (Eds.), *Universities in Transition. The Changing Role and Challenges for Academic Institutions* (pp. 307–325). Ottawa: Springer.

Cassiolato, J. E., Lastres, H., & Couto, M. C. (2014). The Brazilian National System of Innovation: Challenges to Sustainability and Inclusive Development. In G. Dutrénit & J. Sutz (Eds.), *National Innovation Systems, Social Inclusion and Development: The Latin American Experience* (pp. 68–101). Cheltenham: Edward Elgar.

de Mello, J. M. C., Maculan, A. M., & Borges Renault, T. (2011). Brazilian Universities and Their Contribution to Innovation and Development. In B. Göransson & C. Brundenius (Eds.), *Universities in Transition. The Changing Role and Challenges for Academic Institutions* (pp. 53–76). Ottawa: Springer.

Didriksson, A., & de la Fuente, J. R. (2015). Perspectives on the University Social Commitment in the Twenty First Century. In E. Aponte Hernández (Ed.), *La Responsabilidad Social de las Universidades: implicaciones para América Latina y el Caribe* (pp. 33–70). San Juan, Puerto Rico: UNESCO-IESALC.

Enders, J., de Boer, H., & Weyer, E. (2013). Regulatory Autonomy and Performance: The Reform of Higher Education Re-visited. *Higher Education, 65*(1), 5–23.

Gokhberg, L., Kuznetsova, T., & Zaichenko, S. (2011). Russia: Universities in the Context of Reforming the National Innovation System. In B. Göransson & C. Brundenius (Eds.), *Universities in Transition. The Changing Role and Challenges for Academic Institutions* (pp. 247–260). Ottawa: Springer.

Göransson, B., & Brundenius, C. (Eds.). (2011). *Universities in Transition. The Changing Role and Challenges for Academic Institutions.* Ottawa: Springer.

Gregersen, B. (2017). Role of Universities for Inclusive Development and Social Innovation: Experiences from Denmark. In C. Brundenius, B. Göransson, & J. M. Carvalho de Mello (Eds.), *Universities, Inclusive Development and Social Innovation. An International Perspective* (pp. 369–386). Ottawa: Springer.

Hayan, W., & Yuan, Z. (2011). China: Challenges for Higher Education in a High Growth Economy. In B. Göransson & C. Brundenius (Eds.), *Universities in Transition. The Changing Role and Challenges for Academic Institutions* (pp. 143–170). Ottawa: Springer.

Holmwood, J. (2011). Introduction. In J. Holmwood (Ed.), *A Manifesto for the Public University* (pp. 1–11). London: Bloomsbury.

IESALC. (2008). *Declaration of the Regional Conference of Higher Education of Latin America and the Caribbean.* Caracas: UNESCO-IESALC.

Jasanoff, S. (2003). Technologies of Humility: Citizen Participation in Governing Science. *Minerva, 41*, 223–244.

Jongbloed, B., Enders, J., & Salerno, C. (2008). Higher Education and Its Communities: Interconnections, Interdependencies and a Research Agenda. *Higher Education, 56*(3), 303–324.

Mwamila, B. L. M., & Diyamett, B. D. (2011). Tanzania: The Evolving Role of Universities in Economic Development. In B. Göransson & C. Brundenius

(Eds.), *Universities in Transition. The Changing Role and Challenges for Academic Institutions* (pp. 171–191). Ottawa: Springer.

Newfield, C. (2008). *Unmaking the Public University. The Forty-Year Assault on the Middle Class.* Cambridge: Harvard University Press.

NIH, National Institutes of Health. (2017). *What We Do. Budget.* https://www. nih.gov/about-nih/what-we-do/budget. Accessed 8 May 2017

Piketty, T. (2014). *Capital in the XXI Century.* Cambridge, MA: Harvard University Press.

Reay, D. (2011). Universities and the Reproduction of Inequality. In J. Holmwood (Ed.), *A Manifesto for the Public University* (pp. 112–126). London: Bloomsbury.

Rhoades, G., Maldonado, A., Ordorika, I., & Velázques, M. (2004). Imagining Alternatives to Global, Corporate, New Economy Academic Capitalism. *Policy Futures in Education, 2*(2), 316–329.

Roper, C. D., & Hirth, M. A. (2005). A History of Change in the Third Mission of Higher Education: The Evolution of One-Way Service to Interactive Engagement. *Journal of Higher Education Outreach and Engagement, 10*(3), 3–21.

Rose, H., & Rose, S. (1972). *The Radicalization of Science. Socialist Register, 9,* 105–132.

Sabato, J., & Botana, N. (1968). La ciencia y la tecnología en el desarrollo futuro de América Latina. *Revista de la Integración* 3 (Buenos Aires).

Sutz, J. (2005, April). The Role of Universities in Knowledge Production. SciDevNet, Policy Briefs. Available at: http://www.scidev.net/global/policy-brief/the-role-of-universities-in-knowledge-production-.html. Accessed 10 May 2017. Published also in *Journal of Himalayan Science, 3*(5), January–June 2005, 53–56.

The Mercury News. (2007, May 31). *Hillary Clinton Brings Innovation Agenda to Silicon Valley.* http://www.mercurynews.com/2007/05/31/hillary-clinton-brings-innovation-agenda-to-silicon-valley/

Tran Ngoc Ca, & Nguyen Vo Hung. (2011). Vietnam: Current Debates on the Transformation of Academic Institutions. In B. Göransson & C. Brundenius (Eds.), *Universities in Transition. The Changing Role and Challenges for Academic Institutions* (pp. 119–142). Ottawa: Springer.

Weerts, D. J., & Sandmann, L. R. (2008). Building a Two-Way Street: Challenges and Opportunities for Community Engagement at Research Universities. *Review of Higher Education, 32*(1), 73–106.

Weiherl, J., & Frost, J. (2016). Professional and Organizational Commitment in Universities: From Judgement to Developmental Performance Management. In J. Frost, F. Hattke, & M. Reihlen (Eds.), *Multi-Level Governance in Universities. Strategy, Structure, Control* (pp. 173–192). Switzerland: Springer.

CHAPTER 8

Academic Roles, Evaluation, and Development

The roles played by universities in National Systems of Innovation (NSI) are conditioned by a broad spectrum of circumstances. Some of these are essentially internal in nature, whereas others are the result of specific characteristics of the innovation system in place, and still others are contingent on the configurations of the academic system at the global level. Consequently, the roles played by universities are quite diverse, responding to the type of stakeholders and the type of demand or expectations involved; they take different forms and are ruled by specific norms. However diverse such roles may be, in almost all cases they involve knowledge-related activities. Universities act, in NSI, as knowledge providers, directly, through faculty acting as research performers, and indirectly, through the knowledge conveyed to students who later will act as problem-solvers in diverse types of organizations.

THE ROLE OF UNIVERSITIES IN INNOVATION SYSTEMS

The role that universities play in innovation systems relates to one of its principal tasks: unleashing creativity by providing a rich learning environment. The Group of Eight emphasizes that "[T]his makes them central to the innovation process, which depends totally on the capabilities of people and on productive interactions between people having different skill sets, knowledge and perspectives. *Innovation is not something that industries do, or firms do or governments do. It is something that the people within those organisations do, not usually as individuals but as teams that nevertheless*

© The Author(s) 2018
R. Arocena et al., *Developmental Universities in Inclusive Innovation Systems*, https://doi.org/10.1007/978-3-319-64152-2_8

draw upon and depend upon the abilities of individual people" (Group of Eight 2011: 8, emphasis added). What people do within the academic system, particularly in universities, is an important part of any innovation system. Such undertakings are closely related to and influenced by the academic incentives in place, to which people get access by following the rules of the game of the research evaluation system. These rules heavily influence which research is done or not done, a central issue for the dynamic of innovation systems. Thus, research evaluation has an important impact on such a dynamic. Therefore, in this chapter, we will elaborate at some length on the issue of research evaluation, fundamental for the role universities play in innovation systems everywhere and particularly so in developing countries. It is, moreover, a fundamental issue whether innovation systems should change direction to encompass Sustainable Human Development.

The features of universities that may be considered mainly internal and that mold the roles they can play in National Innovation Systems (NISs) include policies for student recruitment, quality of teaching, quality of research, and how the university is positioned vis-à-vis society. The ways in which the last three features relate to NIS are rather obvious; the first is not so evident, though. Universities with high barriers to entrance—whether academic or monetary (and the two are often intertwined)—foster the continuity of the social and political status quo through the reproduction of the elites. This may be highly instrumental in the prevailing knowledge relations within a given innovation system, but it becomes a barrier to changing such relations and to expanding the type of problems currently addressed by research and by innovation. It is worth noting that the universalization of advanced Higher Education, of lifelong Higher Education for all, is not a unanimous goal, even at a discursive level. The UNESCO World Conference on Higher Education, held in 2009, did not accept this as an aim, notwithstanding all the effort in that direction of Latin American countries (Arocena and Sutz 2016).

It is generally accepted that the speed of technical change renders much of the training obtained at Higher Education prone to rapid obsolescence. This leads to recognizing the need for lifelong learning. To broaden Higher Education, attempting to make access to the university universal, is an ambitious goal indeed. It would imply, for instance, overcoming bureaucratic certification of capacities and allowing people with DUI expertise (acquired by Doing, Using and Interacting) (Jensen et al. 2007) to be certified in their capacities to follow university studies. It will require the deployment of different strategies to teach to different people and openness to diverse learning trajectories. Innovation systems in societies where most of the population has the opportunity to study at an advanced level will exhibit a different dynamic than those where only a small part of the citizens has been trained in universities. In particular, a fundamental feature of universities as part of innovation systems, its connectedness with society at large, will be different.

The roles universities and university systems can play in NISs are not only influenced by some of its internal features. They are also shaped by the perception that powerful actors within the innovation system have of what universities should do. More generally, the innovation system structure, its functioning, and prevailing orientations strongly condition the roles of universities. This conditioning acts in two directions. A first direction affects the level of autonomy of universities, particularly public ones, mainly through budgetary allocations and, in some cases, imposition of governance structures. Related decisions usually come from high-level actors in the innovation system, like ministries of science and technology or governmental research councils. Almost thirty years ago, it was heralded that the research system, mainly the university research system, was in transition. Toward where was an open question, but similar symptoms of change were recognized everywhere in highly industrialized countries. Leveling off of the funding for research was the most salient feature of a wider movement toward renegotiating the "social contract" between science and society (Cozzens et al. 1990).

Some analysts posit that a reinvigorated social embeddedness of universities through the "comprehensive mass education facilities of the late twentieth century" explains why the roles universities play have become a concern for broader segments of society, particularly governments and business firms (Brundenius and Göransson 2011: 348). Be that as it may, the roles that universities should play in the innovation system are being renegotiated. Such renegotiation includes, in many countries, measures taken to foster the adoption of goals that are defined externally. The orientation of this process has been called the "marketization" of the university system (Dobbins and Knill 2014). Marketization, in some countries, includes the freedom of universities to choose their students, denying access that earlier was assured by national regulations. More freedom is also given to choosing sources of funding, like selling services, setting tuition fees, owning patents, and the like. The rationale behind these changes is to allow universities to do their best. This usually implies a stratification of universities at the national level. State support is distributed accordingly. In France, where universities were funded on egalitarian principles, changes in the described direction were fostered under Sarkozy's government: "...funds will not be distributed evenly but instead will support the government's policy of creating bigger, more autonomous universities that focus on excellence, have modernised governance, and are highly productive" (see Hazelkorn and Ryan 2013: 90).

Conflicts usually accompany these processes. The ways in which the conflicts are managed and how university roles end up changing are influenced by the characteristics of the "national" part of innovation systems. The national setting continues to be highly influential even in the midst of global pressures toward homogenization. Comparative analyses of how similar pushes for change are "digested" by different university systems confirm the importance of how history structured them and their relations with the broader innovation systems (Dobbins and Knill 2014; Göransson and Brundenius 2011; Mowery and Sampat 2005).

A second direction in which NISs condition the roles that the university may play relates to the flow of knowledge demand stemming from productive and social activities. In science-based and innovation-driven economies, such a flow is intense. Knowledge demand may come from national or international mega-projects—like the Human Genome Project or, before that, the Manhattan Project—or from public technology procurement (Edquist and Hommen 1999). It also comes from business firms that perform internal research and development (R&D) or requisition external research. The latter have become the heaviest R&D spenders in highly industrialized countries, showing the dynamism of the private demand for knowledge. When (i) different actors with purchasing power demand different types of knowledge, (ii) the universities are recognized as valuable knowledge partners by those actors, and (iii) universities are stimulated to become partners through organizational and legal transformations, it can be said that the innovation system fully incorporates universities into the system. However, this does not imply that such an incorporation exploits the cognitive strengths of universities in the best way. It may be quite the contrary, as several accounts of the failures and dangers stemming from a poor understanding of the economic role of universities have stressed (Mowery and Sampat 2005; Lundvall 2010; Mazzoleni and Nelson 2007; The Group of Eight 2011).

The role that universities are expected to play by the rest of the innovation system influences what they do internally and consequently what they can do externally. The expectations that innovation systems in developing countries place on universities are not too high. Professionals are needed, Higher Education is required to provide them, it is generally accepted that Higher Education must be accompanied by research to ensure an adequate level of professional training, but neither governments nor business firms seem to expect that the capacities for knowledge production accumulated in universities may be important for their activities. The internal response to such meager external expectations is—caricaturing to some extent—to develop a sort of academic self-referenced research agenda, a trend that evolves into a self-fulfilled prophecy in relation to how governments and business firms in immature, incomplete, or fragmented innovation systems perceive the role of universities.

The modern academic world is to a great extent a global endeavor. The international community of peers forms the task force of the "organized skepticism" that validates research outputs, dubbed by Robert Merton an essential part of the scientific ethos. An international task force of postgraduate students working in countries different than their own forms the back-bone of much of the research done, particularly in the Global North, with a strong participation of young researchers from the Global South. Even at the undergraduate level, efforts have been made to propitiate international exchanges among universities, of which the European Union Erasmus Program is a telling example. Until relatively recently, this global character did not prominently interfere with the roles that universities played in their own NISs. This situation has changed, though. A complex web of circumstances and features at a global level fostered changes. "Marketization" of Higher Education is paramount among them: "[T]raditionally, postsecondary education has been seen as a *public good*, contributing to society through educating citizens, improving human capital, encouraging civil involvement and boosting economic development. In the past several decades, Higher Education has increasingly been seen as a *private good*, largely benefiting individuals, with the implication that academic institutions, and their students, should pay a significant part of the cost of postsecondary education. (…) Higher Education systems and institutions are increasingly responsible for generating larger percentages of their own revenue. This debate has intensified due (…) to a more widespread political inclination toward greater privatization of services once provided by the state" (Altbach et al. 2009: xii).

Some time ago, this trend had a definite Anglo-Saxon flavor, but today it has spread all over the world. What is posited for the United States is recognizable as an important opinion everywhere, perhaps not always dominant but nonetheless influential: "[C]onventional wisdom says that (USA) public colleges will never again have the public funding they used to assume, so they must economize, commercialize, marketize, and finan-cialize. They must be closer to business and be more like business. They must focus on multiple revenue streams. Universities have, in this view, been protected from the market economy and must move teaching and research towards workforce demands and economic needs. Nearly all senior university officials, whether or not they like this model, felt obliged to adapt to it" (Newfield 2016: 3).

The trends just mentioned raise two questions to our argumentation. First, do such trends imply a change in the roles played by universities in NISs? Second, are those trends related to some configurations of the aca-demic system at a global level? The first question could easily receive as an answer that universities' roles are not changing: teaching, research, and knowledge transfer in diverse forms continue to be performed. However, changes in the perception of how decisions about what to research and to teach should be taken and by whom, accompanied by a renewed hierarchy of stakeholders in which private interests have the upper hand, may trans-form the roles universities play in innovation systems. It would be quite difficult to establish a clear causal link between any change in the innova-tive dynamics and transformations in the knowledge production system. But it is observable that the proposed transformations are vigorously fos-tered precisely to avoid the grim possibility that, by not being embedded enough in market concerns, universities fail to deliver the golden eggs that innovation needs. It is worth noting, then, that opinions warning against this type of reasoning were formulated more than two decades ago: "...there does not seem to be an adequate appreciation of the vulnerability of the science-technology systems in the West today, for all the frequency with which their importance to the modern economy and polity is acknowl-edged; nor of the basic features that are common to these variegated insti-tutional and cultural structures, and which render all of them susceptible to destabilizing and potentially damaging experiments which may soon be embarked upon in the earnest hope of more fully mobilizing the respective national scientific research communities in the service of national economic security – the successor goal to military security – that is now being pro-moted under the euphemism of 'competitiveness'" (Dasgupta and David 1994: 490). Furthermore, "[U]nder conditions approaching the state of 'universally privatized science' that such ideologues call for, an unbalanced research regime might continue to generate economic growth through the exploitation of the scientific and technological knowledge base, but sooner or later, economic progress almost certainly would lose the sustained character that has been taken by many scholars to distinguish ours from previous historical epochs" (Op. cit.: 515).

Later, we will discuss the ways in which research agendas—that is, the questions that research seeks to answer—are influenced by the changes just mentioned. For the moment, what we can assert is that a main justification put forward for transforming the role of the academic system is the claim that a more vibrant innovation system will be the outcome.

In regard to the second question, it can be asserted that there are some salient features of the academic system at a global level that are reinforcing the trends toward the marketization of universities. The main point is that "the global academic system" is a way of referring to an extremely heterogeneous set of institutions with similar goals but different characteristics, modes of governance, and academic outputs. So for those willing to "buy" any of the products offered by the global academic system—particularly students deciding where to invest their money and efforts—comparative information is important. This information came at a global level with the first university rankings in 2003. The impact of such rankings in universities all over the world, driven by internal reactions and by governmental reactions, has been immense. In an Organisation for Economic Co-operation and Development (OECD) report of 2007, precisely titled "How do rankings impact Higher Education" (Hazelkorn 2007), it is said that "…the frenzy provoked by publication of the Shanghai Jiaotong Academic Ranking of World Universities and Times QS World University Rankings gives an indication of the seriousness with which many Higher Education institutions (HEIs), policymakers and the media attach to them. Their increasing credibility derives from their simplicity and provision of 'consumer-type' information independent of the HE sector". As a consequence, a "gladiator obsession" (Ibid) with the place that national universities achieve in the first positions of international rankings acquired the feature of a State affair.

International rankings, which encompass national rankings, department rankings as well as individual researcher rankings, try "to simulate market competition but in reality it looked more like Soviet planning" (Burawoy 2011: 29). Moreover, "[J]ust as the Soviet planners had to decide how to measure the output of their factories, how to develop measures of plan fulfilment, so now universities have to develop elaborate indices of output, KPIs (key performance indicators), reducing research to publications, and publications to refereed journals, and refereed journals to their impact factors. Just as Soviet planning produced absurd distortions, heating that could not be switched off, shoes that were supposed to suit everyone, tractors that were too heavy because targets were in tons or glass that was too thick because targets were in volume, so now the monitoring of Higher Education is replete with parallel distortions that obstruct production (research), dissemination (publication) and transmission (teaching) of knowledge" (Ibid: 30).

The literature warning about the flaws of the measurements on which such rankings are based has done little to diminish their practical importance. Universities scramble to institute changes that may help them climb the rankings' ladder. Governments change their policies toward universities to push them further in that direction. The role that universities play in NISs is being influenced by new features of the globalizing academic system.

CONNECTED AUTONOMY

To produce socially valuable knowledge, universities, at least public universities, need to be autonomous in the sense of not being directly subordinated to concrete external powers, be they economic, political, or religious in nature. Autonomy in this sense means, in particular, freedom to pursue research in directions internally decided, using appropriate methodologies, and communicating the obtained results regardless of who may find them inconvenient or harmful to their interests. But university autonomy is by no means fully defined by these features. It may be achieved with a total disregard for the society in which the university is inserted, claiming that the best to be done is to perform high-quality research defined exclusively in their own ways. Alternatively, autonomy may be conceived in such a way that, along with the fulfillment of its defining traits, the aim orienting academic activities is to better serve society by taking into account voices that are outside academia. The first way of conceiving autonomy, the "ivory tower" way, is akin to autarchy. The second one, which implies dialogues with different stakeholders and before that to recognize the existence of legitimate "external" university stakeholders, may be named connected autonomy: "...the notion of connected autonomy leads to reject the university subordination to the great powers that be, and positions itself at the antipodes of autarchy" (Arocena 2015: 8, our translation). "When universities pay scant attention to its commitment to efforts aimed at more social justice and less inequality, autonomy tends to become autarchy. In such a case, the more or less legitimate particular interests of internal groups, and the conflicts among them, acquire a decisive influence in the life of the institution. What can be called internal particularism prevails. Any relatively complex organization knows this problematic, that probably does not have a definitive solution anywhere. But such configurations of interests and groupings are not static. If universities become connected, working actively with other collective actors, collaborating in a fruitfully and non-subordinated way to the achievement of desirable social changes, other configurations become possible" (Ibid).

Universities, not without internal tensions, recognize that "... working on the supply side of the knowledge economy is necessary and valuable but not sufficient. That is why the University seeks also to work on the demand side. Such work, or 'engagement', is responsive in nature, and is determined not only by the curiosity of the researcher, but also by issues and opportunities arising from within and across global society" (Brink and Hogan 2016: 240). Engagement and academic freedom, connectedness, and autonomy—to make them work together is the aim of a growing number of universities, even if the ways to do so show slow progress.

The concept of connected autonomy resembles Evans's (1995) concept of "embedded autonomy". Of course, there are important differences between both concepts, the most salient of which is that in one case it refers to universities whereas in the other it refers to the "developmental state", as Johnson (1982) denominated the state responsible for the spectacular Japanese economic growth based on knowledge and innovation after the Second World War. The differences between universities and states in relation to the combination of autonomy and connectedness or embeddedness derive primarily from the different possibilities to exert power over their stakeholders. What states can do, especially if we refer to stakeholders external to the organization, universities cannot. However, all the differences notwithstanding, the link between the two characteristics is important also for universities, and for similar reasons. "A state that were only autonomous would lack both sources of intelligence and the ability to rely on decentralized private implementation. Dense connecting networks without a robust internal structure would leave the state incapable of resolving 'collective action' problems, of transcending the individual interests of its private counterparts. Only when embeddedness and autonomy are joined together can a state be called developmental" (Evans 1995: 12).

Autonomy is needed to prevent institutional capture by stakeholders with sufficient power to impose policies, behaviors, or ideologies to their advantage: this holds, even if in different forms, for universities and for states. But shielding may be asphyxiating as well, leading to an institution that only serves itself. Evans (1995: 41) puts it as follows: "[T]he problem is separating the benefits of insulation from the costs of isolation". To avoid isolation, some ways for immersing in society are needed, but strong voices against such immersion arise in both cases. For states, some voices said that being friendly with markets is all that they need to do to achieve an optimal social output and that any deviation (for instance, having an explicit industrial policy) will lead to committing costly mistakes. For universities, some voices said that following the pursuit of knowledge for their own sake is the way of maximizing the harvest of high-quality knowledge to be put at social disposal and that any deviation will submerge universities in a mess of contradictory and short-term requirements that harm the scientific enterprise. Universities have sometimes tried to shield themselves from the prevailing powers, which in actual terms means the state and one of its most conspicuous stakeholders, economic interests: this has proven to be increasingly complicated, though. Balanced outcomes are always difficult to achieve, tensions and conflicts accompany attempts to reach them, and they remain unstable amid changing circumstances. Moreover, again following Evans (1995: 19), it is important not to reify institutions by ascribing them a type of volition of their own: "[I]n practice 'the state wants' because some group of individuals within the state apparatus has a project. This does not mean the project is merely a reflection of their personal biographies or individual maximizing strategies. It does mean that their project may well be opposed by others elsewhere in the state and that the definition of what the state 'wants' is the result of internal political conflict and flux".

If this is true for the state, it is at least as true for universities. What "universities want"—looked at from the perspective of what universities proclaim they want to do and of what they do—is the outcome of a complex web of interactions and power relations involving different internal groups, the governance system including the financial regime, and the kind and strength of the university relations with the rest of society. There is one more feature of potential conflict and power contest that is specific to the academic realm, a feature that importantly influences what the "university wants" and, in a more down-to-earth formulation, "what university people want/need to do": the academic prestige regime. "Prestige" is not a given but a social construct. Its assigning criteria change when circumstances change and power relations inside and outside academia are strong enough. Currently, and related to the general adoption of New Public Management (NPM) in the management of academic pursuits, such criteria are associated with what has been called the "rituals of verification" (Power 1999). This specific aspect, the research evaluation systems and its influence on the roles universities play in NISs, is addressed in the next and last section of this chapter. We now come back to the notion of "connected autonomy" to explore it a bit further and to show how it is related to the prestige regime and the research evaluation system.

There are striking differences in the ways in which states build their embeddedness and universities their connectedness, besides the obvious fact that states have powers to induce behaviors that universities do not have. Embeddedness "…represents something more specific than the fact that the state grows out of its social milieu. It is also more specific than the organic interpenetration of state and society that Gramsci called hegemony. Embeddedness (…) implies a concrete set of connections that link the state intimately and aggressively to particular social groups with whom the state shares a joint project of transformation" (Evans 1995: 59). Universities may have projects for internal transformations; they may aim at such transformations to be better able to contribute to a broader social transformation. But its relations with society differ from being linked to particular social groups with which they share projects of transformation. Universities are knowledge producers and knowledge disseminators. Connectedness is the outcome of considering the knowledge needs of different social actors when fulfilling knowledge production and dissemination. This may be done by means of the settings of research agendas, the contents of teaching, and the efforts to make knowledge available to those different actors. In democratic and plural societies, universities should be connected to a whole gamut of social actors. This clearly is not the case. When David Hess (2007) talks of un-done science, he refers to social actors that need knowledge support for their aims and concerns and cannot find it because the academic system does not connect with them, as if they were invisible to it. This is an expression of lack of connectedness: there is an actor who knows that it needs knowledge but has not enough power to render its demands acknowledged and taken on board by the university. A more complicated expression of lack of connectedness appears when social actors who would benefit from a specific cognitive approach to their problems are not able to identify research as a tool for solving them: the most deprived part of the population is usually in this situation. On the other side, there are actors with power to have their knowledge demands taken on board, like big business firms in knowledge-intense sectors and diverse sections of the state apparatus. The connectedness between the university and such actors is often built by the initiative of the latter: in exchange for the university services they need, they offer material or symbolic resources that the university requires for its functioning. An old example shows this clearly: "IBM has a manpower problem now; they know it will be severe in ten years. Their problem is twofold. They need professionally trained people to help sell their product. They want their customers to have professionally trained people to use their product properly. IBM has" presented "650's to over 50 universities by now under the condition (among others) that a couple of courses in data processing and numerical analysis be given. (…) It is fair to say that, in many cases, to the extent that a university computer activity has a purpose at all, it has been made for them by IBM" (Fein 1959: 10).

Two similarities between the embeddedness of the state and the connectedness of the university are worth mentioning. First, both need the initiative of these institutions. It is not a question of expecting other actors to come and establish the links, even if this may happen in some occasions: state and universities need to build the conditions for these linkages to get established, as well as to set the rules of the game that will govern them. Second, this building needs to be done in a way that preserves autonomy, avoiding the capture of the institutions by particular interests. "Without autonomy, the distinction between embeddedness and capture disappears. *Autonomy by itself does not necessarily predict an interest in development*, either in the narrow sense of economic growth or in the broader sense of improved welfare. The secret of the developmental state lies in the amalgam" (Evans 1995: 59, emphasis added). The same holds for universities. Connecting with society is the more difficult problem, a problem that needs to be solved because "capacity without connection will not do the job" (Op. cit.: 245). This also holds for universities, where the expression may be expanded as "capacity without connection derives into ivory towers, and this will not do the job". At least if the job is understood as maximizing the social usefulness of the knowledge produced, taught, and disseminated. To what extent universities, or some of its academic constituent parts, become socially connected is in part an outcome of internal struggles, but also an outcome of how the innovation system behaves. In this sense, expectedly, universities are weaker than states. States, in Evans's parlance, can "build" actors with which they become embedded: they may help them to emerge through a "midwifery" role and then they may help them to grow and play a transformative role through a "husbandry" role. This is something universities cannot do. The incentives for non-academic actors to become connected to universities stem from the functioning of the national system of innovation, and what universities can do in this respect is limited. The involvement of universities themselves in connecting with social actors relies fundamentally on their internal organization and on how they build a system of incentives where connectedness with diverse actors is appropriately valued without losing autonomy.

The system of incentives may be seen as a disciplining device that works in the sense of building coherence in an institutional milieu where silo-like behavior is more the rule than the exception. Any system of incentives signals which behaviors should be rewarded. In the academic realm, such a system is not unitary and homogeneous; on the contrary, it is like a patchwork made from different pieces, some material and some symbolic. This implies a series of tensions and conflicts for individual academics. Moreover, the pieces of the patchwork of academic incentives are not at the same level in terms of its perceived importance: academic prestige is particularly high in the hierarchy. Academic prestige rewards by conferring academic citizenry. Keeping this citizenry is fundamental for researchers. For this they need a mixture of material resources to perform research, a set of academic relationships to be aware of the state of the art in what they are doing, verifiable quality assurance of the results obtained, and, eventually, verifiable assurance of the social usefulness of such results. Systems of incentives and connectedness are related issues. When getting resources for the university is considered a hallmark of academic seniority and is rewarded with attributes of prestige, connections with commercial partners are encouraged through measures like opening technology transfer offices, allowing faculty to get additional income through consultancy activities, or allowing the privatization of results against previous norms of open disclosure (Murray 2006). The other way around, when universities want to get more connected to social actors who were historically at arm's length from the academy, they need to accommodate the incentive system to legitimate the related activities.

In summary, connected autonomy refers to the capacity of universities to forge their way as actors in NISs. The academic incentives regime is a main source of legitimacy for what university people do. The scope of the connectedness of universities is thus influenced by academic evaluation through the value given to the different activities they perform. The influence of such evaluation on the configuration of universities as actors in innovation systems justifies paying close attention to this issue, to which we turn in the following section.

MAIN CHARACTERISTICS AND INFLUENCE OF PREVAILING ACADEMIC EVALUATION SYSTEMS

Around a hundred years ago, Argentinean students taking part in the Cordoba reform movement discussed above wrote what became an influential text for Latin American universities, the Cordoba Manifesto. They were against the rule of the faculty cast, the mediocrity of the teaching, and its poor academic content. They reclaimed a radical democratization of the universities, in terms of both governance and its role in society. Amid the romantic rhetoric of the text, fundamental roles for the university were proposed: to be "creators of truth, beauty and good".

Every modern university must perform research, "create truth", but to what extent and how they should also work for the "good" are neither consensual nor clear. For the "entrepreneurial university", it means direct collaboration of universities with the capitalization of knowledge (Etzkowitz 2004); for the "engaged university", it means community engagement (Weerts and Sandmann 2008); for the "civic university", it includes "an understanding of not just what it is good at, but what it is good for" (Goddard et al. 2016: 10). The idea of a "developmental university" refers to commitment to fostering development processes (Coleman 1986; Arocena et al. 2014, 2015).

University research policies acknowledge the need to combine the "truth" and the "good". Academic researchers, accordingly, aspire to legitimacy on the double ground of high-quality science and of socially useful science. This is never easy, and contextual factors may further impede harmonization. The research evaluation system, which gives testimony of "quality", may be more or less tuned to "social usefulness" depending on the relative economic, social, and political power of those demanding knowledge. Recent literature suggests that prevailing research evaluation procedures related to quality assessment and research productivity exert a powerful influence in the setting of research agendas. They not only perform ex-post assessment but also serve as a compass indicating what types of research efforts are worth pursuing, in this way influencing future research.

Evaluation does not necessarily constitute a coherent whole: a university researcher may be evaluated in her department, by some more general university body, and by a national organization, all using different criteria; this usually gives rise to tensions and conflicts. Moreover, diverse demands over universities' missions, from within and from outside, may add to these tensions if the harmonization of different research orientations and academic tasks is neglected. In developing countries, where relatively small research communities struggle to survive and grow in the midst of all types of scarcities, such tensions may have severe consequences. If addressing developmental problems is seen by the research community, particularly by young scholars, as making it even more difficult to find a place in the "certified knowledge" world, then the role universities may play in development will be diminished: "[E]ngagement is seen as rhetorically correct; but inside the tenure committee, nobody cares about it. It's business as usual. I'm wrestling with the contradiction between the rhetoric and reality of outreach on this campus" (See Weerts and Sandmann 2008: 92).

Evaluation of individual academic work as an institutionalized practice is, roughly speaking, two centuries old. The appearance of new disciplines and sub-disciplines and a more collective research work led to a proliferation of researchers and research orientations. Appraising academic merits became a serious research policy issue, rendering "evaluation (…) an integral part of the research system" (Frederiksen et al. 2003: 155). Evaluation is an evolving process: "…routine verification may well have been adequate for the purposes of maintaining the stability of administrative accountability in Higher Education, but only so long as the Higher Education system in its entirety was **not** seen as a prime lever for economic or social change" (Neave 1998: 269, emphasis in the original). Accompanying the recognition of the immediate strategic value of knowledge, intermediary evaluation bodies started assessing research quality, inspired by NPM. Around two decades ago, governments in several countries, including the USA and many in Europe, started to consider public universities as state agencies, thus amenable to be under the NPM style of ruling as any other agency. Thus, the working hypothesis and its consequence were as follows: "…if state agencies are faced with clearly formulated goals and a set of incentives and sanctions that are invoked in response to actual behavior, then efficiency will increase. When the emphasis is moved from rule production and rule adherence to goal formulation and performance control, evaluation becomes a core activity…" (Bleiklie 1998: 94).

The "value for money" type of auditing of publicly sponsored research led to "a marked tendency to base trust on the use of quantitative information" (Frederiksen et al. 2003: 155). As a direct result of the adoption of an NPM perspective of the functioning of universities, "…the notion of academic performance has been redefined from one in which its inherent quality is emphasized to one in which measurable quantitative aspects are prominent. In the latter case, qualitative considerations are presumed to be implied by the performance indicators that are used. This makes academic activity open to external scrutiny by superior administrative authorities. Disciplinary competence is thus no longer required in order to evaluate disciplinary performance, as performance indicators such as the number of candidates produced and published books and articles in respected journals all provide simple, standard information that is fairly easy to understand" (Bleiklie 1998: 95).

This trend needs to be explained because it does not derive logically from the renewed importance of research and Higher Education.

The increased relevance of activities connected with advanced knowledge and education implies that more actors become involved and that different interests may collide. Consequently, it may not be easy even for the more powerful sectors to impose their goals by means of consistent practices. As a result, prevailing evaluation patterns are characterized by uncertainty concerning their real consequences. However, they have expanded quickly. Perhaps that contradiction illustrates the notion of (mimetic) isomorphism, understood as a process of change that mimics models of institutional behavior dubbed successful, like NPM. The proponents of the notion put forwards the hypothesis that "the greater the extent to which technologies are uncertain or goals are ambiguous within a field, the greater the rate of isomorphic change" (Di Maggio and Powell 1983: 156). In regard to research specifically, it is stated that "[A]mong the effects of governance taken into account by any anticipatory or reflexive governance, changes in the content of research are the most opaque" (Gläser 2012: 3).

Powerful actors—particularly governments and entrepreneurial elites—are directly interested in changing the governance of knowledge production and use. Their concrete goals are not always clear, and the actual results of prevailing procedures are not well understood. But such procedures seem to be fostered by the powers that be. Thus, they are quickly copied. Poor understanding of methods, combined with clear awareness of who is in command, fosters mimetic isomorphism. It is difficult to imagine how results emanating from such a one-size-fits-all model can be accepted without serious reservations. It seems that academia has been reached by a general trend, as damaging there as in society in general: "[T]he audit society is a society that endangers itself because it invests too heavily in shallow rituals of verification at the expense of other forms of organizational intelligence" (Power 1999: 123).

It is quite clear that the prevailing evaluation system is not unanimously accepted by the academy. The literature involved with assessing the impacts of current research evaluation practices is steadily increasing, highlighting different types of worries and conflictual situations. This literature has in common the concern for a trend that may be weakening academic performance: "[I]nstitutions are measured against other institutions, researchers compete with one another for funds and universities for students. This leads to a permanent state of war between all the parties, destroying the social fabric of the university [...] Of all tasks in the academic workplace, teaching is the least appreciated and has to be outsourced as soon as possible, allowing people to focus on the battle for coveted research money" (Halffman and Radder 2015: 168). A lot of factual evidence supports the last quote.

The following assertion is probably not (very) controversial: "[T]he current situation is characterized by a tension between administrative needs for simple measures and more easy evaluation methods and researchers request for fair and comprehensive assessments of scientific quality" (Aksnes and Rip 2009: 905). Moreover, "...the peer-review system is near its limits due to overload stemming partly from the increasing pressure to publish" (Nowotny 2016: 157).

Such an assertion goes a long way toward the explanation of why the great shift in evaluation favored quantitative methods. In a word: simplicity. The "administrative needs for simple measures" have engendered a very specific system "supported by general and abstract tools (...) that can be used in fairly standardized ways across different substantial areas of activity" (Dahler-Larsen 2013: 31). It is even asserted that such evaluation systems don't have as their basic function the verification of what happens in a particular area of activities but to build a definition of those activities such that some verification is possible (Dahler-Larsen 2007: 99).

Prevailing evaluation patterns, strongly based on bibliometrics, use the Social Sciences Citation Index (SSCI) for the social sciences. Hicks (2006) asserts that "SSCI-only analyses are easier and cheaper" but also particularly dangerous. This is so because in the social sciences there are four distinct literatures: "international journal articles, books, national and enlightenment publications" and only the first one is indexed in the SSCI. If this index is the main basis for evaluation, the contribution of social scientists "to understanding their own societies and communicating their insights to the public" (Hicks 2006: 162) becomes undermined: "[I]t would be a tragedy if the intellectual development of the social sciences and its contribution to society were to be stunted. But that may be the ultimate result if in becoming accountable to narrow measures the enterprise is forced into the straight jacket of one of its historical four modes of scholarship and communication" (Ibid). To this evaluation bias is to be added that social sciences, along with humanities and the arts, are not seen as the main sources of support to economic growth. "Compared to 'hard' sciences, humanities and social sciences' (HASS) social benefits and services are more diffuse and less easily enumerated and capitalized. Likewise, their 'clients' or beneficiaries often are public bodies, non-profit organisations, and other community groups with lower purchasing power" (Benneworth and Jongbloed 2010: 568).

Understanding their own societies and communicating their insights to the public are activities neglected in prevailing research evaluation. They are often related to social critiques. Perhaps most governments and other powers that be are not unhappy with that.

The "Leiden Manifesto for research metrics" posits that "[T]he problem is that evaluation is now led by the data rather than by judgment. Metrics have proliferated: usually well intentioned, not always well informed, often ill applied" (Hicks et al. 2015: 429). Such damaging applications affect universities directly: "[A]cross the world, universities have become obsessed with their position in global rankings (such as the Shanghai Ranking and *Times Higher Education*'s list), even when such lists are based on what are, in our view, inaccurate data and arbitrary indicators" (Idem: 430).

But the problem is even more complicated: "[A]ll measured aspects of a university's activities and duties—education and research—are squeezed into one single measure, while another aspect—societal impact—is even neglected" (Kronman 2013: 96). A single measure may serve perhaps the interests of a well-defined group, but it is surely ill suited to gauge the different activities that universities must accomplish in collaboration with different actors and moreover in different contexts. Should the activities of a private university in a very rich city be estimated by the same measures as those of a public university in a poor country? No wonder that "societal impact" is neglected.

The priority given to rankings leads to a concentration of resources in those dimensions that help to raise them: (i) areas of knowledge that are highly valued by rankings, thus neglecting others, like social sciences; (ii) certain activities, neglecting, for example, university collaboration with society; (iii) limited segments of students, thus fostering social inequality; and (iv) specific regions, thus fostering geographic inequality.

A general evaluation system based on quantification and the increased role of management seem to be fostering the market value of Higher Education. The notion of Higher Education as a public good is contested. Universities used to be conceptualized as a very special type of institution but this seems not to be the case anymore.

Let us pause to recapitulate. Academic evaluation has been a systematic activity for a long time. A great shift in this activity has taken place in recent decades. Evaluation activities grew quickly, and procedures have become increasingly formalized and quantitative. Given the enormous quantitative growth of advanced knowledge and Higher Education as well as its qualitative diversification, evaluation seems to be unmanageably complex and time-consuming. A modicum of simplicity and time-saving is provided by formalized quantitative methods. Now, even if the above-sketched argument could go a long way to explain why the great shift took place, it would not be sufficient to understand why the new dominant evaluation system persists, given that far from generating consensus it promotes great concern in the academy.

Some elements for an answer have already been examined. In a nutshell, the new economic and social role of knowledge fosters a change in the dominant perception of the university. From being cultural institutions shaped by academic incentives, universities are changing to "economic corporations" shaped by market incentives. Consequently, public policies for research and Higher Education are oriented by NPM viewpoints. The corresponding evaluation system, even if it generates doubts and resistances in the academy, is a source of certainty and a guarantee of good results for governments. A closer look at those aspects is needed. That will be attempted next by focusing attention on what traits of universities are really fostered or hampered by actual evaluation procedures.

How Evaluation Systems Foster
or Hamper University Models

Evaluation is usually seen as a source of certainty, often "regarded as an apolitical phenomenon, a formalized approach to accountability" (Schwandt 2012: 220). Thus, "the determination of quality is exempt from any kind of moral-political or normative debate; quality simply *is* performance (...), and performance simply *is* measurable against agreed-upon standards and traceable through indicators" (Ibid). This has been contested in the scholarly literature, defying "the straightforward view that such measurement essentially constitutes a politically neutral, rational instrument facilitating the effective monitoring, and ultimately managing, of performances" (Woelert 2015: 75).

What are the real consequences of the new prevailing evaluation patterns? Frederiksen et al. (2003: 161) assert that "[I]t sometimes appears that because of the difficulties of measuring the desirable phenomena, there is a tendency to focus on what the indicators show, i.e. on the figures rather than the underlying processes. A consequence of this can be changes in behaviour, but in the opposite direction than intended".

Since the relation between what is measured and what needs to be evaluated is poorly understood, some degree of certainty is obtained by "mimetic isomorphism" (that is, by doing what others do). That contributes to the persistence and expansion of the dominant evaluation system even when there is good reason to doubt its real effects. In any case, "performance measurement works through social and political rather than mechanical channels and hence has winners and losers and is extremely consequential" (Lewis 2015: 11). Losers not only include academics who are not selected in contested calls but also stakeholders in society at large who are not taken into account although they are actually or potentially related to—or may benefit from—the generation and use of advanced knowledge. If knowledge is power, more than ever, increasing conflicts concerning knowledge control can be expected. What type of university is fostered by prevailing evaluation patterns and related conflicts?

At least two main types of university are usually considered: the Humboldtian or Academic University and the Entrepreneurial University. The latter, proclaimed by management to "provide economic salvation" (Halffman and Radder 2015: 172), has become the leading model for transforming the university worldwide; fostering it can be seen then as an intended consequence of evaluation patterns.

However, beyond intentions, such patterns point in a different direction: "[B]y valuing some research more highly than other research, rankings—and similar systems of research assessment—reproduce classical conceptions of knowledge and power relations. They encourage a return to 'ivory tower' research conducted by elites in selected institutions at a time when complex global problems and policy objectives require the involvement of interdisciplinary teams with diverse perspectives and experiences" (Hazelkorn 2009: 11). Rather than promoting the Entrepreneurial

University, the actual result seems to reinforce the Academic University. More specifically, it is suggested that performance-based research funding systems enhance control by professional elites and, since they aim for excellence, they will compromise equity or diversity while not enhancing the economic value of research (Hicks 2012).

Nevertheless, it is not obvious that the prevailing criteria are good, in the long run at least, even from the point of view of the Academic University: "[I]f researchers only focus on delivering short-term accountable results and managing their publication assets, what will happen with the long-term basic research that may deliver results that are important in 20–30 years?" (Kronman 2013: 124).

The consequences of academic evaluation are often different from those intended by public policies. A strong and specific statement points in that direction: "[W]e do know that performance-based university research funding systems neglect application of research, although research application is a long-standing concern of governments" (Hicks 2013: 85).

Prevailing evaluation patterns seem to be empowering academic elites, a trend that implies a shift in the internal distribution of power: "…what once was considered to be a functional imperative for all competent researchers – autonomous problem choice – is gradually turning into the privilege of academic elites" (Gläser 2010: 363). The British Research Assessment Exercise shows that "it has largely enhanced the authority of established scientific elites rather than orienting academic research towards economic goals and what the state considered to be user needs" (Whitley 2010: 37).

Again, why does the prevailing evaluation system persist? On the one hand, governments and (some) universities aim at promoting the Entrepreneurial University, but it is not evident that this will be a strong consequence of prevailing evaluation patterns. On the other hand, an actual consequence is the empowerment of academic elites. Perhaps there exists a sort of implicit agreement that keeps the system working: governments can show an example of their commitment to NPM while academic elites are satisfied with what really is a means of enhancing their worldview and power. Governments seeking validation and elites seeking influence converge in fostering a small set of "world class universities". It is worth recalling some of the consequences: "[A] university considered to be *world class* is less likely to stress teaching, public service, providing access to underserved populations, or other important social services" (Altbach et al. 2009: 11). Perhaps the more or less tacit agreement between governments and academic elites hypothesized above protects evaluation patterns that are, at least in the long run, academically damaging.

The last assertion has a tentative character. On the contrary, it is almost beyond doubt that the dominant evaluation system hampers the social commitment of universities: "[L]ong-term involvement with society, which is both complex and uncertain, sits at odds with an academic career progression that values a constant stream of research outputs" (Trencher et al. 2013: 20).

The reward system gives rise to strong disincentives for academic engagement in joint work with communities and non-academic collective actors, even if the latter is seen as "rhetorically correct". A case study showed that "promotion and tenure policies were the strongest barrier to faculty engagement with the community" (Weerts and Sandmann 2008: 91).

The academic situation is even more worrying in the South; the peripheral condition of universities there is also seen in connection with validation and evaluation of academic work: "[T]he Third World looks to the North for validation of academic quality and respectability. For example, academics are expected to publish in Northern academic journals in their disciplines. Promotion often depends on such publication. Even where local scholarly publications exist, they are not respected. While it is understandable that small and relatively new academic systems may wish to have external validation of the work of their scholars and scientists, such reliance has implications for the professoriate. For example, internationally circulated journals are often highly competitive, and journal editors may not place much value on research topics relevant in developing countries. Moreover, it is always more difficult for authors to write in a language that is not their own. Journal editors, for their part, must be guided by the methodological and topical predilections of their immediate colleagues and are as a result less interested in work done by Third World authors" (Altbach 2003: 6).

The result of this trend is clear enough: "[I]mposing an evaluation system that privileges international citations will force scholars to choose topics that interest foreign academics. Over time this poses the danger of forcing non-English language scholars out of the disciplinary core and into a fringe of colourful topics in the hope of attracting the international attention so valued by their governments" (Hicks 2013: 79).

It follows that, if the prevailing evaluation system makes it difficult for academics in the North to work in connection with problems of their communities while being recognized and rewarded as academics, the system makes that even more difficult in the South.

On Alternative Research Evaluation
Systems and Metrics

University systems around the world vary substantially, to such an extent that fundamental concepts, such as autonomy, acquire different meanings in different systems. The Latin American concept of autonomy of public universities implies that universities should be ruled without interference from the national government: the university decision-making bodies are elected by different combinations of internal stakeholders, usually including at least students and faculty. The arm's-length relationship between governments and universities has been fueled by a long-standing ideological struggle opposing oligarchic or neoliberal political rulers and left-wing university student movements, timidly accompanied by faculty, constrained in its activities by very low budgets allocated to knowledge production. The recent transformations fostered in European universities, on the other hand, put a different concept of autonomy forward: universities are freed from governmental rules regarding how to choose students, for instance, but they are tightly disciplined by governmental prioritization and evaluation with concomitant budget allocation. This hampers the traditional conceptualization of autonomy: "[T]he implementation of funding and regulatory frameworks which are introducing neo-liberal forms of market funding and governance mechanisms are reported to be undermining academic autonomy. The common critique is that this erodes the critical space and disempowers academics". It is also said that such frameworks mainly re-shape academic activities in order to promote the entrepreneurial university (Brennan and Naidoo 2008: 297).

Even if at the discourse level universities everywhere see their roles in NISs re-conceptualized, their institutional integration in those systems is extremely diverse, and so it is difficult to compare the impact of evaluative practices on universities across the globe. This diversity narrows drastically when we refer to university people as individuals: prevailing evaluation systems, which are highly globalized and homogenized, exhibit remarkable similar impacts on academics at an individual level in spite of important differences regarding Higher Education systems and NISs.

This does not mean that academics play on an even field. There are hierarchies of prestige related to disciplines, to research topics, to the language in which results are communicated, to the journals in which such results are published, and to the university in which scholars work. But in every corner of academic life, measures of success and above all the incentives that are based on them shape what academics try to do: "[I]f we start to measure research in certain ways and allocate funding according to the results, researchers will adapt to this and the measurements will start to be an incitement, driving research in directions towards the measurable" (Kronman 2013: 123).

The incentives derived from the prevailing ways of measuring research show similar consequences on scholars in very different settings. An example of this can be seen from an analysis of such consequences in Great Britain and in Mexico. The cases are not exactly comparable: the British Research Assessment Exercise (RAE) is directed to universities, and the Mexican National System of Researchers (NSR) is directed to individual scholars. However, given that the analysis of the RAE includes its impact at an individual level, comparisons are nonetheless meaningful. Both analyses are furthermore comparable given that they take a long-term perspective, assessing impact after more than 20 years of application of the instruments.

In the Mexican case, analysts of the NSR posit that "...the NSR stimulus act against the activities more directly related to institutional objectives different from research. (...) Our science and technology system is evolving towards a unimodal one, meaning that the institutional diversity is being reduced, with serious consequences for the integral goals and the joint productivity of the system" (Foro Consultivo Científico y Tecnológico y Academia Mexicana de Ciencias 2005: 50, our translation) and "...20 years later, the NSR is inhibiting the quality and the creativity of researchers (...). Researchers simply comply with the requisites of the NSR. Researchers do not want to enter into much more risky projects in which they may pass 3, 4 or 5 years without publishing anything because the project they get involved with is too complex and will not allow to have in time the scientific publication required by the NSR" (Op. cit.: 54, our translation).

In the case of RAE, the assessment is not less direct.

(i) In terms of the future of research orientation, "...the current approach to research assessment in UK universities is reductionistic and primitive, and almost certainly counterproductive in terms of generating a wide variety of intellectual innovations in the longer term" (Martin and Whitley 2010: 75). The RAE signals pointed to what is more rewarding: basic rather than applied research; shorter-term rather longer-term research; incremental rather than more ambitious or open-ended "pioneering" research; mainstream rather than "alternative" research or research in a highly specialized sub-field; monodisciplinary rather than inter- or multidisciplinary research; "academic" rather than "professional" research (for instance, in medicine, management, law, and planning); research that yields journal articles rather than books; and research where the results can be published in "top" journals rather than more specialized (and generally lower status) ones (Ibid: 70).

(ii) In terms of driving academic activities toward a "unimodal" system where research is paramount, "...the RAE has reduced the willingness of faculty to engage in other academic activities such as reviewing, editing, translating, contributing to reference works, writing popular books, engaging in clinical medicine or community service, providing policy advice, and so on...[...] Many universities and departments now struggle to persuade faculty to give due attention to teaching or administration. The emphasis on the RAE means that individuals (especially 'leading researchers') tend to devote less time to lecture preparation or to meetings with students" (Ibid: 71).

(iii) Impact on personal life: "[T]he RAE has been a factor encouraging overwork and adding to levels of stress. It has disadvantaged those (predominantly women) who have taken time off for family or other reasons, resulting in a 'gap' in their published output" (Ibid: 72).

Moreover, "[A]s a result of the RAE, knowledge has, therefore, being increasingly fettered by the narrow standards of the peer reviewed article (...) Correspondingly, research now lacks variety as a pool for renewal..." (Munch 2014: 74).

In China, concern with research evaluation is growing for similar reasons: "[S]ince the evaluation of a teacher's work highlights research achievements in many universities, more and more teachers devote themselves to research work, at the expense of their teaching, and indirectly cause the deterioration of teaching quality" (Haiyan and Yuan 2011: 163).

The answer proposed earlier to the question why this apparently dysfunctional academic evaluation system prevails seems to hold: more power to the academic elites and compliance with the new managerial logic by governmental—and, in some cases, universities'—bureaucracies. In particular, what Martin and Whitley call the "regulatory capture" of the evaluation process by academic elites (2010: 73) seems to be resistant to attempts to foster "un-done science", even when such science is demanded by actors with purchasing power. The regime of prestige, translated into compelling actions through the regulatory capture by academic elites, tends to be more powerful than other signals competing for research orientation. This is particularly so in developing countries, where internal knowledge demand from business firms and from the state is structurally weak, and research communities, small and fragile, seek in the compliance with the international evaluation system a source of the legitimacy that they do not find at home.

Individual researchers are usually exposed to different research evaluation procedures as long as they receive funds from different organizations. The particular aims of those organizations are usually diverse, and so their evaluation criteria may differ. Researchers suffer the tensions derived from this situation in terms of hard choices. Some of them relate to their academic career vis-à-vis their willingness to put their research capabilities in direct contact with societal challenges and to fulfill the whole range of their academic tasks.

Faculty as well as students—particularly post-graduate students—need to feel supported when they devote time and efforts to pursue research directions that may take more time than average to show progress because, among other reasons, they involve non-academic actors. That is related to "the need for a substantially new type of university, at least in the South, the Developmental University" (Brundenius and Göransson 2011: 348). In a nutshell and as discussed at length above, a Developmental University is characterized by the joint promotion of teaching, research, and extension activities in cooperation with several actors with the overall purpose of contributing to Sustainable Human Development, with special attention given to the democratization of knowledge. Developmental universities can also be partially characterized as those where the social involvement of student and faculty receives formal academic status and where there is room for research agendas to pursue roads directly linked to problems of development. It is important to stress that the issue is not to substitute one type of agenda for another, either at the university level or at the individual level. It is a question of building academic legitimacy beyond the prevailing regulatory capture by disciplinary academic elites, with its consequence of exclusionary quantitative measurements.

Developmental research agendas, unlike purely academic research agendas, require a rich variety of stakeholders; such stakeholders should together build the problems that those research agendas will contain. This is closely related to Elinor Ostrom's idea of coproduction as well as the seminal proposal by Amartya Sen of considering people as agents and not as patients (Ostrom 1996; Sen 1999).

It follows that developmental research agendas depend crucially on the level of connectedness of universities. Connectedness is related to the concept of "third mission" that "refer[s] to all activities concerned with the generation, use, application and exploitation of knowledge and other university capabilities outside [the] academic environment" (Molas-Gallart and Castro-Martínez 2007: 321). Declared commitment to connectedness may be considered well established, irrespectively of what concrete university and national policies are really fostering. How connectedness may be depicted and assessed, however, is more elusive. Table 8.1 depicts in a stylized way how universities are connected to main stakeholders. This is done for universities in the South, in an obviously rough generalization. We suspect that the table would look different in the North for some stakeholders, mainly government and firms, but would present similarities regarding other stakeholders. Repeated testimonies on how social commitment is disregarded by prevailing research evaluation criteria back this presumption.

Table 8.1 Some characteristics of universities' connections to main external stakeholders (in the Global South)

Stakeholders	Are universities aware of stakeholders' knowledge demands/needs?	Have/are stakeholders able to get resources to pay for demands?	Do stakeholders take initiative to become connected to universities?	Do universities pro-actively seek connectionswith stakeholders?
Government	Usually yes	Yes	Usually yes	Yes
Knowledge-based firms*	Sometimes	Usually yes	Sometimes	Yes
Non-knowledge based firms	Usually no	Usually no	Usually no	
Focused groups/ Movements	Sometimes	Usually no	Sometimes	
Vulnerable social groups	No	No	No	

Source: By authors
[a]We understand knowledge-based firms as those that have university graduates performing technical work. A more classic characterization, related to having formal R&D laboratories and important budgetary allocation to R&D, would be too restrictive in the Southern landscape

The gray cells of the table indicate uncertainty. When the university (i) is not aware of the demands or needs of a social actor, (ii) this actor has no capacity to pay for research done around his or her problems or interests (meaning that the university or a governmental body has to provide the resources), and (iii) is not able to take initiative to become connected to universities, those actors will be invisible for research agendas unless universities take a pro-active stance. If specific challenges faced by marginalized actors are to be considered in research agendas, the complex process of dialoguing, searching, understanding, translating, and co-constructing problems that this entails needs explicit support from the university.

There are diverse modalities through which universities may pro-actively seek connection with "neglected stakeholders". They may, for instance, provide funds for researchers who propose to explore how their expertise may be put to work for solving social problems so far not systematically addressed by academic research. They may foster a university culture where research, teaching, or outreach may merge in practice, instead of being, as often, in separated bunkers. But they also need to allow the emergence of a counter-hegemonic prestige regime because this relates to a fundamental part of researchers' academic identity. The latter leads directly to the research evaluation system because, ultimately, what research is carried out results from decisions taken by individual researchers who need to be recognized for what they do. An evaluation system may punish, in terms of going down in the prestige ladder, academics who embark on research that takes more time than average to produce results or that is communicated in local languages and is not related to trendy topics, defined as such by business firms, governments or academia. Such an evaluation system will lead universities to a connectedness biased toward powerful stakeholders, academics, and non-academics.

Research agendas are built around and influenced by diverse interests and incentives. Academic evaluation is a particularly powerful influence: prevailing criteria, emphasizing unilaterally academic status, hamper more than foster the developmental role of universities (Bianco et al. 2016). New, more balanced, and "pluralistic" evaluation systems are needed in order to foster both academic quality and social engagement. New conceptualizations of research are in the air, like Responsible Research and Innovation, "an ambitious challenge for the creation of a Research and Innovation policy driven by the needs of society and engaging all societal actors via inclusive participatory approaches" (European Commission 2012: 3). No policy of this sort can be fulfilled without deep changes in the prevailing research evaluation system.

What would a "developmental" research evaluation metrics, aiming at putting knowledge at the service of Sustainable Human Development, look like?

It will need to avoid some discouraging effects, encourage some other effects, and carefully take into account the context in which the social process of knowledge production is taking place. Evaluation should be related to the aim of universities and not the other way around. So we may take the following three points of departure, shared by other approaches to research evaluation.

First, a developmental university must perform first-rate research to promote creativity among its students and to address with some success the challenging problems that affect the society in which it is inserted. Such research needs to be rooted in strong disciplinary performance, but research associated with the demanding problems that societies are currently experiencing has increasingly a socially collective and academically interdisciplinary nature. So a developmental evaluation system should avoid "discouraging measurements", formally stated or customarily applied, that punish interdisciplinary work, joint definition of research problems with non-academic stakeholders, attention paid to local problems of little interest for international mainstream science, or adventurous intellectual endeavors with uncertain outcomes. What metrics may embed this?

Second, a developmental research evaluation system should include "encouraging measurements" related to normative aims. Operationalizing normative aims in research is different from stating how many children should attain a full vaccinating scheme in a given period. Developmental aims usually cannot be related to research agendas and research outputs straightforwardly. The difficulties in defining and applying comparable criteria to assess university-society collaborations have been acknowledged (Bölling and Eriksson 2016; Molas-Gallart and Castro-Martínez 2007). The importance of working toward the building of criteria to permit such an assessment has been put forwards: "[T]o ensure the success of this approach (referring to the civic university), it is critical that resources and prestige are dedicated to teaching, research and engagement, and the integration of these, and that appropriate metrics are developed to identify and evaluate engagement, particularly where it is integrated into teaching and research" (Bernard and Bates 2016: 195). In particular, research impacts the fulfillment of the envisaged aims through mediations that are outside academia. The latter notwithstanding, the orientation of research does play a role in such fulfillment. How can a metric appreciate this?

Third, a developmental research evaluation system should bear in mind that context matters. John Moulton, addressing the 2016 International Conference on Science, Technology and Innovation (STI) Indicators, "Peripheries, frontiers and beyond", stated: "[S]o our indicators are not neutral to context. In fact, the vast majority of current STI indicators have their origins in the North and typically reflect the properties of the science systems in these regions. Unless we make an attempt to understand what a specific indicator means in context, we are likely to draw hugely implausible conclusions (that may have far-reaching conclusions for policy and strategy)" (Moulton 2016). Moreover, research performance indicators that originated in the North are contested even there. How can a metric consider the context in which research is done without fostering an "isolationist research culture" that would lead to little more than self-justifying mediocre research?

To approach these questions, it is worth asking another one: which are the strongest constraints that prevailing evaluation systems put on development-related research? They are basically pressures of time and pressures of prestige. The latter are particularly strong: "[A] commitment to branding as a civic university carries risks in terms of international reputation. The biggest risk of adopting the ethos and branding of a civic university is to be seen as inferior. 'Serious' universities are expected to follow a Cambridge type approach of pursuing excellence and to take a purist 'curiosity-led' approach to research. Institutions that do not follow this model risk being seen as 'second-rate'. Further, the effort required to engage with civil society and to use societal challenges as the fundamental platforms for much of the work can actually distract from the raw pursuit of academic excellence" (Brink and Hogan 2016: 252–253).

Countervailing these constraints cannot—and should not—be done by disregarding concerns over research productivity and international visibility. But productivity should be understood differently from counting the number of papers produced. Performing meaningful developmental research involves devoting time to building the research problem and to ensure the fulfilment of the correct methodological conditions for research itself. So productivity should measure not only the outputs of research but the inputs to research that the researcher must construct. And care should be taken not to, even inadvertently, burden those who want to connect to society: "...at least take the obstacles away for those who like to work on societal impact in the academic setting, and facilitate their work" (Borg et al. 2016: 216). Again, which metric may give an account of this?

The prestige issue is more complicated to deal with. Building a counter-hegemonic prestige regime, even if not aiming at substituting the prevailing one but only offering a complementary one, will face fierce opposition. It is something neither universities nor governments can do individually; they will need to join forces. Different stakeholders may have an influence on this, from international organization to grassroots movements working from below. Metrics will be able to capture alternative prestige criteria but only once they have been put in place. It is a bit like a chicken-and-egg issue, but if a metric is established that stimulates development-related research even against the prevailing prestige regime, the latter will be easier to replicate.

Taking into account the above considerations, a new metric should:

i) allow for flexible shifts from prevailing metrics to "devmetrics"; this means that researchers may work for a period being evaluated by one metric and for another period evaluated by the other, depending on the working program they commit themselves to pursue;
ii) value the time devoted to help widening the cognitive connectedness of the university as research time;
iii) offer prizes for the best research outcomes that help solving societal problems; devise specific calls for research aimed at finding this type of solution.

What would the identifying characteristics of a "devmetric" look like?

i) The evaluation period for individual researchers' performance allows for the time needed to build research problems with external stakeholders.
ii) During the period to be evaluated, the researcher is required to show her capacity to do good research by having at least one publication in a good journal, but neither the number of publications nor the place of the related journals in the journal's prestige ranking will be considered.
iii) During the period to be evaluated, the researcher is required to give a detailed account of (a) the strategy that she followed to build a research project with external stakeholders or that takes stakeholders' needs into account; (b) the results achieved in research terms, including formal papers as well as "grey" knowledge products; and (c) the results achieved in developmental terms. The last

point is difficult to objectivize; it can be approached only through preliminary results and subjective appreciation. Knowing this beforehand, and so not being fooled by any illusory objectivity, may help to perform a reasoned and convincing research evaluation exercise.

In summary, a developmental research evaluation system would need to assess quality but not by counting papers; this is the only way to make room and provide time for developmental research concerns. The list of what should not be done in this respect is being put forwards more often and openly these days than ever before: the Leiden Manifesto is good proof of this. But the prevailing research evaluation system is resilient; the evidence and voices raised against it tend to be ignored, neglected, or even accepted but without real impact on current practices. It has been proposed that what is needed is a change in the uses or functions of evaluation, shifting from the present emphasis on "justifying decisions better" to "making better decisions". For this, research evaluation needs to be conceptualized as a tool "to improve or shape the research contents" (Ràfols et al. 2016: 3).

A developmentally oriented research evaluation, accompanied by a consistent metric, should recognize that it is high time to give precedence over measuring, controlling, punishing, selecting, comparing, and ranking, to encouraging and facilitating the dialogue with society around problems and how research and innovation can be part of their solutions. Some would say that "second-rate science" will be the outcome of developmental research evaluation systems and of "devmetrics". Many more will probably say that the outcome will be that the "truth" and the "good" of the Cordoba Manifesto may have a chance to reach a fair balance. Achieving this is indeed a difficult challenge. More researchers, all over the world, are uniting and organizing themselves to face this challenge. In the following two sections, we will briefly discuss how two countries—one from the Global South, Uruguay, and one from the North, Sweden—are coping with the internal and external pressures brought on by the prevailing academic evaluation system.

Tensions Derived from Conflicting Evaluation Systems: A Uruguayan Example

Uruguay has a very high institutional concentration in terms of knowledge production. Around 80% of FTE (full-time equivalent) researchers work in the standardized category of Higher Education, a high figure even in South America; those working in Business Enterprises, including public enterprises, represent less than 2%. But the unique feature is that one institution, the public University of the Republic (UR), accounts for around three quarters of the research done in the country. It is not an exaggeration to state that in Uruguay—with the exception of the life sciences and to some extent agricultural research, where more institutional diversification exists—what is not researched at the UR is hardly researched at all.

The overall organization of UR resembles a loose agglomeration of different schools more than a single institution governed by a common set of rules regarding teaching and research. Amid this federate tradition, two institutions aimed at promoting university research were built at a central level: the Full-Time Regime (FTR) in 1958 and the University Research Council in 1991. A main characteristic of both organizations is that they established common rules, valid for all faculty regardless of which college they belong to. The first entails a salary increase; the second provides funds to perform research activities.

A new institution of national coverage was launched in 2008: the National System of Researchers (NSR). The NSR evaluates researchers through a normalized CV model; those selected in any of the four categories of the system receive a monthly stipend.

Three quarters of all researchers belonging to the NSR belong to the university FTR as well; the other way around, 82% of researchers belonging to the FTR regime belong to the NSR as well. So the overlap is substantial and potential conflicts affect a high proportion of university researchers. The FTR is fifty years older than the NSR; the latter, even if designed and fostered mainly by highly prestigious researchers belonging to the UR, has different aims, considers other issues, and has a different evaluation approach.

Two important characteristics shared by the FTR and the NSR are that entrance is granted if merit allows—there is not a fixed number of admissions—and that the continuity in both schemes depends on evaluation. The differences are striking, though:

(i) <u>Main aim</u>: Give better conditions for accomplishing an academic life, particularly research activities (FTR); classify researchers and encourage publications in refereed journals (NSR);

(ii) <u>Evaluation scope</u>: past activities and proposed future work (FTR); past activities (NSR);

(iii) <u>Required activities to belong to the incentive scheme</u>: publications and post-graduate students' supervision (FTR and NSR); institutional building, outreach, and undergraduate teaching (FTR);

(iv) <u>Work burden and period of evaluation</u>: moderate, time for evaluation is flexible (applications come at any time and the work is
spread over the year); 5 years (FTR); high, time for evaluation is
rigid (applications come at a given date in great numbers and are
studied simultaneously); 4 years for senior researchers and 3 years
for junior researchers (NSR);

(v) <u>Monetary reward</u>: FTR is three times higher than NSR.

A scholar belonging to the two schemes may end up feeling a tension in
terms of her academic choices given the mutually exclusionary effects of
some required features. However, the puzzling question is why these tensions should appear at all for university researchers in the FTR, given that it
is clearly more convenient than the NSR in economic terms. The answer
relates to the relative reputation weight of the two schemes: most researchers
see the NSR as conferring more academic prestige, particularly because it
stems from regulations set by the academic elite. This explains the increasing
frenzy for publishing, given that this is the main NSR criterion for valuing
researchers and particularly for comparing researcher among themselves.

As indicated by the agency that provides the funds for the NSR, the
National Agency for Research and Innovation (ANII), "[T]he evaluation
criteria of the NSR are steadily being adopted by the academic community, contributing to the establishment of standards. (…) Researchers,
especially the youngest that represent the entrance door to the NSR, want
to respond to the requirements of the instrument, which gives it an important normative power" (ANII 2012: 7, our translation).

The "normative power" establishes standards that push for more publications, regardless of other possible aims of the institutions in which researchers work. Moreover, the NRS currently uses the journal impact measurement
(H index) as a proxy to academic visibility of research outputs (Ibid: 16).

This is at odds with what the Uruguayan community of exact and
natural scientists proposed some time ago as an evaluation system to
judge their own work: "[I]t is currently a quite diffused practice among
certain areas to quantify the impact of a scientific journal on the community through the 'impact index'. (…) We found it a poor approximation
to reduce to a number assigned to the journal where it has been published the diverse and rich facets that the potential impact of a scientific
contribution has. This criterion has received multiple criticisms from the
international scientific community and its use should be discouraged"

(Programa de Desarrollo de las Ciencias Básicas, PEDECIBA 2004: 4, our translation).

Given the smallness of the Uruguayan research community, the burden of qualitative assessment is high. The frequent, massive, and tightly scheduled evaluation procedures of the NSR make quantitative proxies to academic value and impact a welcome shortcut. The PEDECIBA recommendations seem to have been forgotten. But concerns aroused by this type of assessment are starting to be voiced again.

A recent institutional attempt to change research evaluation criteria involved the university research policy as a whole. Fostering such a change was part of the effort of making universities less elitist, particularly by democratizing access, by articulating research with social needs, and by promoting the relations between the university and social movement and vulnerable groups. Perhaps the traditional way of evaluating faculty in the FTR could have coped with these changes without much contradiction given its traditional qualitative style of assessment. Nevertheless, the wide superposition of faculty belonging to the FTR and to the NSR introduced tensions at an individual level.

Recognizing that the problem was institutional more than individual, the University Research Council organized in 2012 a wide discussion around how faculty in the FTR should be evaluated. The most original recommendation regarding research was to avoid a rush to produce papers by asking to have at least one paper published in a reference journal in the 5-year evaluation period. The idea behind this proposal is that if a researcher can prove that she is able to publish what is counted normally as a good piece of work, she may dedicate part of the remaining period to do research that may not lead to more papers, without being punished academically. Research problems defined together with non-academic actors or of mainly local interest may then be taken on board more easily.

The university's main authority accepted the proposal. The reactions of the university faculty, however, oscillated between indifference and hostility. Few voices rose up in its support and some pointed at the possibility of endangering research efforts by taking "non-publishable" research too much into consideration. The recent literature on engaged or civic universities has as a common concern the lack of encouragement at an institutional level, monetary and symbolic, of efforts toward connecting universities with social problems by co-working with non-academic actors. Opening legitimate academic spaces for good-quality work related to problems that need to be unearthed from society, in different ways and for different reasons, may become an international collective endeavor of university people committed to rescuing the social responsibility associated with knowledge production.

What may happen in Uruguay? The "status group" role of the NSR is strong, because this is what it aims for: signaling who are the best researchers. Fostering good and locally relevant research is, for the time being, a weak competitor in terms of awarding academic status. However, the negative effects of research efforts strategically geared toward entering and staying in the NSR are increasingly being recognized in different institutions, even if the concerns tend to be voiced as anecdotes. There is a long way to go from this malaise to an organized movement able to legitimize an alternative research evaluation system, but signals pointing in this direction are discernible.

Agreeing on What Is Wrong but Not How to Fix It: Some Reflections from Sweden

R&D has received high priority for the last several decades in the Swedish research policy community, resulting in a consistently high level of funding for R&D regardless of which political parties have been in power. In 2013, Swedish R&D amounted to 3.30% of GDP, one of the highest figures among OECD countries.

The business enterprise sector accounted for 69% of total R&D activities in 2013, while universities and other Higher Education institutions accounted for 27% (SCB 2015). The private business sector finances R&D up to around 60%; almost all of these R&D funds go to companies.

The state directly (through the budget) funds most of the research activities in the Higher-Education sector. In 2013, this core funding amounted to almost half of the R&D revenues of this sector; the rest was accounted for by research councils and other external sources such as SSF (strategic research), Mistra (strategic environmental research), KK-foundation (knowledge and competence development), and STINT (internationalization of Higher Education and research).

There are four main research councils responsible for financing research:

- the Swedish Research Council (VR)—funding basic research in science, technology, medicine, the humanities, and social sciences;
- the Swedish Research Council for Health, Working life and Welfare—funding basic and needs-driven research;

- the Swedish Research Council (Formas)—funding basic and needs-driven research in the areas of Environment, Agricultural Sciences, and Spatial Planning;
- the Swedish Governmental Agency for Innovation Systems (Vinnova)—funding needs-driven research in technology, transport, communication, and working life.

The high consensus achieved concerning the need for a high and sustained level of funding for research has not reached the governance, organization, and form of research, though. This reflects partly the constantly evolving discourse on the nature of knowledge and the knowledge creation process. This notwithstanding, governments of different political shades have, in recent decades, instituted a clear shift toward marketization of knowledge production (Fischer 2015). This has been done through funding steering mechanisms as well as other measures to better align academic research with market forces. Increasingly, the objective of the government to achieve higher direct relevance of research for societal problems has resulted in a lowering of core funding—governed by the university researchers themselves—and an increase in external funding, often targeted or earmarked for strategic or needs-driven research or both. Thus, the relative level of core funding from government to universities has decreased from around 70% of total funding in 1995 to well below 60% in 2003 and around 50% today.

With half of the funding for academic research coming from core funding and half from external sources, the respective evaluation systems determining who gets access to the resources become critical. Moreover, incompatibilities in the systems may give rise to disincentives.

The competition for core funding rests on performance-based ex-post evaluation by academic peers. Already in 1997, in a seminal paper, Wennerås and Wold pointed to the nepotism and sexism inherent in the peer-review system for post-doctoral fellowship at the then–Swedish Medical Research Council and called for "a scientific evaluation of the scientific evaluation system" that would scrutinize the biases in rewarding particular persons or subject matters over others (Wennerås and Wold 1997). More recently, Hammarfelt and de Rijcke (2015), in a study of effects of the Swedish research evaluation systems on publication practices, concluded that the implementation of a performance-based research evaluation system has resulted in an increased number of publications in English (rather than Swedish) and in peer-reviewed high-ranked journals. In particular, younger researchers appear to have understood the implications and devote most of their time to publishing, lest they perish. Such an evaluation system may divert research interest away from problem areas that are perceived as not interesting or as too local by the peer-reviewers in the editorial staff of prestigious international journals. Moreover, as van Dalen and Henkens (2012) found in a worldwide survey of demographers, the pressure for publishing has resulted in a move away from policy and translating research outcomes for the public, toward publications intended for academic circles. They conclude that "a strong focus on academic publications tends to crowd out activities that may increase the amount of information available to policy-makers and the general public" (van Dalen and Henkens 2012: 1292).

Given that securing funding from external sources allows academic staff to reduce teaching requirements and increase research time, thus advancing his or her academic career, the pressure to compete for external funding is intense. Even tenured professors are expected to raise at least 50% of their salary from external sources to complement the university core funding. This puts a heavy load on the research councils to evaluate and select projects to support; the approval rate can be as low as 8–12% of the applications, as in the case of the humanities and social sciences at the Swedish Research Council.

The ex-ante evaluation of research proposals takes into account "the academic quality and the applicants' competence" and likelihood of success. The review is carried out by review boards reflecting the research society at large and consists of prominent researchers in respective areas. As Lamont (2009) notes, however, review panels are inclined to act on personal preferences and disciplinary orientation, where elitism, gender bias, and populism can lead to non-diversity and "business as usual" (Lamont 2009). A research evaluation system that prioritizes the "best" researchers (which tend to be old and male) often leads to what Merton (1968) dubbed the Matthew effect (the recognized researchers get appropriations because of their reputation and newcomers are crowded out), to gender imbalance, and to a paucity in the width of research projects.

The evaluation systems for core funding and external funding exhibit some overlap but both contribute to the weeding out of certain projects. In particular, it would seem like multidisciplinary projects have problems in finding appropriate funding instruments.

The tensions among and between the internal and external evaluation systems is further exacerbated by the pressure on researchers, departments, faculties, and universities to publish in first-rate international journals in order to climb in university rankings.

The universities as well as research councils are well aware of the unintended consequences of the evaluation systems. In the research policy discourse, there is a general agreement that (a) the balance between free basic research and commercial research continues to be skewed in favor of the latter, (b) increasing short-term external funding precludes new and bold research initiatives and leads to the emergence of universities as research hotels, and (c) too much strategic research leads to conformity and conceptual inbreeding.

The research councils have instituted a number of measures to counteract drawbacks in the peer-review evaluation system. In its policy, the Swedish Research Council recognizes the risk of conflicts of interest in the rather small research community in Sweden as well as the risk of mainstream research being favored over innovative and multidisciplinary research. The measures include an expressed intention to fund younger researchers, to encourage multidisciplinary research, and to mainstream gender in project calls.

At universities and at the faculty level, the responses have been of a more ad hoc nature. The awareness of and knowledge about challenges associated with evaluations are broad at all levels of the university system, but there is less consensus on what needs to be done. A recent study of the evaluation model for university-society collaboration confirms the broad general knowledge about difficulties associated with evaluation; it finds that discussions tends to focus on how to construct relevant indicators rather than on the fundamental objectives and goals of the collaboration to be evaluated (Bölling and Eriksson 2016).

Why do the prevailing evaluation systems with their focus on more or less relevant quantitative indicators persist? The tentative answer offered in a preceding section may have some relevance to the case of Sweden: that there exists a sort of implicit agreement that maintains the status quo in the evaluation system so governments can point to examples of their commitment to NPM while the academic elite continues to exert their power and propagate their worldview.

References

Aksnes, D., & Rip, A. (2009). Researchers' Perceptions of Citations. *Research Policy, 38*(6), 895–905.

Altbach, P. (Ed.). (2003). *The Decline of the Guru. The Academic Profession in the Third World*. New York: Palgrave Macmillan.

Altbach, P., Reisberg, L., & Rumbley, L. (2009). *Trends in Global Higher Education: Tracking an Academic Revolution*. Paris: UNESCO.

ANII. (2012). *Evaluación del impacto del Sistema Nacional de Investigadores.* Available at: http://www.anii.org.uy/institucional/documentos-de-interes/4/informes-de-evaluacion/. Accessed 12 July 2016.

Arocena, R. (2015). *La autonomía de la 'Universidad para el Desarrollo'* (núm 66, pp. 7–18). México: Universidades, UDUAL.

Arocena, R., & Sutz, J. (2016). Universidades para el Desarrollo, Policy Brief for the First Open Forum on Science of the Americas and the Caribbean. Available at: http://www.unesco.org/new/fileadmin/MULTIMEDIA/FIELD/Montevideo/pdf/PolicyPapersCILAC-UnivParaDesarrollo.pdf. Accessed 10 May 2017.

Arocena, R., Göransson, B., & Sutz, J. (2014). Universities and Higher Education in Development. In B. Currie-Alder, S. M. R. Kanbur, D. Malone, & R. Medhora (Eds.), *International Development: Ideas, Experience, and Prospects.* Oxford: Oxford University Press.

Arocena, R., Göransson, B., & Sutz, J. (2015). Knowledge Policies in Developing Countries: Inclusive Development and the 'Developmental University'. *Technology in Society, 41,* 10–20.

Benneworth, P., & Jongbloed, B. (2010). Who Matters to Universities? A Stakeholder Perspective on Humanities, Arts and Social Sciences Valorisation. *Higher Education, 59*(5), 567–588.

Bernard, J., & Bates, C. (2016). Dublin Institute of Technology: Moving, Merging, and Managing the Civic Engagement Mission. In J. Goddard, H. Hazelkorn, L. Kempton, & P. Vallance (Eds.), *The Civic University. The Policy and Leadership Challenges* (pp. 180–200). Cheltenham: Edward Elgar.

Bianco, M., Gras, N., & Sutz, J. (2016). Academic Evaluation: Universal Instrument? Tool for Development? *Minerva, 54*(4), 399–421.

Bleiklie, I. (1998). Justifying the Evaluative State: New Public Management Ideals in Higher Education. *Journal of Public Affairs Education, 4*(2), 87–100.

Bölling, M., & Eriksson, Y. (2016). "Collaboration with Society: The Future Role of Universities?" Identifying Challenges for Evaluation. *Research Evaluation, 25*(2), 209–218.

Borg, H., Galema, A., Mulder, H., & Steenbeek, S. (2016). The University of Groningen: An Engaging University. In J. Goddard, H. Hazelkorn, L. Kempton, & P. Vallance (Eds.), *The Civic University. The Policy and Leadership Challenges* (pp. 201–221). Cheltenham: Edward Elgar.

Brennan, J., & Naidoo, R. (2008). Higher Education and the Achievement (and/or Prevention) of Equity and Social Justice. *Higher Education, 56*(3), 287–302.

Brink, C., & Hogan, J. (2016). Newcastle University and the Development of the Concept of a World-Class Civic University. In J. Goddard, H. Hazelkorn, L. Kempton, & P. Vallance (Eds.), *The Civic University. The Policy and Leadership Challenges* (pp. 240–256). Cheltenham: Edward Elgar.

Brundenius, C., & Göransson, B. (2011). The Three Missions of Universities: A Synthesis of UniDev Project Findings. In B. Göransson & C. Brundenius (Eds.),

Universities in Transition. The Changing Role and Challenges for Academic Institutions (pp. 329–352). Ottawa: Springer.

Burawoy, M. (2011). Redefining the Public University: Global and National Contexts. In J. Holmwood (Ed.), *A Manifesto for the Public University* (pp. 27–41). London: Bloomsbury.

Coleman, J. S. (1986). The Idea of the Developmental University. *Minerva, 24*(4), 476–494.

Cozzens, S. E., Healey, P., Rip, A., & Ziman, J. (Eds.). (1990). *The Research System in Transition*. Dordrecht: Kluwer Academic Publishers.

Dahler-Larsen, P. (2007). ¿Debemos evaluarlo todo? O de la estimación de la evaluabilidad a la cultura de la evaluación. *Evaluación de Políticas Públicas, 836*, 93–104.

Dahler-Larsen, P. (2013). Evaluation as a Situational or a Universal Good? Why Evaluability Assessment for Evaluation Systems Is a Good Idea, What It Might Look Like in Practice, and Why It Is Not Fashionable. *Scandinavian Journal of Public Administration, 16*(3), 29–46.

Dasgupta, P., & David, P. (1994). Toward a New Economics of Science. *Research Policy, 23*(3), 487–521.

Di Maggio, P., & Powell, W. (1983). The Iron Cage Revisited: Institutional Isomorphism and Collective Rationality in Organizational Fields. *American Sociological Review, 48*(2), 147–160.

Dobbins, M., & Knill, C. (2014). *Higher Education Governance and Policy Change in Western Europe. International Challenges to Historical Institutions*. London: Palgrave Macmillan.

Edquist, C., & Hommen, L. (1999). Systems of Innovation: Theory and Policy for the Demand Side. *Technology in Society, 21*(1), 63–79.

Etzkowitz, H. (2004). The Evolution of the Entrepreneurial University. *International Journal of Technology and Globalization, 1*(1), 64–77.

European Commission. (2012). *Responsible Research and Innovation. Europe's Ability to Respond to Societal Challenges*. Available at: https://ec.europa.eu/research/swafs/pdf/pub_public_engagement/responsible-research-and-innovation-leaflet_en.pdf. Accessed 10 May 2017.

Evans, P. (1995). *Embedded Autonomy. States and Industrial Transformation*. Cambridge, MA: Princeton University Press.

Fein, L. (1959). The Role of the University in Computers, Data Processing, and Related Fields. *Communications of the ACM, 2*(9), 7–12.

Fischer, J. (2015). *Knowledge Compromise(d)? Ways and Values of Coproduction in Academia*. Doctoral dissertation, Lund University.

Foro Consultivo Científico Tecnológico y Academia Nacional Mexicana de Ciencias. (2005). *Una Reflexión sobre el Sistema Nacional de Investigadores a 20 Años de su Creación*. Available at: http://www.coniunctus.amc.edu.mx/libros/20_sni_final.pdf. Accessed 10 May 2017.

Frederiksen, L. F., Hansson, F., & Wenneberg, S. B. (2003). The Agora and the Role of Research Evaluation. *Evaluation, 9*(2), 149–172.

Gläser, J. (2010). From Governance to Authority Relations? In R. Whitley, J. Gläser, & L. Engwall (Eds.), *Reconfiguring Knowledge Production: Changing Authority Relationships in the Sciences and Their Consequences for Intellectual Innovation* (pp. 357–369). New York: Oxford University Press.

Gläser, J. (2012). *How Does Governance Change Research Content? On the Possibility of a Sociological Middle-Range Theory Linking Science Policy Studies to the Sociology of Scientific Knowledge.* The Technical University Technology Studies Working Papers, TUTS-WP-1. Available at: https://www.ts.tu-berlin.de/fileadmin/fg226/TUTS/TUTS-WP-1-2012.pdf. Accessed 10 May 2017.

Goddard, J., Hazelkorn, H., Kempton, L., & Vallance, P. (2016). Introduction: Why the Civic University? In J. Goddard, H. Hazelkorn, L. Kempton, & P. Vallance (Eds.), *The Civic University. The Policy and Leadership Challenges* (pp. 3–15). Cheltenham: Edward Elgar.

Göransson, B., & Brundenius, C. (Eds.). (2011). *Universities in Transition. The Changing Role and Challenges for Academic Institutions.* Ottawa: Springer.

Group of Eight. (2011). *Role of Universities in the Innovation Systems* (Discussion Paper). Available at: https://www.go8.edu.au/publication/role-universities-national-innovation-system. Accessed 10 May 2017.

Halffman, W., & Radder, H. (2015). The Academic Manifesto: From an Occupied to a Public University. *Minerva, 53*(2), 165–187.

Hammarfelt, B., & de Rijcke, S. (2015). Accountability in Context: Effects of Research Evaluation Systems on Publication Practices, Disciplinary Norms, and Individual Working Routines in the Faculty of Arts at Uppsala University. *Research Evaluation, 24*(1), 63–77.

Haiyan, W., & Yuan, Z. (2011). China: Challenges for Higher Education in a High Growth Economy. In B. Göransson & C. Brundenius (Eds.), *Universities in Transition. The Changing Role and Challenges for Academic Institutions* (pp. 143–170). Ottawa: Springer.

Hazelkorn, E. (2007). How Do Rankings Impact on Higher Education?, OECD Programme on Institutional Management in Higher Education.

Hazelkorn, E. (2009). *Impact of Global Rankings on Higher Education Research and the Production of Knowledge.* UNESCO Forum on Higher Education, Research and Knowledge (Occasional Paper 18). Paris: UNESCO.

Hazelkorn, E., & Ryan, M. (2013). The Impact of University Rankings on Higher Education Policy in Europe: A Challenge to Perceived Wisdom and a Stimulus for Change. In P. Zgaga, U. Teichler, & J. Brennan (Eds.), *The Globalization Challenge for European Higher Education: Convergence and Diversity, Centres and Peripheries* (pp. 79–100). Frankfurt: Peter Lang.

Hess, D. (2007). *Alternative Pathways in Science and Industry. Activism, Innovation, and the Environment in an Era of Globalization.* Cambridge, MA: The MIT Press.

Hicks, D. (2006). The Dangers of Partial Bibliometric Evaluation in the Social Sciences. *Economia Politica, XXIII*(2), 145–162.

Hicks, D. (2012). Performance-Based University Research Funding Systems. *Research Policy, 41*(2), 251–261.

Hicks, D. (2013). One Size Doesn't Fit All: On the Co-evolution of National Evaluation Systems and Social Science Publishing. *Confero, 1*(1), 67–90.

Hicks, D., Wouters, P., Waltman, L., de Rijcke, S., & Rafols, I. (2015). The Leiden Manifesto for Research Metrics. *Nature, 520*(23), 429–431.

Jensen, M., Johnson, B., Lorenz, E., & Lundvalll, B. A. (2007). Forms of Knowledge and Modes of Innovation. *Research Policy, 36*, 680–693.

Johnson, C. (1982). *MITI and the Japanese Miracle. The Growth on Industrial Policy 1925–1975.* Stanford: Stanford University Press.

Kronman, U. (2013). Managing Your Assets in the Publication Economy. *Confero, 1*(1), 91–128.

Lamont, M. (2009). *How Professors Think. Inside the Curious World of Academic Judgment.* Cambridge, MA: Harvard University Press.

Lewis, J. M. (2015). The Politics and Consequences of Performance Measurement. *Policy and Society, 34*, 1–12.

Lundvall, B. Å. (2010). Postcript: Innovation System Research – Where It Comes from and Where It Might Go. In B. A. Lundvalll (Ed.), *National Systems of Innovation. Towards a Theory of Innovation and Interactive Learning* (pp. 317–366). London: Anthem Press.

Martin, B., & Whitley, R. (2010). The UK Research Assessment Exercise: A Case of Regulatory Capture? In R. Whitley, J. Gläser, & L. Engwall (Eds.), *Reconfiguring Knowledge Production: Changing Authority Relationships in the Sciences and Their Consequences for Intellectual Innovation* (pp. 51–79). New York: Oxford University Press.

Mazzoleni, R., & Nelson, R. (2007). Public Research Institutions and Economic Catch-Up. *Research Policy, 36*, 1512–1528.

Merton, R. (1968). The Matthew Effect on Science. *Science, 159*(3810), 56–63.

Molas-Gallart, J., & Castro-Martínez, E. (2007). Ambiguity and Conflict in the Development of "Third Mission" Indicators. *Research Evaluation, 16*(4), 321–330.

Moulton, J. (2016, September). *The Deep Structure of STI Indicators: Contextual Knowledge and Scientometrics.* Key-Note speech, 21th International Conference on STI Indicators, Valencia, Spain.

Mowery, D., & Sampat, B. (2005). Universities in National Innovation Systems. In J. Fagerberg, D. Mowery, & R. Nelson (Eds.), *The Oxford Handbook of Innovation* (pp. 209–239). Oxford: Oxford University Press.

Munch, R. (2014). *Academic Capitalism. Universities in the Global Struggle for Excellence.* London: Routledge.

Murray, F. (2006). *The Oncomouse that Roared: Resistance and Accommodation to Patenting in Academic Science*. Paper presented at the Toronto Conference "Bringing Science to Life". Available at: http://fmurray.scripts.mit.edu/docs/THE_ONCOMOUSE_THAT_ROARED_FINAL.pdf. Accessed 10 May 2017

Neave, G. (1998). The Evaluative State Reconsidered. *European Journal of Education, 33*(3), 265–284.

Newfield, C. (2016). *The Great Mistake. How We Wrecked Public Universities and How We Can Fix Them*. Baltimore: John Hopkins University Press.

Nowotny, H. (2016). *The Cunning of Uncertainty*. Cambridge, UK: Polity.

Ostrom, E. (1996). Crossing the Great Divide: Coproduction, Synergy, and Development. *World Development, 24*(6), 1073–1087.

PEDECIBA. (2004). *Criterios, herramientas y procedimientos generales para la evaluación de la actividad académica de los investigadores*. Available at: http://www.pedeciba.edu.uy/docspd/CritEvalInv04.pdf. Accessed 12 July 2016.

Power, M. (1999). *The Audit Society. Rituals of Verification*. Oxford: Oxford University Press.

Ràfols, I., Molas-Gallart, J., Chavarro, D., & Robinson-García, N. (2016, June 2–3). On the Dominance of Quantitative Evaluation in "Peripheral" Countries: Auditing Research with Technologies of Distance. Paper presented at *Excellence policies in science*, Leiden.

SCB. (2015). Statistics Sweden. *Research and Development in Sweden 2013*. UF 16 SM 1501 (in Swedish).

Schwandt, T. A. (2012). Quality, Standards and Accountability: An Uneasy Alliance. *Education Inquiry, 3*(2), 217–224.

Sen, A. (1999). *Development as Freedom*. New York: Anchor Books.

Trencher, G., et al. (2013). Beyond the Third Mission: Exploring the Emerging University Function of Co-creation for Sustainability. *Science and Public Policy, 41*(2), 151–179.

van Dalen, H. P., & Henkens, K. (2012). Intended and Unintended Consequences of a Publish-or-Perish Culture: A Worldwide Survey. *Journal of the American Society for Information Science and Technology, 63*(7), 1282–1293.

Weerts, D. J., & Sandmann, L. R. (2008). Building a Two-Way Street: Challenges and Opportunities for Community Engagement at Research Universities. *Review of Higher Education, 32*(1), 73–106.

Wennerås, C., & Wold, A. (1997). Nepotism and Sexism in Peer-Review. *Nature, 387*, 341–343.

Whitley, R. (2010). Reconfiguring the Public Sciences: The Impact of Governance Changes on Authority and Innovation in Public Science Systems. In R. Whitley, J. Gläser, & L. Engwall (Eds.), *Reconfiguring Knowledge Production: Changing Authority Relationships in the Sciences and Their Consequences for Intellectual Innovation* (pp. 3–47). New York: Oxford University Press.

Woelert, P. (2015). The 'Logic of Escalation' in Performance Measurement: An Analysis of the Dynamics of a Research Evaluation System. *Policy and Society, 34*, 75–85.

Discussion and book launch

Developmental Universities in Inclusive Innovation Systems

Alternatives for Knowledge Democratization in the Global South

Authors Judith Sutz and Rodrigo Arocena
(Universidad de le Republica,Uruguay), and
a panel of distinguished speakers join SPRU
faculty members and researchers to discuss
the topic of this important new book.

Wednesday 16 May
17:00 – 18:30
Room 155, School of Business,
Management and Economics
Jubilee Building

Book a place
sussex.ac.uk/spru/newsandevents/events?id=44166

UNIVERSITY
OF SUSSEX

SPRU
SCIENCE POLICY
RESEARCH UNIT

CHAPTER 9

What Does the Future Hold?

Can universities be developmental, up to a significant level? A positive answer in a given case would mean that such a university is a potentially strong actor in an inclusive innovation system. Can universities help in the task of overcoming exclusion? Benneworth asserts that "[I]ntuitively, universities should be able to help solve problems faced socially by excluded communities. On one hand, universities are home to a range of disciplines which have detailed understandings of the kinds of problems, and the potential solutions to those problems, faced by excluded communities. On the other hand, universities can help integrate those communities and individuals back into the knowledge society, equip individuals and communities to re-engage with the knowledge society. However, this raises the question of whether universities can fit that activity into a set of demands by key stakeholders around the narrower outputs demanded by their primary missions" (Benneworth 2013: 21).

Is the notion of Developmental University useful in a meaningful sense? The question can be analyzed from at least three different angles. Empirically, we conjecture that the notion has some value in describing phenomena that are really happening, albeit on a rather limited scale. Prospectively, the notion is useful for discussing possible futures. From a propositional point of view, we assert that the concept of Developmental University is valuable for organizing, in a systematic way, answers to the question "What should be done?" in order to foster knowledge democratization.

© The Author(s) 2018   225
R. Arocena et al., *Developmental Universities in Inclusive Innovation Systems*, https://doi.org/10.1007/978-3-319-64152-2_9

POTENTIAL CONTRIBUTIONS OF UNIVERSITIES
TO KNOWLEDGE DEMOCRATIZATION

Above, it was suggested that some actual processes exemplify the notion of Developmental University. That may be illustrated by the following appreciation of a relevant case: "[T]he Nordic countries [...] seem to be mimicking the US research governance model, with strong position for universities, a high profile in growing research areas, and strong ties between the research system and high-technology firms and sectors. Contrary to the development in USA and the UK, however, this governance model has been combined with a strong public support of research areas with connections to low-technology industries and to mature industrial fields such as food, engineering and the transport industry. Furthermore, the drive to concentrate resources to fewer recipients and fields has been balanced by regional considerations: the Nordic countries, with the partial exception of Denmark, have all made major investments in peripheral universities. Hence, the Nordic countries face the challenge of combining policy goals: resource concentration and adaption of research system to economic and regional interests" (Benner 2011: 20).

The above quote may be interpreted as saying that Nordic universities are fostering the geographic and productive diffusion of the benefits and power of knowledge. They do that, for example, by investing in peripheral regions and by promoting research that is not restricted to high-tech sectors.

Such evolution goes against prevailing orientations for university reform and knowledge policies. Those orientations contribute to the concentration of benefits and resources related to knowledge in geographically, productively, and socially restricted sectors. It can be said that some traits akin to the notion of Developmental University are emerging in Nordic countries. Going from the factual to the prospective approach, given the relevant achievements and wide reputation of the Nordic social model, such a trend deserves close attention. If it gets consolidated, better perspectives would be opened for fighting knowledge-based inequality.

Three main threads may guide universities to contribute to knowledge democratization: (i) inclusive access, (ii) inclusive research and innovation agendas, and (iii) involvement of multiple stakeholders in addressing social problems. This statement gives rise to some questions to be addressed below: why are those three threads important for knowledge democratization? Are they recognized as such in policy discourses?

A fundamental and related question is the following: why and how can the material and intellectual interests of faculty and students foster developmental tasks and partnerships? What examples can be given in which such material and intellectual interests were expressed? We conjecture that developmental tasks may attract both faculty and students, by combining professional and ethical concerns.

Committing universities to the democratization of knowledge, particularly in the Global South, implies finding ways through which many more young people coming from all strata of society can access Higher Education.

This is also important for the North since it is a way of diminishing inequality and social exclusion: "[I]mproving the education system is also important from the point of view of preventing social segmentation and social exclusion. This problem has become severe in the context of rapid structural change which is accelerated by the application of high technology in production. It has both saved labour and shifted labour demand towards high-skilled labour. A part of the labour force is thus in danger of being excluded from the labour market" (Kaitila and Kotilainen 2008: 398).

Transforming internal structures and procedures as well as external relations in order to cooperate in generalizing access and success in Higher Education can be seen as a major contribution of universities to the expansion of capabilities and freedoms.

Such a task should be oriented not only toward young people but toward the citizenry at large. It can be seen as a major contribution to diminishing inequalities and particularly to fostering participation in collective decisions: "[E]ducation appears to have the greatest impact on political participation [...] and education is loosely correlated with other resources: occupation, income, and access to organizations. Since it would be preposterous to reduce inequalities in political resources by imposing a ceiling on education, the alternative is substantially to increase the minimum level of education, which would require a far larger allocation of resources than at present to the task of reeducating the less educated" (Dahl 1982: 171).

Committing universities to the democratization of knowledge also implies fostering the engagement of faculty and students in research and innovation related to different types of social and developmental issues. Connections between Higher Education and innovation processes deserve more attention: "until now innovation scholars have hardly addressed the educational system. Research in the requirements the knowledge society asks from the educational system is scarce" (Shapira et al. 2010: 462).

Connecting universities with innovation requires working with several different stakeholders in a way akin to Ostrom's notion of "coproduction"; more often than not, the research and innovation agenda should be "coproduced". This again reminds us that democratization of knowledge cannot be effective if isolated: "coproduced agendas" need public policy support to be pursued and applied. More broadly speaking, it is difficult to expect that such agendas will survive and expand if the Innovation System in which they try to exist is not favorable.

The "coproduction" point of view in knowledge democratization is connected with the way Helga Nowotny (n.d.) uses the concepts of integration, contextualization, and implication: "[I]f joint problem solving is the aim, then the means must provide for an integration of perspectives in the identification, formulation and resolution of what has to become a shared problem". Consequently, "we should go beyond value-added; we should start to speak about value-integrated. There is something of a societal value that needs to be integrated into the definition of good science". The context needs to be considered. "Contextualisation means bringing people into knowledge production by asking one question: 'where is the place of people in our knowledge?'" That leads to implication. "Asking the question about the place of people in our knowledge also implies an additional dimension, namely that researchers move not only in the context of application, but that they need to start thinking about the context of implication. What are the implications of what we are doing, of formulating problems in this particular way?"

Often all of this means working on issues that have weak or no commercial demand or whose results are too specific or heterodox to be published in mainstream journals. As already argued at some length, this type of commitment requires another one that aims to transform prevailing academic incentives and reward systems.

Committing universities to the democratization of knowledge also implies dedicating time and efforts to cooperating with different organisms and collective actors in interactive learning spaces where different types of knowledge are combined in order to solve social problems with priority given to those of the most deprived sectors. Such commitments are not favored by prevailing trends and policies as already examined. But those trends and policies are not the only game in town. Important examples point in quite different directions.

The Project-Based Learning System in Denmark connects community problems with student and faculty concerns (Gregersen and Rasmussen 2011). The D-Lab of the Massachusetts Institute of Technology has been able to put to work a significant number of students and faculty around technological developments aimed at solving challenging problems in ways that take into account the contexts of poor regions in the Global South.

Many other examples all over the world make the following assertion quite plausible: "[U]niversities may in the future tend to adopt a more holistic perspective, predicated on the synergies between their scientific and social missions. This should translate into a greater diversity and diversification of curricula, with the aim of becoming more attuned and responsive to the combined, yet diverse, social and scientific needs and expectations of different groups of their students" (Nowotny et al. 2001: 91).

The Humboldtian project opened quite wide possibilities for fostering active teaching (that is, for making students fundamental protagonists of learning processes). That stems from the insertion of teaching activities in contexts of professionalized research; there, teachers and researchers were often the same persons; and those persons, by relating their teaching with their research, favored the transformation of studying in a quite creative activity. Such prevailing attitudes matched well with another trait of the Humboldtian project that fostered an enduring function of universities as a generator of cultural norms (Nowotny et al. 2001: 93). Those norms are related not only to ethical duties of people belonging to universities as communities but also to the cognitive foundations of research: "[P]erhaps the epistemological core, the source of reliable knowledge, is to be found more in these general rules of conduct than in detailed methodologies" (Ibid).

This notion of reliable knowledge resulting from general rules of conduct is powerful. It should be seen as a fundamental orientation for democratization of knowledge, particularly when research agendas are radically opened in ways associated with coproduction, integration, contextualization, and implication as previously discussed. In this sense, the Developmental University is a notion inspired by the best tradition of the academic university.

INDICATORS OF THE DEVELOPMENTAL ROLE OF UNIVERSITIES

Models are just models. They can also be called "ideal types" or "stylized facts", remembering that in their elaboration the emphasis goes to some few dynamics, considered to be highly influential, while a lot of things are left aside. Seen from the point of view of those abstractions, realities are usually messy things that, at best, show some important similarities with one of the models or with more than one. Everybody knows that really existing universities are quite complex and heterogeneous organizations. Especially if we are considering big public universities, we should not expect to be able to describe them neatly by means of one model. When contrasting models are compared with realities, what is found is probably some mixture of different models, albeit with different proportions in their respective components.

The fundamental assertion of this book is that an alternative model, different from the prevailing one, is needed to study and foster the positive connections of universities in the context of inclusive innovation systems. As noted, we do not expect to find pure examples of Developmental Universities, but with that notion in mind, we will analyze the feasibility, ways, and extents of the contribution of universities to development. Such analyses can be shaped as a set of questions about what happens today and what the future possibilities are concerning the main components of the notion.: "[A] conception is an idea with empirical content. If the idea is too large for the content, you are tending to the trap of grand theory; if the content swallows the idea, you are tending towards the pitfall of abstracter empiricism" (Mills 1971: 138). The indicators we consider in the following may give empirical content to the idea of the Developmental University.

The Crucial Challenge

A first indicator of the contribution of universities to Human Sustainable Development is offered by what they do to promote the generalization of access to Higher Education. There is an enrollment gap between "North" and "South"—stressed several years ago by the World Bank—that makes generalizing advanced education a much more pressing issue in underdevelopment than elsewhere. The contribution of a "Southern" university to closing the enrollment gap is a major indicator of its developmental character. Maybe it is also significant in the North; it should be remembered that "the skill premium has shown a strong increase in most advanced countries during the past twenty years" (Milanović 2016: 47).

Expanding access and success in Higher Education is a necessary condition, even if evidently not a sufficient one, for democratization of knowledge all around the world.

When proposing some answers to the question "How Can Inequality in Rich Welfare States Be Reduced?", Milanović (2016: 221) writes: "To reduce inequality in endowments, more widely spread ownership of capital needs to be combined with more equal distribution of education. By that I mean not only making sure that everyone has the same number of years of schooling, but equalizing meaningful access to education".

Concerning Higher Education in Europe, it is asserted that "the number of students is decreasing due to low birth rates and an ageing society" (Schmoch 2011: 277). Assuming that enrollment in universities should decrease because of demographic trends is a thoroughly outdated conception of education as something that should end at some stage of life. Moreover, to accept that the majority of the population is going to finish their studies before they are twenty years old or shortly after is a sure way to failure in the realm of production and beyond. The opposite perspective should be embraced: "[T]he student experience in the 21st century will likely be characterized by more years of engagement with education over the course of a lifetime, as well as greater options in terms of what, when, and how to study" (Altbach et al. 2009: 109). Moreover, "[S]tudents must be primed to engage in learning activities across many more phases of their lives, and institutions must be prepared to meet the needs of a wide range of nontraditional learners" (Altbach et al. 2009: 111).

When characterizing the teaching mission of the Developmental University in Chapter 7, we stated that in our time Higher Education must be "seen as lifelong advanced learning of increasing quality and increasingly connected with work, citizen activities, cultural expansion, and, in general, freedoms and capabilities for living lives that people value and have reason to value".

From such a perspective, lifelong advanced learning does not refer to a more or less scattered supply of occasional courses: it is the core of education transformation for knowledge democratization. Such a transformation is a clue both for improving economic performance and, perhaps even more so, for recovering and enhancing social cohesion. It requires investing great efforts in improving teaching: "[M]oving toward the goal of generalized, life-long Higher Education requires demanding and providing new content to principles of active teaching, according to which learners are individually and collectively the principal protagonists. Active, permanent, and high-level teaching is only possible if it is closely and innovative linked to the exercise of citizenship, active performance within the work place, and access to the diversity of cultures" (IESALC 2008: 53).

Although that way of understanding active teaching can be traced to very old theories and practices, it has not been dominant in Higher Education: "traditional university teaching was knowledge centered rather

than student centered. [...] The prevailing conception of teaching emphasized what teachers did, not what students learned" (Altbach et al.
2009: 113). That conception is apparent when speaking of knowledge
transmission as synonymous to education. That is alien to the main normative guide of seeing people as agents. It also seems to be factually
wrong: "[T]he idea deriving from constructivist psychology [is] that
knowledge is not transmitted by a teacher but is constructed by students
through their own learning activities" (Altbach et al. 2009: 119). But routines and entrenched interests hamper the advance of active teaching:
"[T]heoretical developments that prioritize learning outcomes have led
some participants in the Higher Education community to shift from a
teacher-centered input model, to one that is student centered and based
on outputs. Good teaching, in other words, would focus less on what
teachers do and primarily on what *students learn*. This paradigm shift is
playing out dynamically in some learning environments but is encounter-
ing obstacles in others" (Altbach et al. 2009: 114).

Working toward the generalization of advanced lifelong learning includes
stressing the value of adult education and vocational training. It is worth
recalling that "Denmark has a long tradition of adult education and
training—including vocational training. [...] the Danish work force is among
the most active when it comes to participating in continuing education and
lifelong learning activities" (Gregersen and Rasmussen 2011: 288).

Vocational training has often been despised in the academy, thereby
safeguarding the survival of a status ethos with aristocratic pretensions.
That promotes the division of post-secondary education into a high way,
connected with theory and the world of the mind, and a low way, where
only directly practical issues find a place. Thus, the ancient stratification
between the intellectual and the manual is recovered and perpetuated in
the "knowledge society". That is both a normative and a political mistake:
it fosters inequality and hurts democracy and at the same time hampers
development based on learning and innovation.

Today, nobody would accept (at least openly) that elementary school
should be divided in two: a "theoretical" or "liberal" one and a "vocational" or "practical" one. Perhaps tomorrow the post-secondary division
of today will also be difficult to accept. Everybody should have access to a
high-quality vocational or professional education in order to be able to
work creatively in conditions that ensure the dignity of work. And everybody needs the capabilities related to general culture and interdisciplinary
teaching in creative contexts. There exists a "global interest in developing

students who are skilled communicators, effective critical thinkers, dynamic problem solvers, and productive team members" (Altbach et al. 2009: 26).

The alternative to a highly stratified Higher Education is to democratize the Humboldtian tradition by upgrading adult education in general in combination with creative activities, not just in educational institutions but in society at large. That means opening several educational trajectories that take into account diversity and, in particular, offer different ways of combining "theory" and "practice", so all those willing can keep learning at advanced levels. The main clue for this seems to be the combination of education and work. The authors just quoted say that, in Denmark in recent years, "an increasing number of employees have participated in part-time further education, mainly at the master's level" (Gregersen and Rasmussen 2011: 294). What Schmoch (2011: 280) says for Germany should be valid in general: "the first mission of the universities, i.e., teaching, will get a new impetus". This is the second indicator for evaluating the developmental role of universities.

We have stated above that expanding access and success in Higher Education are necessary conditions for democratizing knowledge all over the world. But access and success do not necessarily go hand in hand. Formal access may be granted to everybody (for instance, by making it possible to enter universities without any payment to all who have finished secondary education). But the academic levels of secondary education may be different; moreover, the levels of effective learning may be extremely different, usually stratified by the socio-economic background of the student's family. If a "one-size fits-all" type of teaching is fixed beforehand, only those with a good learning and knowledge baggage from secondary education will succeed. Many of those who access university from more disadvantaged backgrounds will fail, experiencing a high dose of frustration. Free access becomes, in these situations that are more the rule than the exception in the Global South, a sort of institutionalized hypocrisy. The university can take steps to address this challenge, devising several forms of accompanying and supporting students who find it difficult to cope with the university learning regime. Some of these forms can rely on inter-peer solidarity, by encouraging students to help other students. How universities take care of the academic success of the more disadvantaged students is a third indicator for evaluating their developmental role.

Now, in order to expand its contribution to access and success in Higher Education, universities need several types of partnerships with other actors. They are needed particularly in order to expand the possibilities so that graduates may find creative work in their own countries. The scarcity of such possibilities has always been a major characteristic of underdevelopment. The collaboration of the university with other institutional and social actors for expanding the opportunities opened to graduates for working in learning and innovative contexts is a fourth indicator of its developmental character.

We have stressed more than once that the number of such spaces can grow only if knowledge demand is expanded. In turn, this requires—in the South and perhaps beyond—that potentially strong social demand for knowledge becomes effective. The attention given by the university to these issues in its research agenda and policies is a fifth indicator of its developmental character.

Knowledge Production and Its Connections

In the characterization of the Developmental University, it was stated above that its research mission "aims at expanding endogenous capabilities for generating knowledge—at local, regional and national levels—, in all the disciplines and in interdisciplinary activities, with international quality and social vocation".

Thus, a sixth indicator to gauge the contribution of the university to development should be the quality of its research, evaluated with cultural amplitude and depth. In this context, it is worthwhile remembering that universities are "the most important incubator of the next generation of researchers" (Nowotny et al. 2001: 91). This is as important concerning research as it is in relation to the strength of innovation in every socially valuable activity; consequently, guaranteeing that the supply of talented people will be systematically growing "(i)ncreasingly (…) becomes one of the most essential, and indispensable, contributions that universities are expected to make" (Ibid).

As discussed in a previous chapter, it is quite usual that academic evaluation systems aim, with more or less accuracy and success, to reward the international quality of research. But it is quite less usual that academic evaluation pays due attention to the very difficult and time-consuming tasks that need to be performed in order to combine the quality of research with social vocation. The challenge is not only to reward outstanding research at an international level but also to "reward scholars who break new ground in their disciplines by working with communities". This "strategy of using community engagement to achieve genuine scholarly insight is better suited [...] than a strategy based on 'service'" (Levine 2007: 262).

Neither is the direct contribution of research to teaching, at the graduate and undergraduate levels, valued as it should be from a Humboldtian point of view.

In general, academic evaluation systems seldom encourage what was characterized above, for the Developmental University, as the third "mission of fostering the socially valuable use of knowledge" by cooperating "with a wide variety of actors in interactive learning processes that upgrade the capabilities for producing goods and services as well as for solving problems, with priority given to the needs of the most deprived sectors".

The connection of such a "third mission" with teaching and research—in a neo-Humboldtian perspective—should be promoted: "[W]hen engagement is high on a university's agenda, the challenge for those in charge of the university is to achieve a situation where community engagement is realised through the core activities of teaching and research and not have it regarded as a residual activity" (Jongbloed et al. 2008: 313).

Such engagement not only needs to be backed by teaching and research. It can also promote both, particularly in the frequently difficult interdisciplinary tasks: "engagement requires cooperation among a variety of disciplinary fields to address societal problems" (Weerts and Sandmann 2008: 81).

Countries with a weak research structure should not wait until it is strengthened before putting it to work in socially valuable issues, like promoting production, protecting the environment, improving health, and coping with social problems such as poverty and violence. From this perspective, it is said that Latin American societies do not seem to be ready to increase resources for research without seeing its concrete benefits (Schwartzman 2008: 1). Surely, that is also true in other regions of the world. The best thing to do is to combine research and application because that is good for knowledge production and because that combination at the same time attracts talents, resources, and social legitimacy.

Cooperation with different actors in the socially valuable use of knowledge should not be seen as "transference of knowledge", which is an equally flawed conception of identifying teaching with transmission of knowledge. Or, in the words of Weerts and Sandmann, "[T]he new philosophy emphasizes a shift away from an expert model of delivering university knowledge to the public and toward a more collaborative model in which community partners play a significant role in creating and sharing knowledge to the mutual benefit of institutions and society" (Weerts and Sandmann 2008: 74).

It is worth stressing that this perspective opens multiple possibilities for universities to become active partners in Innovation Systems at different levels.

We would thus suggest that a seventh indicator of the developmental contributions of universities could be to what extent they work with development-oriented evaluation systems that foster the combination of teaching, research, and cooperation with society in valuable uses of knowledge.

Who Governs and for Whom?

Why would universities give priority to developmental concerns? The question brings us to the issue of university governance: "[H]istorically, the right of the university to govern itself has always been an important though contested issue [...] and was intimately tight to the issue of the professional autonomy of academics [...], i.e. their role and powers in the self-governance of the university as well as their academic freedom to pursue teaching and research without fear of intervention or punishment. The modern conception of the university embraced the idea of the university as a distinctive social institution which deserves special status in terms of autonomy and academic freedom based on a 'social compact' that evolved between Higher Education, the state and society. The belief that the university requires autonomy from substantial political or corporate influence to function optimally was in turn linked to the role of the state as the guardian of the university in substantive matters, guaranteed state funding, at least in continental Europe, strong professional self-governance and protection of academic freedom" (Enders et al. 2013: 3). Moreover, "[S]tate-university relationships developed a specific form characterized by a strong role of the state as well as of the academic profession. On the one hand, the state functioned as a strong regulator and funder of universities exercising bureaucratic control over procedural matters. On the other hand, the state protected the autonomy of the university as a social institution, academic freedom as well as academic self-governance, and substantial matters were delegated to academics within a broad state framework" (Enders et al. 2013: 4).

The former dominant model—the Humboldtian university—included a type of governance in its ideal formulation. It praised academic autonomy or, perhaps more precisely, the autonomy of universities as understood by the leading academic strata. For good or for bad reasons, it was asserted that the advance of knowledge in such a way would be better guaranteed than by other institutional schemes. Of course, from ideals to realities there is always some bigger or lesser distance.

More often than not, in Germany and beyond, governing structures were built and often re-built in ways that can be seen as working combinations of professional self-control and political regulation, thus making the interests of academic elites compatible with the general orientations of governments.

That traditional organization is in no small measure the opposite of the now prevailing guides for university governance, the New Public Management model, which "is characterized by the call for more market orientation, less regulation, and strong leadership" (Schmoch 2011: 275). The idea of viewing universities as production organizations is catching on in most parts of the world. For example, "Dutch universities are nowadays confronted with a new regulatory regime of control in which their managerial autonomy is supposed to be instrumental in aligning them to governmental goals and performance expectations. This is what we call 'regulatory autonomy'" (Enders et al. 2013: 17).

In the case of the United States, from where a strong push for the incorporation of the New Public Management philosophy comes, this "regulatory autonomy" has resulted in an important shift in terms of the structure of university personnel: "…at the University of California between 1994 and 2009, the ratio of senior managers to ladder-ranked faculty has risen from 3:7 to 1:1, and the salary structure has been distorted accordingly. The President of the university now expects to earn the equivalent of a corporate executive salary (…). All managerial and administrative salaries are stretched accordingly, and salaries within the university become ever more unequal, varying with the marketability of the associated knowledge and the credentials they produce" (Burawoy 2011: 28). This author posits that universities are facing changes toward the coexistence of two models, both inspired by the introduction of the New Public Management guidance to university governance: the commodification model and the regulation model. In regard to the former, its consequences have been that "[M]arkets have invaded every dimension of the university, and its 'autonomy' now means only that it can choose the way to tackle budget deficits, whether through restructuring its faculties, employing temporary instructors, outsourcing service work, raising student fees, moving to distance learning, etc." (Burawoy 2011: 29).

It can be said that "the old model" of governance privileged the (direct) role of government and the interests of academic elites but that "the new model", closely connected with the idea of the Entrepreneurial University, privileges a different (and rather indirect) role of government as well as the external interests of market elites and the internal interest of academic administrators. Are feasible alternatives necessarily limited to those types of scarcely democratic arrangements? An affirmative answer would leave a very small margin for committing universities to knowledge democratization. But history shows other possibilities: "[S]ince the Reformation in 1536, universities in Denmark have been state institutions, but with some degree of autonomy. This means that a collegial governance system based on the professors through a senate has governed the university. Starting 1968, the students demanded more influence on decision making within the universities, and in the beginning of the 1970s, the governance structure that functioned during the next couple of decades was passed by the parliament. In this act, the university senate consisted of a share of 50% professors, 25% students, and 25% technical administrative staff. Their constituencies within the university elected their members of the senate, and the same constituencies in the same proportions elected the rector" (Gregersen and Rasmussen 2011: 291).

That Danish University Reform appears as a clear example of "autonomy and co-government". This has been the traditional plight of those public Latin American universities shaped by the Latin American Movement for University Reform that started in 1918. In this tradition, autonomy has at least three related but different meanings. First, it means not being subordinated to governments, seen as frequent partners of privileged social sectors. Second, it refers to what is sometimes called "technical autonomy" of the university to determine the orientations of teaching and research; it is based on the specific capabilities of academic bodies and thus akin to autonomy in the Humboldtian project. Third, it opens the possibility of transforming universities, in particular by the direct incorporation of student representatives in the governing bodies. The last is what co-government means. In the Latin American ideal of university, such direct participation of students was seen as the major tool for democratizing the university. In turn, that would be the way both to weaken ties with dominant sectors and build partnerships with popular sectors. The latter was pursued mainly by promoting extension activities and by committing students and even universities as such in popular struggles.

Changes in universities have not always being considered as something that starts in the center countries and then is transferred to the peripheries.

In 1968, when "co-government" was demanded in the agitated universities in the North, in Paris and beyond, Carlos Quijano, a leading intellectual of the Latin American Movement for University Reform, wrote that European students were joining the long march started half a century before by their Latin American comrades. By then, student movements in Latin America were fighting for democracy in society at large against authoritarian governments.

At the same time, also concerning "co-government", a professor at Columbia University wrote the following: "[I]f [...] the student is a client, he is a special variety of client: the apprentice. And as apprentice, he is a member—to be sure, the most junior member in breadth of experience and length of service—of the university as a professional organization. The undergraduate student, the liberal-arts student, is an apprentice in the ways of the educated man. The graduate student, the student in the professional schools, is an apprentice in a professional community. In both cases the student is not a mere client. To define him as a mere client is to define the university as an economic institution selling services in the marketplace. Insofar as this has even been asserted to be the case, the guardians of the idea of university have always vigorously denied it. But to deny this image is to accept the membership of the student in the university community. To accept the membership of the student in the university community is to accept his right to participate in some meaningful way in the governance of the university, and particularly in its policy planning" (Wallerstein 1969: 95).

Participating in the governance of the university is, in our view, a right of the students and of every member of the university as a community. This view is akin to the normative conception of development as the expansion of freedoms and capabilities. The stress of such a conception on agency suggests seeing also that type of enlarged participation as a potential means for fostering knowledge democratization. As a right, it should be as valuable today as half a century ago; as a potential means, it is today more relevant than in 1968 and much more than in 1918, simply because the power of knowledge has grown steadily, particularly in the last century and a half.

Concerning student participation, it is asserted that "[F]inding ways to protect students' rights and enhance their roles in governance and decision making will be especially important if Higher Education is to respond effectively to changing students profiles and needs the world over" (Altbach et al. 2009: 109).

What could be said fifty years ago about the possibilities of participation in general and how do they look today? "[T]he governance of the university has thus become for the first time in a long time a major item on the agenda of society. The achievement of internal democratization is clearly a long-term and difficult task. It will be resisted strongly by forces within and without the university. But it is clear that university itself is the main arena in which the political battle will be fought out, and it is probable that the legitimacy of such democratization will eventually be widely accepted. In this sense, time is in the side of the forces of progress" (Wallerstein 1969: 104).

Several comments are in order. First, it was not "the first time in a long time" that the governance of the university rose high in the agenda of society; as already recalled, that had been happening in Latin America since 1918. And if democratic governance of the university was erased by the military governments of the American south in the 1970s, the item came back to the collective agenda with the democratization processes of the 1980s, in which student movements often had a recognized role. Thus, when dictatorships ended, often (though not always) some amount of "autonomy and co-government" was restored. In that sense, the legacy of the Latin American University Reform is still a reference, particularly when the winds of change blow in quite a different direction.

In fact, as foresighted in Wallerstein's quote, democratization of the university was strongly resisted by internal and external forces. And concerning that issue, today it is not easy to say that time was "in the side of the forces of progress". In fact, what has been happening in the North concerning university governance looks more like a Counter-Reform than a democratization process. The prevailing model combines the New Public Management with a "Hierarchical Top-Down System" such as the one operating in Denmark, where in 2003 a "university board with a majority of external members from business, cultural institutions and foreign universities formally got most of the power that hitherto had been located in the senate. Furthermore, the rector, the deans, and the heads of the departments are appointed, not elected" (Gregersen and Rasmussen 2011: 292).

This Counter-Reform is detrimental in at least two substantive issues. First, it weakens the contribution of the university to the education of citizens by means of participation: "[U]niversities in the knowledge society are not merely a source of knowledge but a means to participate. However, governance transformation is changing their capacity to deliver that vital contribution" (Benneworth 2013: 12). Second, it does not foster the contribution of Higher Education as a public good to society at large since "[U]niversity societal engagement only weakly fits with performance management measures and targets" (Benneworth 2013: 13).

Successes and failures of more or less autonomous and democratic universities, as well as ups and downs of internal democracy itself, pose difficult problems. Are attempts to democratize the university and to weaken its ties with dominant elites doomed to fail? If some measure of autonomy and self-government is obtained, can it foster strong connections with different collective actors in ways that strength Inclusive Innovations Systems? Or, on the contrary, is the most probable evolution toward variants of autarchy where decisions are slow and changes are small because the particular interests of academic elites and other internal groups prevail?

Questions similar to those posed above shape what can be called the problem of the connected autonomy of a (truly engaged developmental type of) university.

Brunner (2011: 145) recalls that university governance has to take into account a wide and differentiated set of stakeholders. Some of them are internal—teachers, students, and administrative personnel—and many are external. Some of the last are quite traditional actors whereas others are emerging as such. Their interests can be related to universities in direct or indirect ways, permanently or transiently, rather positively or otherwise. An incomplete list of external stakeholders includes governments (national, regional, local), public agencies, graduates, firms and employers, trade unions, non-governmental organizations, communities, and different movements of civil society. The same author says that from such context a vision emerges of the responsibilities of public universities that is wider and more complex than the usual ones. That leads the university to combine its collegial and self-government traditions with the multiple demands posed by external stakeholders.

Under such conditions, there is probably no general solution to the problem of the connected autonomy of universities that can be given in formal terms. It is difficult to institutionalize relations involving such a wide set of very different external stakeholders. Perhaps only transient and approximate solutions can be offered, combining general principles with context-dependent organizations. Principles include commitment to Sustainable Human Development and democratic participation. The last notion, like agency in Sen's conception, is both a normative end and a means. It requires a relevant degree of autonomy of the university, particularly to make the best use of its capabilities and to allow significant involvement of internal stakeholders. At the same time, autarchy must be systematically confronted. That entails taking into account external stakeholders. But it is not easy to do so in an institutionalized way. Furthermore, "[E]xternal stakeholders also can come in many shapes. When the university regards their claims as important, their voice may be heard via external representatives in the university's internal decision-making bodies. An interesting question here is whether the external representatives are representing themselves or representing a wider group. For instance, who can speak for external stakeholders such as the small and medium-sized enterprises?" (Jongbloed et al. 2008: 312).

Surely a more difficult question is: who can speak for neglected regions or deprived sectors or affected communities? The general commitment to a "third mission" characterized by "horizontal" types of collaboration with different social and institutional actors should inspire wide and systematic consultations as well as more articulated and specific "project-based" ways of participation of external stakeholders.

The above considerations suggest an eighth indicator of the developmental role of universities, namely the actual possibilities opened by its governance to combine their autonomous work and initiatives, a wide set of connections with civil society, and involvement in public policies—if contributing to Human Sustainable Development—without subordination to the interests of external elites or equating autonomy with the rule of internal elites.

How well are the universities of the world faring in contributing to Human Sustainable Development? The developmental role of universities is to a high degree of a qualitative nature and thus difficult to measure. Moreover, conventional indicators may paint a confusing picture with widely different outcomes in and between countries. In some countries, the introduction or increases in tuition or other hindrances to access to Higher Education can be found alongside affirmative action programs and government support to students. However, in one aspect of inclusiveness in Higher Education, it seems that the development is fairly uniform around the world—the enrollment in Higher Education. In the North as well as the Global South, enrollment rates have generally increased in recent decades as a result of the expansion of Higher Education. In a study of 11 developed and developing countries on the extent to which Higher Education institutions are socially inclusive, it was found that all countries experienced a steady or even considerable increase in the level of tertiary enrollment between 2000 and 2014 (Brundenius 2017). Positive as this development may be, the real contribution of universities to Human Sustainable Development will depend on how socially inclusive the Higher Education system is and to what extent it can accept the challenge of democratization of knowledge.

BACK TO THE PROSPECTIVE APPROACH

In Chapter 2, we sketched a prospective approach to Human Sustainable Development. Referring to that elaboration, we want to mention some factors that will probably be highly influential concerning the strengthening or weakening of the developmental contributions of universities. Of course, in order to consider the possibilities of some outcomes, the interactions between those factors must be studied in each specific context.

Given the increasing role of advanced knowledge in social relations in general, the first factor taken into account should be the different knowledge demands and the power that backs them. Not surprisingly, today the stronger demands are those stemming from dominant economic and social actors. But the ensuing dynamics are fostering inequality within most countries, while prevailing ways of using knowledge contribute to damaging the environment and to raising the probabilities of climatic threats. The developmental role of universities could become stronger if environmental and social concerns challenge the dominant modes of producing and using knowledge.

Since knowledge is widely seen as an engine of growth, prevailing economic policies and the models that orient them will keep being a very influential factor concerning the orientation of universities and innovation in general. Here, the distinction between explicit and implicit policies is important; it was made famous by Amílcar Herrera forty years ago in Latin America when analyzing science, technology, and development issues. In fact, in underdeveloped countries, the knowledge policy, beyond the written words, is often a non-existent policy. That is not mainly a consequence of ignorance but of a combination of the actual weak economic relevance of knowledge with the absence of a strategy for development that goes beyond standard recipes for "catching up". So in the Global South at least, the inflection in knowledge policies that environmental and social dangers may trigger would also need deep ideological changes.

Of course, public policies for education in general will greatly influence the evolution of universities. Governments frequently give priority to universalizing Secondary Education. Their success in this realm is evidently a major requisite for generalizing Higher Education. But the last demands specific policies, substantial monetary resources, and—perhaps above all—innovation capabilities concerning ways and places of teaching. Strong social and political support for such tasks is not evident. But at least the purpose and means for democratizing access to advanced learning have risen in the political agenda of some countries, North and South. Related issues will not wither away, because "the social base in Higher Education will continue to broaden, along with uncertainty about how this will affect inequalities of educational opportunities between social groups" (Altbach et al. 2009: xix).

The constellation of (material and ideal) interests concerning the above issue is perhaps not very different from the one shaping the academic reward system. In any case, such a system, as shaped today by the interaction of "internal" and "external" influences, does not strongly foster the developmental role of universities. That will be difficult to change without new "alliances" of external and internal actors whose interests are different from those of economic and academic elites.

International academic relations are fundamental for every university and simply vital for a university in an underdeveloped country. Without international cooperation, it cannot do much to improve teaching or knowledge generation and use. But an obvious tension appears here since the so-called internationalization of Higher Education fosters not only intellectual collaboration but research agendas, evaluation systems, and academic values prevailing in the North that—to say the least—are not always well suited for development in the South (Bianco et al. 2016). This, in particular, is a main factor propelling the new dominant model for universities in the world at large.

When potential factors of change within universities are analyzed, prevailing student attitudes become relevant. What do they expect or demand (or both) from universities? Often students are seen, and even see themselves, as clients. That helps to consolidate the entrepreneurial university—and academic capitalism in general. But the client attitude cannot be seen as the only game in town in the past or today. Today, as in the past, a fair number of students get involved in university decision-making processes or in demanding a place in such processes. Many of them and perhaps a larger proportion of other students get involved in extension and service activities. Their motivations and projects deserve close attention when calibrating the possibilities for change within universities and in their relations with external actors.

Thus, we arrive at a crucial issue for the prospect of changes in universities. What happens with social movements concerning advanced knowledge? Estrangement seems a frequent attitude, particularly in the Global South, often combined with distrust and even hostility. Nevertheless, some more or less informed positive expectations can also be detected. Examples can be given even of some "popular actors" willing to get involved in policies and actions that foster knowledge democratization. But it is very difficult to imagine that such anecdotal evidence can expand into being a relevant trend. Bridges between, on the one hand, the academy and advanced knowledge and, on the other hand, social organizations truly representing "popular" or deprived sectors are obviously difficult to build.

The organizing question for a prospective approach to the Developmental University can thus be briefly formulated: who are the stakeholders? The issue could be analyzed in the context of the general trends and alternative possibilities that were considered above. Attention should be paid to which groups, strata, and movements, inside and above all outside universities, are such that the dynamics of knowledge open possibilities for articulating their material and ideal interests in ways that promote the developmental tasks of universities and knowledge democratization in general.

THE INNOVATION SYSTEM AND THE UNIVERSITY

In a nutshell, the decisive indicator of the developmental role of a given university is its contribution to building the stronger and more inclusive systems of innovation that are needed in underdevelopment and surely not only in the Global South.

We have already suggested that a form of innovation that connects knowledge production and use with increasing employability and service provision can be an outcome of innovation policies seen as social policies. Here, we want to remember its connection with the problem of stakeholders and add that such policies may be a component of a specific productive strategy: "[I]n the case of innovation policies considered as social policies, given that the articulating role of the state is still more important and needs to connect more diverse actors than in other innovation policies, [… we must inquire] which sectors of the state apparatus may be willing to promote these tasks of connection and articulation. This begs the question of which economic interest may promote the emergence of organized networks involving these innovation policies. In this respect, an analogy can be made with the protection of 'infant industries'. This would point to a type of specialization with high added value in the form of knowledge and skills related to social inclusion" (Arocena and Sutz 2014: 31). Concerning the feasibility of such a "pattern of specialization", Cuba is a telling example. There, some fundamental issues of health have been tackled by a systematic policy of endogenous research with international quality. That allowed Cuba to cope with some fundamental needs, weakly attended to in several parts of the Global South by importing scarcely affordable medicines. In that way, Cuba became an exporter of medicines (Núñez et al. 2011: 105; Lage 2011).

The connections between social policies, technological dynamics, and productive strategies appear to be crucial for fostering inclusive Innovation Systems.

They are closely related to an interpretation of the dynamics of inequality: "[T]he three forces that we view as broadly shaping the evolution of inequality, namely, technology, openness (or globalization), and policy (or politics), which we shall bundle together under the acronym TOP" (Milanović 2016: 76). In Latin America, during the first years of this century, two of those forces contributed to diminishing inequalities. The dynamics of globalization, mainly by increasing the role of China in industrial production and international trade, generated a high demand of commodities. The ensuing economic boom in Latin America led to the expansion of employment, particularly of less qualified types, that improved the situation of poor people. The commodity boom also increased the margins for distributional policies.

When the boom withers, those two equalizing factors lose steam. And some huge problems are (again) evident. More or less similar situations can be seen in other regions of the Global South. We can briefly describe some of them by referring to the three "forces" considered by Milanovic. First, states have fewer resources for widening or even maintaining distributional policies. Second, the changes in the international economy imply that now globalization is not favoring commodity producers but rather that the contrary can happen. As a consequence, those countries that were unable to upgrade their productive structure once again see their external position weakening, with quite obvious internal consequences. So, third, technology comes into play against equality.

The last cannot be seen as a necessary outcome. Perhaps the Latin American situation would be brighter today if the prosperity of yesterday had been managed not only to foster distribution but to combine it with upgrading innovation and external economic insertion. No small effort was made for that purpose in some countries of the continent, but on the whole, the balance looks disappointing.

Much more can be said concerning the actual situation in the Global South. But let us pause to insert the above remarks in the general approach of this book. The recent commodity boom did not mean that the emergence of a knowledge-based and innovation-driven economy in some places of the world is not the fundamental structural change of our time. On the contrary, the global expansion of such an economy multiplied the industrial production in large peripheral and poor areas, mainly in East Asia, and, as a consequence, the demand of food and primary products from that area rose. Industrialization of Western Europe during the nineteenth century fostered the commodity-based prosperity of countries like Argentina and Uruguay, but that did not mean that industry was not becoming an indicator of economic development; on the contrary. That became evident in these countries only when external demand of primary products fell abruptly in the 1930s. What could we say today?

In those regions where the economy is dependent more on extractive activities than on advanced knowledge and qualifications, the after-boom will probably not only affect social indicators negatively but also deepen the environmental damages. Countervailing powers that more or less control such damages in mining, logging, massive cultivations, and unbalanced agriculture will weaken. States will increasingly need the resources they are offered by firms promoting such activities, and environmental controls will tend to be less severe. Poor people will be more in need of jobs, and it will become harder for them to protect working conditions or to resist the degradation of natural surroundings. Equality and sustainability are prone to suffer.

Such possible outcomes will mainly affect deprived sectors and underdeveloped regions, but as shown by migrations and climatic changes, their consequences will be truly global. Perhaps it will now become more evident than yesterday that prevailing knowledge policies are flawed. Since they are driven primarily by commercial demand, they are not very attuned to social and environmental problems. They mainly favor those who can pay for knowledge: generally speaking, those sectors and regions that are already knowledge-strong. Problems of other people are frequently neglected. Improving the social situation of a vast part of the world population is hampered because inequalities in access to and use of knowledge are not counteracted. Perhaps an even greater problem is posed because prevailing ways of generating and using knowledge are dominated by the interests of minorities, thus making it difficult to really take into account the sustainability problems of humankind as such. In this sense, our contention is that Human Sustainable Development needs knowledge democratization.

Inclusive Innovation Systems are those where such democratization takes place. A fundamental condition for that is the positive interaction between states, knowledge producers, and social sectors that are normally neglected. A needed axis for such interaction is identifying the potentially huge knowledge demand stemming from collective problems and concerns. We contend that Developmental Universities should and could be important actors in Inclusive Innovation Systems. But, reciprocally, it is almost impossible for universities to contribute to Human Sustainable Development if they are isolated or embedded in Innovation Systems from which weak and marginalized social groups are in fact disconnected and without their incorporation being pursued by public policies.

Conclusion: Knowledge Democratization, South and North

The first two "key messages" of the World Social Science Report 2016 are the following: "[E]conomic and political power are increasingly concentrated in the hands of a small number of people. This can threaten growth, social cohesion and the health of democracies; Global economic inequality declined during the first decade of this century, largely due to the reduction of poverty in countries like China and India. This favourable trend could however be reversed if inequality within countries continues to increase" (ISSC, IDS and UNESCO 2016: 26).

Inequality lies at the heart of human problems, North and South. A book we have quoted more than once ends by saying, "[I]t is true that since 1980 we have seen an 'Inequality Turn' and that the twenty-first century brings challenges in terms of the ageing of the population, climate change, and global imbalances. But the solutions to these problems lie in our own hands. If we are willing to use today's greater wealth to address these challenges, and accept that resources should be shared less unequally, there are indeed grounds for optimism" (Atkinson 2015: 308). Knowledge is a fundamental resource; it is far from evident that the powers that be are willing to share it less unequally. Democratization of knowledge is needed but it will not take place by itself. History suggests that significant democratization processes happen only when the agency of unprivileged sectors rises above ordinary levels.

This book aims to contribute to the theoretical and practical search for alternative strategies for the transformation of universities in the Global South in order to promote knowledge democratization for Human

Sustainable Development. Such strategies must be plural and highly dependent on their specific contexts. At the same time, it is fundamental to learn by comparing contexts and by cooperation between actors located in different geographies, South and North. That is so not only because some problems are similar but above all because a common purpose worldwide should be to foster knowledge democratization as a means of expanding capabilities and freedoms of people seen not as patients but as agents.

REFERENCES

Altbach, P., Reisberg, L., & Rumbley, L. (2009). *Trends in Global Higher Education: Tracking an Academic Revolution*. París: UNESCO.

Arocena, R., & Sutz, J. (2014). Innovation and Democratisation of Knowledge as a Contribution to Inclusive Development. In G. Dutrenit & J. Sutz (Eds.), *National Innovation Systems, Social Inclusion and Development. The Latin American Experience* (pp. 15–33). Cheltenham: Edward Elgar.

Atkinson, A. B. (2015). *Inequality: What Can Be Done?* Cambridge, USA: Harvard University Press.

Benner, M. (2011). In Search of Excellence? An International Perspective on Governance of University Research. In B. Göransson & C. Brundenius (Eds.), *Universities in Transition. The Changing Role and Challenges for Academic Institutions* (pp. 11–24). Ottawa: Springer.

Benneworth, P. (2013). University Engagement with Socially Excluded Communities. Towards the Idea of 'the Engaged University'. In P. Benneworth (Ed.), *University Engagement with Socially Excluded Communities* (pp. 3–31). Netherlands: Springer.

Bianco, M., Gras, N., & Sutz, J. (2016). Academic Evaluation: Universal Instrument? Tool for Development? *Minerva, 54*(4), 399–421.

Brundenius, C. (2017). Challenges of Rising Inequalities and the Quest for Inclusive and Sustainable Development. In C. Brundenius, B. Göransson, & J. M. Carvalho de Mello (Eds.), *Universities, Inclusive Development and Social Innovation. An International Perspective* (pp. 9–48). Ottawa: Springer.

Brunner, J. J. (2011). Gobernanza universitaria: tipología, dinámicas y tendencias. *Revista de Educación, 355*. Mayo-Agosto, 137–159.

Burawoy, M. (2011). Redefining the Public University: Global and National Contexts. In J. Holmwood (Ed.), *A Manifesto for the Public University* (pp. 27–41). London: Bloomsbury.

Dahl, R. A. (1982). *Dilemmas of Pluralist Democracy: Autonomy Vs. Control*. New Haven/London: Yale University Press.

Enders, J., de Boer, H., & Weyer, E. (2013). Regulatory Autonomy and Performance: The Reform of Higher Education Re-visited. *Higher Education, 65*(1), 5–23.

Gregersen, B., & Rasmussen, G. (2011). Developing Universities: The Evolving Role of Academic Institutions in Denmark. In B. Göransson & C. Brundenius (Eds.), *Universities in Transition. The Changing Role and Challenges for Academic Institutions* (pp. 283–306). Ottawa: Springer.

IESALC. (2008). *Declaration of the Regional Conference of Higher Education of Latin America and the Caribbean.* Caracas: UNESCO-IESALC.

ISSC, IDS and UNESCO. (2016). *World Social Science Report 2016, Challenging Inequalities: Pathways to a Just World.* Paris: UNESCO Publishing.

Jongbloed, B., Enders, J., & Salerno, C. (2008). Higher Education and Its Communities: Interconnections, Interdependencies and a Research Agenda. *Higher Education, 56*(3), 303–324.

Kaitila, V., & Kotilainen, M. (2008). Not Just Nokia: Finland. In C. Edquist & L. Hommen (Eds.), *Small Country Innovation Systems Globalization, Change and Policy in Asia and Europe* (pp. 355–402). Cheltenham: Edward Elgar.

Lage, A. (2011). Global Pharmaceutical Development and Access: Critical Issues of Ethics and Equity. *MEDICC Review, 13*(3), 16–22.

Levine, P. (2007). Collective Action, Civic Engagement, and the Knowledge Commons. In C. Hess & E. Ostrom (Eds.), *Understanding Knowledge as Commons. From Theory to Practice* (pp. 247–275). Cambridge, USA: The MIT Press.

Milanović, B. (2016). *Global in Equality: A New Approach for the Age of Globalization.* Cambridge, MA: Harvard University Press.

Mills, C. W. (1971). *The Sociological Imagination.* London, UK: Pelican Books (Original: 1959).

Nowotny, H. (n.d.). *The Potential of Transdisciplinarity.* Available at: http://www.helga-nowotny.eu/downloads/helga_nowotny_b59.pdf. Accessed 9 May 2017.

Nowotny, H., Scott, P., & Gibbons, M. (2001). *Re-thinking Science. Knowledge and the Public in an Age of Uncertainty.* Cambridge, UK: Polity Press.

Núñez, J., Montalvo, L. F., Pérez Ones, I., Fernández, A., & García Cuevas, J. L. (2011). Cuba: University, Innovation and Society: Higher Education in the National System of Innovation. In B. Göransson & C. Brundenius (Eds.), *Universities in Transition. The Changing Role and Challenges for Academic Institutions* (pp. 97–118). Ottawa: Springer.

Schmoch, U. (2011). Germany: The Role of Universities in the Learning Economy. In B. Göransson & C. Brundenius (Eds.), *Universities in Transition. The Changing Role and Challenges for Academic Institutions* (pp. 261–282). Ottawa: Springer.

Schwartzman, S. (2008). Introducción. Educación Superior, Investigación Científica e Innovación en América Latina. In S. Schwartzman (Ed.), *Universidad y desarrollo en Latinoamérica: experiencias exitosas de centros de investigación* (pp. 1–25). Bogotá: IESALC-UNESCO.

Shapira, P., Smits, R., & Kuhlmann, S. (2010). An Outlook on Innovation Policy, Theory and Practice. In R. Smits, S. Kuhlmann, & P. Shapira (Eds.), *The Theory and Practice of Innovation Policy* (pp. 449–466). Cheltenham, UK: Edward Elgar.

Wallerstein, I. (1969). *University in Turmoil. The Politics of Change.* New York: Atheneum.

Weerts, D. J., & Sandmann, L. R. (2008). Building a Two-Way Street: Challenges and Opportunities for Community Engagement at Research Universities. *Review of Higher Education, 32*(1), 73–106.

REFERENCES

Abrol, D. (2014). Pro-Poor Innovation Making, Knowledge Production, and Technology Implementation for Rural Areas: Lessons from the Indian Experience. In V. R. Shyama (Ed.), *Innovation in India. Combining Economic Growth with Inclusive Development* (pp. 337–378). Delhi: Cambridge University Press.

Abrol, D. (2017). The Honey Bee Network. In A. Smith, M. Fressoli, D. Abrol, E. Around, & A. Ely (Eds.), *Grassroots Innovation Movements* (pp. 145–164). New York: Routledge.

Aguirre-Bastos, C., Aliaga Lordeman, J., Garrón Védia, I., & Rubín de Célis Cedro, R. (2016). National Innovation System in Bolivia: Making Research and Innovation Matter. In B. Göransson, C. Brundenius, & C. Aguirre (Eds.), *Innovation Systems for Development: Making Research and Innovation in Developing Countries Matter.* Northampton: Edward Elgar Publishing.

Aksnes, D., & Rip, A. (2009). Researchers' Perceptions of Citations. *Research Policy, 38*(6), 895–905.

Altbach, P. (Ed.). (2003). *The Decline of the Guru. The Academic Profession in the Third World.* New York: Palgrave Macmillan.

Altbach, P., Reisberg, L., & Rumbley, L. (2009). *Trends in Global Higher Education: Tracking an Academic Revolution.* París: UNESCO.

Alzugaray, S., Mederos, L., & Sutz, J. (2012). Building Bridges. Social Inclusion Problems as Research and Innovation Issues. *Review of Policy Research, 29*(6), 776–796.

Amaral Filho, J. (2006). Pingo D'água: un arranjo innovativo no semi-árido do ceará. In H. Lastres & J. Cassiolato (org.), *Estratégias para o desenvolvimento: um enfoque sobre arranjos produtivos locais do Norte, Nordeste e Centro-Oeste Brasileiros* (pp. 49–66), e-papers, Río de Janeiro.

© The Author(s) 2018

R. Arocena et al., *Developmental Universities in Inclusive Innovation Systems*, https://doi.org/10.1007/978-3-319-64152-2

Amsden, A. (1989). *Asia's Next Giant. South Korea and late Industrialization.* New York/Oxford: Oxford University Press.

Anand, S., & Sen, A. (2000). Human Development and Economic Sustainability. *World Development, 2812,* 2029–2049.

Anderson, R. D. (2004). *European Universities from the Enlightenment to 1914.* Oxford: Oxford University press.

Andersen, E. S., & Lundvall, B.-Å. (1988). Small National Innovation Systems Facing Technological Revolutions: An Analytical Framework. In C. Freeman & B.-Å. Lundvall (Eds.), *Small Countries Facing the Technological Revolution.* London: Pinter Publishers.

ANII. (2012). *Evaluación del impacto del Sistema Nacional de Investigadores.* Available at: http://www.anii.org.uy/institucional/documentos-de-interes/4/informes-de-evaluacion/. Accessed 12 July 2016.

Arocena, R. (2015). *La autonomía de la 'Universidad para el Desarrollo'* (núm 66, pp. 7–18). México: Universidades, UDUAL.

Arocena, R., & Sutz, J. (2000a). *Interactive Learning Spaces and Development Policies in Latin America* (Druid Working Paper 00–13). Denmark: Aalborg University. Available at: http://www3.druid.dk/wp/20000013.pdf. Accessed 10 May 2017.

Arocena, R., & Sutz, J. (2000b). Looking at National Systems of Innovation from the South. *Industry and Innovation, 7*(1), 55–75.

Arocena, R., & Sutz, J. (2001). Changing Knowledge Production and Latin American Universities. *Research Policy, 30*(8), 1221–1234.

Arocena, R., & Sutz, J. (2010). Weak Knowledge Demand in the South: Learning Divides and Innovation Policies. *Science and Public Policy, 37*(8), 571–582.

Arocena, R., & Sutz, J. (2011). Uruguay: Higher Education, National System of Innovation and Economic Development in a Small Peripheral Country. In B. Göransson & C. Brundenius (Eds.), *Universities in Transition. The Changing Role and Challenges for Academic Institutions* (pp. 77–96). Ottawa: Springer.

Arocena, R., & Sutz, J. (2012). Research and Innovation Policies for Social Inclusion: An Opportunity for Developing Countries. *Innovation and Development, 2*(1), 147–158.

Arocena, R., & Sutz, J. (2014). Innovation and Democratisation of Knowledge as a Contribution to Inclusive Development. In G. Dutrenit & J. Sutz (Eds.), *National Innovation Systems, Social Inclusion and Development. The Latin American Experience* (pp. 15–33). Cheltenham: Edward Elgar.

Arocena, R., & Sutz, J. (2016a). Innovación y Sistemas Nacionales de Innovación en procesos de desarrollo. In A. Erbes y D. Suárez (comp.), *Repensando el desarrollo : una discusión desde los sistemas de innovación* (pp. 69–102). Argentina: Universidad Nacional de General Sarmiento. Available at: http://www.ungs.edu.ar/ms_publicaciones/wp-content/uploads/2016/08/9789876302449-completo.pdf. Accessed 11 May 2017.

Arocena, R., & Sutz, J. (2016b). Universidades para el Desarrollo, Policy Brief for the First Open Forum on Science of the Americas and the Caribbean. Available at:

http://www.unesco.org/new/fileadmin/MULTIMEDIA/FIELD/ Montevideo/pdf/PolicyPapersCILAC-UnivParaDesarrollo.pdf. Accessed 10 May 2017.

Arocena, R., Göransson, B., & Sutz, J. (2014). Universities and Higher Education in Development. In B. Currie-Alder, S. M. R. Kanbur, D. Malone, & R. Medhora (Eds.), *International Development: Ideas, Experience, and Prospects.* Oxford: Oxford University Press.

Arocena, R., Göransson, B., & Sutz, J. (2015). Knowledge Policies in Developing Countries: Inclusive Development and the 'Developmental University'. *Technology in Society, 41*, 10–20.

Astronomo, R., & Burton, D. (2010). Carbohydrate Vaccines: Developing Sweet Solutions to Sticky Situations? *Nature Reviews, 9*, 308–324.

Atkinson, A. B. (2015). *Inequality: What Can Be Done?* Cambridge, USA: Harvard University Press.

Bairoch, P. (1982). International Industrialization Levels from 1750 to 1980. *Journal of European Economic History, 11*, 269–333.

Bairoch, P. (1993). *Economics and World History. Myths and Paradoxes.* Chicago: The University of Chicago Press.

Baker, E. (2005). The Reform of the Intellectual Property, [online] *Post-Autistic Economic Review*, (32), first article. Available at: http://www.paecon.net/ PAEReview/issue32/Baker32.htm. Accessed 11 May 2017.

Balaji, V. (2005). Sustainability Issues in Rural Asian Telecenters. In R. Davison, R. Harris, S. Qureshi, D. Vogel, & G.-J. de Vreede (Eds.), *Information Systems in Developing Countries. Theory and Practice.* Hong Kong: City University of Hong Kong Press.

Bell, M., & Pavitt, K. (1997). Technological Accumulation and Industrial Growth: Contrasts Between Developed and Developing Countries. In D. Archibugi & J. Michie (Eds.), *Technology, Globalization and Economic Performance* (pp. 83–137). Cambridge: Cambridge University Press.

Ben-David, J. (1984). *The Scientist's Role in Society.* Chicago: The University of Chicago Press.

Benner, M. (2011). In Search of Excellence? An International Perspective on Governance of University Research. In B. Göransson & C. Brundenius (Eds.), *Universities in Transition. The Changing Role and Challenges for Academic Institutions* (pp. 11–24). Ottawa: Springer.

Benneworth, P. (2013). University Engagement with Socially Excluded Communities. Towards the Idea of 'the Engaged University'. In P. Benneworth (Ed.), *University Engagement with Socially Excluded Communities* (pp. 3–31). Netherlands: Springer.

Benneworth, P., & Jongbloed, B. (2010). Who Matters to Universities? A Stakeholder Perspective on Humanities, Arts and Social Sciences Valorisation. *Higher Education, 59*(5), 567–588.

Bernard, J., & Bates, C. (2016). Dublin Institute of Technology: Moving, Merging, and Managing the Civic Engagement Mission. In J. Goddard, H. Hazelkorn, L. Kempton, & P. Vallance (Eds.), *The Civic University. The Policy and Leadership Challenges* (pp. 180–200). Cheltenham: Edward Elgar.

Bianco, M., Gras, N., & Sutz, J. (2016). Academic Evaluation: Universal Instrument? Tool for Development? *Minerva, 54*(4), 399–421.

Bleiklie, I. (1998). Justifying the Evaluative State: New Public Management Ideals in Higher Education. *Journal of Public Affairs Education, 4*(2), 87–100.

Bloch, M. (1969). Advent and Triumph of the Water Mill. In M. Bloch (Ed.), *Land and Work in Medieval Europe* (pp. 136, 168). New York: Harper and Row.

Block, F. L., & Keller, M. R. (Eds.). (2011). *State of Innovation: The U.S. Government's Role in Technology Development*. Boulder: Paradigm Publishers.

Bölling, M., & Eriksson, Y. (2016). "Collaboration with Society: The Future Role of Universities?" Identifying Challenges for Evaluation. *Research Evaluation, 25*(2), 209–218.

Borg, H., Galema, A., Mulder, H., & Steenbeek, S. (2016). The University of Groningen: An Engaging University. In J. Goddard, H. Hazelkorn, L. Kempton, & P. Vallance (Eds.), *The Civic University. The Policy and Leadership Challenges* (pp. 201–221). Cheltenham: Edward Elgar.

Bound, K., & Thornton, I. (2012). *Our Frugal Future: Lessons from India's Innovation System*. Available at: https://www.nesta.org.uk/sites/default/files/our_frugal_future.pdf. Accessed 11 May 2017.

Brem, A., & Wolfram, P. (2014). Research and Development from the Bottom Up – Introduction of Terminologies for New Product Development in Emerging Markets. *Journal of Innovation and Entrepreneurship, 3*, 9. Available at: http://innovation-entrepreneurship.springeropen.com/articles/10.1186/2192-5372-3-9. Accessed 10 May 2017.

Brennan, J., & Naidoo, R. (2008). Higher Education and the Achievement (and/or Prevention) of Equity and Social Justice. *Higher Education, 56*(3), 287–302.

Brink, C., & Hogan, J. (2016). Newcastle University and the Development of the Concept of a World-Class Civic University. In J. Goddard, H. Hazelkorn, L. Kempton, & P. Vallance (Eds.), *The Civic University. The Policy and Leadership Challenges* (pp. 240–256). Cheltenham: Edward Elgar.

Broad, W., & Wade, N. (1982). *The Betrayers of the Truth*. New York: Simon and Schuster.

Brundenius, C. (2017). Challenges of Rising Inequalities and the Quest for Inclusive and Sustainable Development. In C. Brundenius, B. Göransson, & J. M. Carvalho de Mello (Eds.), *Universities, Inclusive Development and Social Innovation. An International Perspective* (pp. 9–48). Ottawa: Springer.

Brundenius, C., & Göransson, B. (2011). The Three Missions of Universities: A Synthesis of UniDev Project Findings. In B. Göransson & C. Brundenius (Eds.), *Universities in Transition. The Changing Role and Challenges for Academic Institutions* (pp. 329–352). Ottawa: Springer.

Brundenius, C., Göransson, B., & Ågren, J. (2011). The Role of Academic Institutions in the National System of Innovation and the Debate in Sweden. In B. Göransson & C. Brundenius (Eds.), *Universities in Transition. The Changing Role and Challenges for Academic Institutions* (pp. 307–325). Ottawa: Springer.

Brunner, J. J. (2011). Gobernanza universitaria: tipología, dinámicas y tendencias. *Revista de Educación, 355.* Mayo-Agosto, 137–159.

Brunner, J. J. (2015). Transformaciones del espíritu comunitario de la universidad: base de la responsabilidad social de la academia. In E. Aponte Hernández (Ed.), *La responsabilidad social de las universidades: Implicaciones para América Latina, IESALC-UNESCO* (pp. 97–114). San Juan: IESALC-UNESCO.

Brynjolfsson, E., & McAfee, A. (2014). *The Second Machine Age. Work, Progress, and Prosperity in a Time of Brilliant Technologies.* New York: Norton and Co.

Burawoy, M. (2011). Redefining the Public University: Global and National Contexts. In J. Holmwood (Ed.), *A Manifesto for the Public University* (pp. 27–41). London: Bloomsbury.

Cassiolato, J., & Couto, M. C. (Eds.). (2015). *Health Innovation Systems, Equity and Development,* e-papers, Río de Janeiro.

Cassiolato, J. E., Lastres, H., & Couto, M. C. (2014). The Brazilian National System of Innovation: Challenges to Sustainability and Inclusive Development. In G. Dutrénit & J. Sutz (Eds.), *National Innovation Systems, Social Inclusion and Development: The Latin American Experience* (pp. 68–101). Cheltenham: Edward Elgar.

Castaldi, C., Cimoli, M., Correa, N., & Dosi, G. (2009). Technological Learning, Policy Regimes, and Growth: The Long-Term Patterns and Some Specificities of a 'Globalized' Economy. In M. Cimoli, G. Dossi, & J. Stiglitz (Eds.), *Industrial Policy and Development: The Political Economy of Capabilities Accumulation* (pp. 39–75). Oxford: Oxford University Press.

Chang, H.-J. (2002). *Kicking away the Ladder: Development Strategy in Historical Perspective.* London: Anthem Press.

Chang, H.-J. (2011). Hamlet Without the Prince of Denmark: How Development Has Disappeared from Today's 'Development' Discourse. In S. Khan & J. Christiansen (Eds.), *Towards New Developmentalism: Market as Means rather than Master* (pp. 47–58). Abingdon: Routledge.

Chataway, J., Hanlin, B., & Kaplisnky, R. (2013). *Inclusive Innovation. An Architecture for Policy Development* (IKD Working Paper No. 65). Milton Keynes: The Open University.

Christensen, J. L., Gregersen, B., Johnson, B., Lundvall, B.-A., & Tomlinson, M. (2008). An NSI in Transition? Denmark. In C. Edquist & L. Hommen (Eds.), *Small Country Innovation Systems Globalization, Change and Policy in Asia and Europe* (pp. 403–441). Cheltenham: Edward Elgar.

Cipolla, C. (1967). *An Economic History of World Population.* Harmondsworth: Penguin.

Clark, B. (1995). *Places of Inquiry: Research and Advanced Education in Modern Universities.* Berkeley: The California University Press.

Clark, B. (1997). The Modern Integration of Research Activities with Teaching and Learning. *The Journal of Higher Education, 68*(3), 241–255.

Clark, B. (1998). *Creating Entrepreneurial Universities: Organizational Pathways of Transformation.* New York: Pergamon Press.

Coleman, J. S. (1986). The Idea of the Developmental University. *Minerva, 24*(4), 476–494.

Collins, R. (2002). *A Global Theory of Intellectual Change.* Cambridge, MA: Harvard University Press.

Collison, C., & Parcell, G. (2001). *Learning to Fly – Practical Lessons from One of the World's Leading Knowledge Companies.* Oxford Capstone.

Cornia, G. A. (2010). Income Distribution under Latin America's New Left Regimes. *Journal of Human Development and Capabilities, 11*(1), 85–114.

Couto, M. C., Scerri, M., & Marhajah, R. (2013). *Inequality and Development Challenges.* London: IDRC-Routledge.

Cozzens, S., & Sutz, J. (2014). Innovation in Informal Settings: Reflections and Proposals for a Research Agenda. *Innovation and Development, 4*(1), 5–31.

Cozzens, S., & Thakur, D. (2014). *Innovation and Inequality. Emerging Technologies in an Unequal World.* New York: Edward Elgar.

Cozzens, S. E., Healey, P., Rip, A., & Ziman, J. (Eds.). (1990). *The Research System in Transition.* Dordrecht: Kluwer Academic Publishers.

Crespi, G., & Dutrenit, G. (2014). *Science, Technology and Innovation Policies for Development: The Latin American Experience.* Dordrecht: Springer.

Currie-Alder, B., Kanbur, R., Malone, D., & Medhora, R. (2014). The State of Development Thought. In B. Currie-Alder, R. Kanbur, D. Malone, & R. Medhora (Eds.), *International Development. Ideas, Experience, and Prospects* (pp. 1–20). New York: Oxford University Press.

D'Este, P., & Perkmann, M. (2007). *Why Do Academics Work with Industry? A Study of the Relationships Between Collaboration Rationales and Channels of Interaction.* Paper presented at the Druid Summer Conference on Appropriability, Proximity, Routines and Innovation, Denmark.

Dahl, R. A. (1982). *Dilemmas of Pluralist Democracy: Autonomy Vs. Control.* New Haven/London: Yale University Press.

Dahl, R. A. (1989). *Democracy and Its Critics.* New Haven: Yale University Press.

Dahler-Larsen, P. (2007). ¿Debemos evaluarlo todo? O de la estimación de la evaluabilidad a la cultura de la evaluación. *Evaluación de Políticas Públicas, 836,* 93–104.

Dahler-Larsen, P. (2013). Evaluation as a Situational or a Universal Good? Why Evaluability Assessment for Evaluation Systems Is a Good Idea, What It Might Look Like in Practice, and Why It Is Not Fashionable. *Scandinavian Journal of Public Administration, 16*(3), 29–46.

Dahlman, C. (2009). Growth and Development in China and India: The Role of Industrial and Innovation Policy in Rapid Catch-Up. In G. Dosi, M. Cimoli, & J. E. Stiglitz (Eds.), *Industrial Policy and Development. The Political Economy of Capabilities Accumulation* (pp. 303–335). Oxford: Oxford University Press.

Dalum, B., Fagerberg, J., & Jorgensen, U. (1988). Small Open Economies in the World Market for Electronics: the Case of the Nordic Countries. In C. Freeman & B.-A. Lundvall (Eds.), *Small Countries Facing Technological Revolution* (pp. 113–138). London: Pinter.

Danish Agency for Science, Technology and Innovation. (2016). *An OECD Horizon Scan on Megatrends and Technology Trends in the Context of Future Research Policy*. Available at: http://ufm.dk/en/publications/2016/files/an-oecd-horizon-scan-of-megatrends-and-technology-trends-in-the-context-of-future-research-policy.pdf. Accessed 10 May 2017.

Dasgupta, P., & David, P. (1994). Toward a New Economics of Science. *Research Policy, 23*(3), 487–521.

David, P. (1985). Clio and the Economics of QWERTY. *The American Economic Review, 75*(2), Papers and Proceedings of the Ninety-Seventh Annual Meeting of the American Economic Association, pp. 332–337.

Davison, R., Harris, R., Qureshi, S., Vogel, D., & de Vreede, G.-J. (Eds.). (2005). *Information Systems in Developing Countries. Theory and Practice.* Hong Kong: City University of Hong Kong Press.

de la Mothe and Paquet, G. (Ed.). (1996). *Evolutionary Economics and the New International Political Economy.* London: Pinter.

de Mello, J. M. C., Maculan, A. M., & Borges Renault, T. (2011). Brazilian Universities and Their Contribution to Innovation and Development. In B. Göransson & C. Brundenius (Eds.), *Universities in Transition. The Changing Role and Challenges for Academic Institutions* (pp. 53–76). Ottawa: Springer.

Deaton, A. (2013). *The Great Escape. Health, Wealth, and the Origins of Inequality.* Princeton: Princeton University Press.

Di Maggio, P., & Powell, W. (1983). The Iron Cage Revisited: Institutional Isomorphism and Collective Rationality in Organizational Fields. *American Sociological Review, 48*(2), 147–160.

Didriksson, A., & de la Fuente, J. R. (2015). Perspectives on the University Social Commitment in the Twenty First Century. In E. Aponte Hernández (Ed.), *La Responsabilidad Social de las Universidades: implicaciones para América Latina y el Caribe* (pp. 33–70). San Juan, Puerto Rico: UNESCO-IESALC.

Dobbins, M., & Knill, C. (2014). *Higher Education Governance and Policy Change in Western Europe. International Challenges to Historical Institutions.* London: Palgrave Macmillan.

Doner, R., & Schneider, B. R. (2016). The Middle-Income Trap: More Politics than Economics. *World Politics, 4,* 608–644.

ECLAC (Economic Commission for Latin America and the Caribbean). (2010). *Time for Equality: Closing Gaps, Opening Trails: Summary* (LC/G.2433(SES.33/4). Santiago, Chile: Economic Commission for Latin America and the Caribbean.

ECLAC (Economic Commission for Latin America and the Caribbean). (2016). *Horizons 2030: Equality at the Centre of Sustainable Development* (LC/G.2660(SES.36/3). Santiago de Chile: Economic Commission for Latin America and the Caribbean.

Edquist, C., & Hommen, L. (1999). Systems of Innovation: Theory and Policy for the Demand Side. *Technology in Society, 21*(1), 63–79.

Edquist, C., & Hommen, L. (Eds.). (2008). *Small Country Innovation Systems. Globalization, Change and Policy in Asia and Europe.* Cheltenham: Edward Elgar.

Enders, J., de Boer, H., & Weyer, E. (2013). Regulatory Autonomy and Performance: The Reform of Higher Education Re-visited. *Higher Education, 65*(1), 5–23.

Etzkowitz, H. (1990). The Second Academic Revolution: The Role of the Research University in Economic Development. In S. E. Cozzens, P. Healey, A. Rip, & J. Ziman (Eds.), *The Research System in Transition* (pp. 109–124). Dordrecht: Kluwer Academic Publishers.

Etzkowitz, H. (1997). The Entrepreneurial University and the Emergence of Democratic Corporatism. In L. Leydesdorff & H. Etzkowitz (Eds.), *Universities and the Global Knowledge Economy* (pp. 141–152). London: Pinter.

Etzkowitz, H. (2004). The Evolution of the Entrepreneurial University. *International Journal of Technology and Globalization, 1*(1), 64–77.

European Commission. (1997). *Building the European Information Society for Us All.* Final Policy Report of the High-Level Expert Group, Brussels.

European Commission. (2012). *Responsible Research and Innovation. Europe's Ability to Respond to Societal Challenges.* Available at: https://ec.europa.eu/research/swafs/pdf/pub_public_engagement/responsible-research-and-innovation-leaflet_en.pdf. Accessed 10 May 2017.

European Commission. (2015). *Call for Tenders: 'Study on Frugal Innovation and Reengineering of Traditional Techniques'.* Available at: https://infoeuropa.eurocid.pt/files/database/000065001-000066000/000065237_2.pdf. Accessed 10 May 2017.

European Commission. (2016). *A Conceptual Analysis of Foundations, Trends and Relevant Potentials in the Field of Frugal Innovation (for Europe).* Interim Report for the Project "Study on frugal innovation and reengineering of traditional techniques" Commissioned to Fraunhofer ISI and Nesta.

Evans, P. (1995). *Embedded Autonomy. States and Industrial Transformation.* Cambridge, MA: Princeton University Press.

Evans, P., & Heller, P. (2015). Human Development, State Transformation and the Politics of the Developmental State. In S. Leibfried, E. Huber, M. Lange, J. Levy, F. Nullmeier, & J. Stephens (Eds.), *The Oxford Handbook of Transformations of the State* (pp. 691–713). Oxford: Oxford University Press.

Fajnzylber, F. (1984). *La industrialización trunca de América Latina*. México D.F.: Centro Editor.

Fayerabend, P. (1988). *Against Method*. London: Verso.

Fein, L. (1959). The Role of the University in Computers, Data Processing, and Related Fields. *Communications of the ACM, 2*(9), 7–12.

Fischer, J. (2015). *Knowledge Compromise(d)? Ways and Values of Coproduction in Academia*. Doctoral dissertation, Lund University.

Flanagan, K., Uyarra, E., & Laranja, M. (2011). Reconceptualising the 'Policymix' for Innovation. *Research Policy, 40*(5), 702–713.

Foro Consultivo Científico Tecnológico y Academia Nacional Mexicana de Ciencias. (2005). *Una Reflexión sobre el Sistema Nacional de Investigadores a 20 Años de su Creación*. Available at: http://www.coniunctus.amc.edu.mx/libros/20_sni_final.pdf. Accessed 10 May 2017.

Foster, C., & Heeks, R. (2013). Innovation and Scaling of ICT for the Bottom-of-the-Pyramid. *Journal of Information Technology, 28*(4), 296–315.

Frederiksen, L. F., Hansson, F., & Wenneberg, S. B. (2003). The Agora and the Role of Research Evaluation. *Evaluation, 9*(2), 149–172.

Freeman, C. (1977). Malthus with a Computer. In A. Teich (Ed.), *Technology and Man's Future* (pp. 82–98). New York: St. Martin's Press.

Freeman, C. (1982). *The Economics of Industrial Innovation* (2nd ed.). London: Pinter.

Freeman, C. (1987). *Technology Policy and Economic Performance – Lessons from Japan*. London: Pinter Publishers.

Freeman, C. (1988). Technology Gaps, International Trade and the Problems of Smaller and Less Developed Countries. In C. Freeman & B.-A. Lundvall (Eds.), *Small Countries Facing Technological Revolution* (pp. 37–66). London: Pinter.

Freeman, C. (1992). Science and Economy at the National Level. In C. Freeman (Ed.), *The Economics of Hope* (pp. 31–49). London: Pinter Publishers.

Freeman, C. (1996). Catching Up and Falling Behind: The Case of Asia and Latin America. In J. de la Mothe & G. Paquet (Eds.), *Evolutionary Economics and the New International Political Economy* (pp. 160–179). London: Pinter.

Freeman, C., & Lundvall, B.-A. (Eds.). (1988). *Small Countries Facing Technological Revolution*. London: Pinter.

Freeman, C., & Soete, L. (1997). *The Economics of Industrial Innovation* (3rd ed.). Cambridge, MA: The MIT Press.

Fuchs, R. (1998, June). *"Little Engines that Did": Case Histories from the Global Telecentre Movement, IDRC*. Available at: https://idl-bnc-idrc.dspacedirect.org/bitstream/handle/10625/12989/108350.pdf?sequence=1. Accessed 15 May 2017.

Garud, R., & Karnøe, P. (2003). Bricolage Versus Breakthrough: Distributed and Embedded Agency in Technological Entrepreneurship. *Research Policy, 32*, 277–300.

Geels, F. W. (2010). Ontologies, Socio-Technical Transitions (to Sustainability), and the Multi-Level Perspective. *Research Policy, 39*(4), 495–510.

Geels, F. W. (2014). From Sectoral Systems of Innovation to Socio-Technical Systems Insights About Dynamics and Change from Sociology and Institutional Theory. *Research Policy, 33*(6–7), 897–920.

Gerth, H., & Wright, C. (1991). *From Max Weber.* Oxford: Routledge.

Gibbons, M., Limoges, C., Nowotny, H., Schwartzman, S., Scott, P., & Trow, M. (1994). *The New Production of Knowledge.* London: SAGE Publications.

Gibson, C., Andersson, K., Ostrom, E., & Shivakumar, S. (2005). *The Samaritan's Dilemma: The Political Economy of Development Aid.* Oxford: Oxford University Press.

Gläser, J. (2010). From Governance to Authority Relations? In R. Whitley, J. Gläser, & L. Engwall (Eds.), *Reconfiguring Knowledge Production: Changing Authority Relationships in the Sciences and Their Consequences for Intellectual Innovation* (pp. 357–369). New York: Oxford University Press.

Gläser, J. (2012). *How Does Governance Change Research Content? On the Possibility of a Sociological Middle-Range Theory Linking Science Policy Studies to the Sociology of Scientific Knowledge.* The Technical University Technology Studies Working Papers, TUTS-WP-1. Available at: https://www.ts.tu-berlin.de/fileadmin/fg226/TUTS/TUTS-WP-1-2012.pdf. Accessed 10 May 2017.

Goddard, J., Hazelkorn, H., Kempton, L., & Vallance, P. (2016). Introduction: Why the Civic University? In J. Goddard, H. Hazelkorn, L. Kempton, & P. Vallance (Eds.), *The Civic University. The Policy and Leadership Challenges* (pp. 3–15). Cheltenham: Edward Elgar.

Gokhberg, L., Kuznetsova, T., & Zaichenko, S. (2011). Russia: Universities in the Context of Reforming the National Innovation System. In B. Göransson & C. Brundenius (Eds.), *Universities in Transition. The Changing Role and Challenges for Academic Institutions* (pp. 247–260). Ottawa: Springer.

Göransson, B. (1993). *Catching Up in Technology—Case Studies from the Telecommunications Equipment Industry.* London: Taylor Graham.

Göransson, B., & Brundenius, C. (Eds.). (2011). *Universities in Transition. The Changing Role and Challenges for Academic Institutions.* Ottawa: Springer.

Government Bill. (2012). Research and Innovation—A Summary of Government Bill 2012/13:30. Government Offices of Sweden

Granath, J. (1998). *Torslanda to Uddevalla via Kalmar: A Journey in Production Practices at Volvo.* Presented at Seminário Internacional Reestruturação Produtiva, Flexibilidade do Trabalho e Novas Competências Profissionais COPPE/UFRJ, Rio de Janeiro, Brasil. Accesible at: https://www.academia.edu/5495539/Torslanda_to_Uddevalla_via_Kalmar_A_journey_in_production_practice_in_Volvo. Accessed 10 May 2017.

Gregersen, B. (2017). Role of Universities for Inclusive Development and Social Innovation: Experiences from Denmark. In C. Brundenius, B. Göransson, & J. M. Carvalho de Mello (Eds.), *Universities, Inclusive Development and Social Innovation. An International Perspective* (pp. 369–386). Ottawa: Springer.

Gregersen, B., & Rasmussen, G. (2011). Developing Universities: The Evolving Role of Academic Institutions in Denmark. In B. Göransson & C. Brundenius (Eds.), *Universities in Transition. The Changing Role and Challenges for Academic Institutions* (pp. 283–306). Ottawa: Springer.

Gronning, T., Moen, S. E., & Sutherland, D. (2008). Low Innovation Intensity, High Growth and Specialized Trajectories. In C. Edquist & L. Hommen (Eds.), *Small Country Innovation Systems Globalization, Change and Policy in Asia and Europe* (pp. 281–318). Cheltenham: Edward Elgar.

Group of Eight. (2011). *Role of Universities in the Innovation Systems* (Discussion Paper). Available at: https://www.go8.edu.au/publication/role-universities-national-innovation-system. Accessed 10 May 2017.

Guarga, R., Mastrangelo, P., Scaglione, G., & Supino, E. (2000). Evaluation of the SIS, a New Frost Protection Method Applied in a Citrus Orchard. In *Proceedings of the 9th Congress of the International Society of Citriculture* (p. 583), Orlando, USA.

Haiyan, W., & Yuan, Z. (2011). China: Challenges for Higher Education in a High Growth Economy. In B. Göransson & C. Brundenius (Eds.), *Universities in Transition. The Changing Role and Challenges for Academic Institutions* (pp. 143–170). Ottawa: Springer.

Halffman, W., & Radder, H. (2015). The Academic Manifesto: From an Occupied to a Public University. *Minerva, 53*(2), 165–187.

Hammarfelt, B., & de Rijcke, S. (2015). Accountability in Context: Effects of Research Evaluation Systems on Publication Practices, Disciplinary Norms, and Individual Working Routines in the Faculty of Arts at Uppsala University. *Research Evaluation, 24*(1), 63–77.

Hazelkorn, E. (2007). How Do Rankings Impact on Higher Education?, OECD Programme on Institutional Management in Higher Education.

Hazelkorn, E. (2009). Impact of Global Rankings on Higher Education Research and the Production of Knowledge. *UNESCO Forum on Higher Education, Research and Knowledge* (Occasional Paper 18). Paris: UNESCO.

Hazelkorn, E., & Ryan, M. (2013). The Impact of University Rankings on Higher Education Policy in Europe: A Challenge to Perceived Wisdom and a Stimulus for Change. In P. Zgaga, U. Teichler, & J. Brennan (Eds.), *The Globalization Challenge for European Higher Education: Convergence and Diversity, Centres and Peripheries* (pp. 79–100). Frankfurt: Peter Lang.

Heeks, R. (2013). Conceptualizing Inclusive Innovation: Modifying Systems of Innovation Frameworks to Understand Diffusion of New Technology to Low-Income Countries. *European Journal of Development Research, 25*, 333–355.

Heeks, R., Foster, C., & Nugroho, Y. (2014). New Models of Inclusive Innovation for Development. *Innovation and Development, 4*(2), 175–183.

Held, D., & Kaya, A. (Eds.). (2007). *Global Inequality. Patterns and Explanations.* Cambridge, UK: Polity Press.

Hess, D. (2007). *Alternative Pathways in Science and Industry. Activism, Innovation, and the Environment in an Era of Globalization*. Cambridge, MA: The MIT Press.

Heyer, J., Stewart, F., & Thorp, R. (2002). *Group Behaviour and Development. Is the Market Destroying Cooperation?* Oxford: Oxford University Press.

Hicks, D. (2006). The Dangers of Partial Bibliometric Evaluation in the Social Sciences. *Economia Politica, XXIII*(2), 145–162.

Hicks, D. (2012). Performance-Based University Research Funding Systems. *Research Policy, 41*(2), 251–261.

Hicks, D. (2013). One Size Doesn't Fit All: On the Co-evolution of National Evaluation Systems and Social Science Publishing. *Confero, 1*(1), 67–90.

Hicks, D., Wouters, P., Waltman, L., de Rijcke, S., & Rafols, I. (2015). The Leiden Manifesto for Research Metrics. *Nature, 520*(23), 429–431.

Hirschman, A. (1958). *The Strategy of Economic Development*. New Haven: Yale University Press.

Hirschman, A. (1981). *Essays in Trespassing. Economics to Politics and Beyond*. Cambridge: Cambridge University Press.

Hodgson, G. M. (2001). *Economics and Utopia. Why the Learning Economy Is Not the End of History*. Hoboken: Taylor and Francis e-Library.

Hodgson, G. M. (2015a). Conceptualizing Capitalism: How the Misuse of Key Concepts Impedes our Understanding of Modern Economies. *BooksandIdeas. net*. Available at: http://www.booksandideas.net/IMG/pdf/20150507_conceptualizing_capitalism.pdf. Accessed 10 May 2017.

Hodgson, G. M. (2015b). *Conceptualizing Capitalism. Institutions, Evolution, Future*. Chicago: The University of Chicago Press.

Holmwood, J. (2011). Introduction. In J. Holmwood (Ed.), *A Manifesto for the Public University* (pp. 1–11). London: Bloomsbury.

Howard, R. (2005). Utopia: Where Workers Craft New Technology. *Technology Review, 88*(3). Reprinted in Z. Pylyshyn & L. Banon (Eds.). (1989). *Perspectives in the Computer Revolution* (pp. 341–350). Ablex Publishing Co.

Howard, T. A. (2006). *Protestant Theology and the Making of the Modern German University*. Oxford/New York: Oxford University Press.

Hubert, A. (2010). *Empowering People, Driving Change: Social Innovation in the European Union*. Report to the European Commission, BEPA, Luxenbourg.

IESALC. (2008). *Declaration of the Regional Conference of Higher Education of Latin America and the Caribbean*. Caracas: UNESCO-IESALC.

Iizuka, M., & Sadre Ghazi, S. (2012). *Understanding Dynamics of Pro-poor Innovation: Mapping the Disputed Areas*. Paper presented at the Dynamics of Institution and Markets in Europe (DIME) Final Conference, 6–8 April 2011, Maastricht.

ILO. (2016). *Non-standard Employment Around the World*. Geneva. Available at: http://www.ilo.org/global/publications/books/WCMS_534326/lang--en/index.htm. Accessed 10 May 2017.

ISSC, IDS and UNESCO. (2016). *World Social Science Report 2016, Challenging Inequalities: Pathways to a Just World.* Paris: UNESCO Publishing.

Jasanoff, S. (2003). Technologies of Humility: Citizen Participation in Governing Science. *Minerva, 41,* 223–244.

Jensen, M., Johnson, B., Lorenz, E., & Lundvalll, B. A. (2007). Forms of Knowledge and Modes of Innovation. *Research Policy, 36,* 680–693.

Johnson, C. (1982). *MITI and the Japanese Miracle. The Growth on Industrial Policy 1925–1975.* Stanford: Stanford University Press.

Johnson, B., & Andersen, A. D. (2012). *Learning, Innovation and Inclusive Development.* Globelics Thematic Report No 1, Denmark. Available at: http://vbn.aau.dk/files/70880770/Learning_Innovation_and_Inclusive_Development.pdf. Accessed 10 May 2017.

Jongbloed, B., Enders, J., & Salerno, C. (2008). Higher Education and Its Communities: Interconnections, Interdependencies and a Research Agenda. *Higher Education, 56*(3), 303–324.

Judt, T. (2008). *Reappraisals. Reflections on the Forgotten Twentieth Century.* New York: The Penguin Press.

Kaitila, V., & Kotilainen, M. (2008). Not Just Nokia: Finland. In C. Edquist & L. Hommen (Eds.), *Small Country Innovation Systems Globalization, Change and Policy in Asia and Europe* (pp. 355–402). Cheltenham: Edward Elgar.

Khan, M., & Blankenburg, S. (2009). The Political Economy of Industrial Policy in Asia and Latin America. In G. Dosi, M. Cimoli, & J. E. Stiglitz (Eds.), *Industrial Policy and Development: The Political Economy of Capabilities Accumulation* (pp. 336–377). Oxford: Oxford University Press.

Kohli, A. (2003). Democracy and Development: Trends and Prospects. In A. Kohli, C.-I. Moon, & G. Sørensen (Eds.), *States, Markets and Just Growth : Development in the Twenty-First Century* (pp. 39–63). New York: The United Nations University.

Kraemer-Mbula, E., & Wunsch-Vincent, S. (Eds.). (2016). *Informal Economy in Developing Nations. Hidden Engine of Innovation?* Cambridge, UK: Cambridge University Press.

Kranzberg, M. (1967). The Unity of Science. *American Scientist, 55*(1), 48–66.

Kronman, U. (2013). Managing Your Assets in the Publication Economy. *Confero, 1*(1), 91–128.

Lage, A. (2011). Global Pharmaceutical Development and Access: Critical Issues of Ethics and Equity. *MEDICC Review, 13*(3), 16–22.

Lamont, M. (2009). *How Professors Think. Inside the Curious World of Academic Judgment.* Cambridge, MA: Harvard University Press.

Landaverde, M., Di Fabio, J. L., Ruocco, G., Leal, I., y de Quadros, C. (1999). Introducción de la vacuna conjugada contra Hib en Chile y Uruguay. *Rev Panam Salud Publica, 5*(3), Washington. Available at: http://www.scielosp.org/pdf/rpsp/v5n3/top200.pdf. Accessed 10 May 2017.

266   REFERENCES

Landinelli, J. (2008). Scenarios of Diversification, Differentiation, and Segmentation of Higher Education in Latin America and the Caribbean. In A. L. Gazzolla & A. Didriksson (Eds.), *Trends in Higher Education in Latin America and the Caribbean.* Caracas: IESALC-UNESCO.

Langrish, J., Gibbons, M., Evans, W. G., & Jevons, F. R. (1972). *Wealth from Knowledge: A Study of Innovation in Industry.* New York: Halsted/John Willey.

Lazonick, W., & Mazzucato, M. (2012). *The Risk-Reward Nexus. Innovation, Finance and Inclusive Growth.* Policy Network Paper, New York.

Lemola, T., & Lovio, R. (1988). Possibilities for a Small Country in High-Technology Production: The Case of Finland. In C. Freeman & B.-A. Lundvall (Eds.), *Small Countries Facing Technological Revolution* (pp. 139–155). London: Pinter.

Levine, P. (2007). Collective Action, Civic Engagement, and the Knowledge Commons. In C. Hess & E. Ostrom (Eds.), *Understanding Knowledge as Commons. From Theory to Practice* (pp. 247–275). Cambridge, USA: The MIT Press.

Lewis, J. M. (2015). The Politics and Consequences of Performance Measurement. *Policy and Society, 34,* 1–12.

Leydesdorff, L., & Van Den Besselaar, P. (1987). What We Have Learned from the Amsterdam Science Shop. In S. Blume, J. Bunders, L. Leydesdroff, & R. Whitley (Eds.), *The Social Direction of the Public Sciences* (pp. 135–162). Dordrecht: D. Reidel Publishing Co.

Long, N. (2001). *Development Sociology. Actor Perspectives.* London: Routledge.

Lorenz, E., & Valeyre, A. (2007). Organizational Forms and Innovative Performance: A Comparison of the EU-15. In E. Lorenz & B. A. Lundvalll (Eds.), *How Europe's Economies Learn. Coordinating Competing Models* (pp. 227, 248). Oxford: Oxford University Press.

Lundell, P. (2005). *Designing Democracy: The UTOPIA-Project and the Role of Labour Movement in Technological Change, 1981—1986, Working Paper No 52.* Stockholm: The Royal Institute of Technology, Centre of Excellence for Studies in Science and Innovation.

Lundvall, B. Å. (1985). *Product Innovation and User-Producer Interaction* (Industrial Development Research Series No. 31). Aalborg: Aalborg University Press.

Lundvall, B. Å. (1988). Innovation as an Interactive Process: from User-Producer Interaction to the National System of Innovation. In G. Dosi, C. Freeman, R. Nelson, G. Silverberg, & L. Soete (Eds.), *Technical Change and Economic Theory* (pp. 349–369). London: Pinter.

Lundvall, B. Å. (Ed.). (1992). *National Systems of Innovation. Towards a Theory of Innovation and Interactive Learning.* London: Pinter.

Lundvall, B. Å. (2002). *Innovation, Growth and Social Cohesion. The Danish Model.* Cheltenham, UK: Elgar.

Lundvall, B. Å. (2007). National Innovation Systems—Analytical Concept and Development Tool. *Industry and Innovation, 14*(1), 95–119.

Lundvall, B. Å. (2010). Postscript: Innovation System Research – Where It Comes from and Where It Might Go. In B. A. Lundvalll (Ed.), *National Systems of Innovation. Towards a Theory of Innovation and Interactive Learning* (pp. 317–366). London: Anthem Press.

Lundvall, B. Å. (2016). Innovation Systems and Development: History, Theory and Challenges. In E. Reinert, J. Ghosh, & R. Kattel (Eds.), *Handbook of Alternative Theories of Economic Development* (pp. 594–612). Cheltenham: Edward Elgar.

Lundvall, B. Å., & Borrás, S. (1997). *The Globalising Learning Economy: Implications for Innovation Policy.* Policy document of the Targeted Socio-Economic Research Program, European Commission, Bruxelles.

Lundvall, B.-Å., & Johnson, B. (1994). The Learning Economy. *Industry and Innovation, 1*(2), 23–42.

Lundvall, B. Å., Joseph, K. J., Chaminade, C., & Vang, J. (2011). *Handbook of Innovation Systems and Developing Countries: Building Domestic Capabilities in a Global Setting.* Northampton: Edward Elgar.

Maclaine Pont, P., van Est, Q., & Deuten, J. (2016). *Shaping Socio-Technical Innovation Through Policy -Essay Commissioned by the Department of Knowledge, Innovation and Strategy of the Dutch Ministry of Infrastructure and the Environment.* The Hague: Rathenau Instituut.

Mani, S. (2005). *Keeping Pace with Globalization. Innovation Capability in Korea's Telecommunications Equipment Industry, Working Paper 370.* Maastricht: UNU-INTECH.

Mann, M. (1986). *The Sources of Social Power, Vol. I, A History of Power from the Beginning to AD 1760.* Cambridge: Cambridge University Press.

Mann, M. (1993). *The Sources of Social Power, Vol. II: The Rise of Classes and Nation-States, 1760–1914.* Cambridge: Cambridge University Press.

Mann, M. (2006). The Sources of Social Power Revisited: A Response to Criticism. In J. Hall & R. Schroeder (Eds.), *An Anatomy of Power. The Social Theory of Michael Mann* (pp. 343–396). Cambridge: Cambridge University Press.

Mann, M. (2012). *The Sources of Social Power, Vol. III (2012): Global Empires and Revolution, 1890–1945.* Cambridge: Cambridge University Press.

Mann, M. (2013a). *The Sources of Social Power. Vol. IV Globalizations, 1945–2011.* Cambridge: Cambridge University Press.

Mann, M. (2013b). The End May Be Nigh, but for Whom? In I. Wallerstein, R. Collins, M. Mann, G. Derluguian, & C. Calhoun (Eds.), *Does Capitalism Have a Future?* (pp. 71–97). New York: Oxford University Press.

Mann, M. (2016). Response to the Critics. In R. Schroeder (Ed.), *Global Powers. Michael Mann's Anatomy of the Twentieth Century and Beyond* (pp. 281–322). Cambridge, UK: Cambridge University Press.

Marglin, S. A. (1974). What Do Bosses Do?: The Origins and Functions of Hierarchy in Capitalist Production. *Review of Radical Political Economics*, 6, 60–127.

Martin, B. (2010). Inside the Public Scientific System: Changing Modes of Knowledge Production. In R. Smits, S. Kuhlmann, & P. Shapira (Eds.), *The Theory and Practice of Innovation Policy* (pp. 25–50). Cheltenham, UK: Edward Elgar.

Martin, B., & Whitley, R. (2010). The UK Research Assessment Exercise: A Case of Regulatory Capture? In R. Whitley, J. Gläser, & L. Engwall (Eds.), *Reconfiguring Knowledge Production: Changing Authority Relationships in the Sciences and Their Consequences for Intellectual Innovation* (pp. 51–79). New York: Oxford University Press.

Mazzoleni, R., & Nelson, R. (2007). Public Research Institutions and Economic Catch-Up. *Research Policy*, 36, 1512–1528.

Mazzoleni, R., & Nelson, R. (2009). The Roles of Research at Universities and Public Labs in Economic Catch-Up. In G. Dosi, M. Cimoli, & J. E. Stiglitz (Eds.), *Industrial Policy and Development. The Political Economy of Capabilities Accumulation* (pp. 378–408). Oxford: Oxford University Press.

Mazzucato, M., & Penna, C. (2015). *The Brazilian Innovation System: A Mission-Oriented Policy Proposal*. Brasília, DF: Centro de Gestão e Estudos Estratégicos.

Merton, R. (1968). The Matthew Effect on Science. *Science*, 159(3810), 56–63.

Merton, R. (1973). The Normative Structure of Science. In R. Merton (Ed.), *The Sociology of Science: Theoretical and Empirical Investigations* (pp. 267–280). Chicago: The University of Chicago Press.

Metropolis, N., Howlett, J., & Rota, G. C. (Eds.). (1985). *A History of Computing in the Twentieth Century*. New York: Academic Press.

Milanović, B. (2011). *The Haves and the Have-Nots. A Brief and Idiosyncratic History of Global Inequality*. New York: Basic Books.

Milanović, B. (2016). *Global in Equality: A New Approach for the Age of Globalization*. Cambridge, MA: Harvard University Press.

Mills, C. W. (1971). *The Sociological Imagination*. London: Pelican Books (Original: 1959).

Mokyr, J. (1990). *The Lever of Riches: Technological Creativity and Economic Progress*. New York: Oxford University Press.

Mokyr, J. (2002). *The Gifts of Athena. Historical Origins of the Knowledge Economy*. Princeton: Princeton University Press.

Mokyr, J. (2005a). Long-Term Economic Growth and the History of Technology. In P. Aghion & S. Durlauf (Eds.), *Handbook of Economic Growth, Vol. 1, Part 2* (pp. 1113–1181). Amsterdam: Elsevier.

Mokyr, J. (2005b). The Intellectual Origins of Modern Economic Growth. *The Journal of Economic History*, 65(2), 285–351.

Molas-Gallart, J., & Castro-Martínez, E. (2007). Ambiguity and Conflict in the Development of "Third Mission" Indicators. *Research Evaluation*, 16(4), 321–330.

Morel, C. (2003). Neglected Diseases: Under-Funded Research and Inadequate Health Interventions, EMBO Reports, Special issue. Available at: https://www.ncbi.nlm.nih.gov/pmc/articles/PMC1326440/. Accessed 10 May 2017.

Mosha, H. J. (1986). The Role of African Universities in National Development: A Critical Analysis. *Comparative Education, 22*(2), 93–109.

Moulton, J. (2016, September). *The Deep Structure of STI Indicators: Contextual Knowledge and Scientometrics.* Key-Note speech, 21th International Conference on STI Indicators, Valencia, Spain.

Mowery, D., & Rosenberg, N. (1998). *Paths of Innovation. Technological Change in 20th-Century America.* New York: Cambridge University Press.

Mowery, D., & Sampat, B. (2005). Universities in National Innovation Systems. In J. Fagerberg, D. Mowery, & R. Nelson (Eds.), *The Oxford Handbook of Innovation* (pp. 209–239). Oxford: Oxford University Press.

Müller, S. (1996). The Advent of the University of Calculation. In J. Müller (Ed.), *Universities in the Twenty-First Century* (pp. 15–23). Oxford: Berghahn Books.

Muller, J. (2010). *Befit for Change: Social Construction of Endogenous Technology in the South.* FAU conference, Gjerrild.

Munch, R. (2014). *Academic Capitalism. Universities in the Global Struggle for Excellence.* London: Routledge.

Murray, F. (2006). *The Oncomouse that Roared: Resistance and Accommodation to Patenting in Academic Science.* Paper presented at the Toronto Conference "Bringing Science to Life". Available at: http://fmurray.scripts.mit.edu/docs/THE_ONCOMOUSE_THAT_ROARED_FINAL.pdf. Accessed 10 May 2017

Mwamila, B. L. M., & Diyamett, B. D. (2011). Tanzania: The Evolving Role of Universities in Economic Development. In B. Göransson & C. Brundenius (Eds.), *Universities in Transition. The Changing Role and Challenges for Academic Institutions* (pp. 171–191). Ottawa: Springer.

National Science Board. (2010). Global Higher Education and Work-Force Trends. In *Science and Engineering Indicators 2010.* Washington, DC: National Science Board.

National Science Board. (2016). *Science and Engineering Indicators 2016.* Washington, DC: National Science Board.

Neave, G. (1998). The Evaluative State Reconsidered. *European Journal of Education, 33*(3), 265–284.

Nelson, R. (1993). *National Innovation Systems.* Cary: Oxford University Press.

Nelson, R., & Winter, S. (1982). *An Evolutionary Theory of Economic Change.* Cambridge: The Belknap Press of Harvard University Press.

Nelson, R., & Rosenberg, N. (1994). American Universities and Technical Advance in Industry. *Policy Research, 3,* 323–348.

Newfield, C. (2008). *Unmaking the Public University. The Forty-Year Assault on the Middle Class.* Cambridge: Harvard University Press.

Newfield, C. (2016). *The Great Mistake. How We Wrecked Public Universities and How We Can Fix Them.* Baltimore: John Hopkins University Press.

NIH, National Institutes of Health. (2017). *What We Do. Budget.* https://www.nih.gov/about-nih/what-we-do/budget. Accessed 8 May 2017

Noble, D. (1977). *America by Design. Science, Technology and the Rise of Corporate Capitalism.* New York: Knopf Books.

Noble, D. (1979). Social Choice in Machine Design: The Case of Numerically Controlled Machine Tools. In A. Zimbalist (Ed.), *Case Studies on the Labour Process* (pp. 18–50). New York: Monthly Review Press.

North, D. (1997). *Some Fundamental Puzzles in Economic History/Development.* Indiana University Working Paper Series. Available at: http://econwpa.repec.org/eps/eh/papers/9509/9509001.pdf. Accessed 10 May 2017.

North, D. (2005). *Understanding the Process of Economic Change.* Princeton: Princeton University Press.

Nowotny, H. (n.d.). *The Potential of Transdisciplinarity.* Available at: http://www.helga-nowotny.eu/downloads/helga_nowotny_b59.pdf. Accessed 9 May 2017.

Nowotny, H. (2016). *The Cunning of Uncertainty.* Cambridge, UK: Polity.

Nowotny, H., Scott, P., & Gibbons, M. (2001). *Re-thinking Science. Knowledge and the Public in an Age of Uncertainty.* Cambridge, UK: Polity Press.

NSF. (2016). *Science and Engineering Indicators 2016* (p. 454).

Núñez, J., Montalvo, L. F., Pérez Ones, I., Fernández, A., & García Cuevas, J. L. (2011). Cuba: University, Innovation and Society: Higher Education in the National System of Innovation. In B. Göransson & C. Brundenius (Eds.), *Universities in Transition. The Changing Role and Challenges for Academic Institutions* (pp. 97–118). Ottawa: Springer.

Nussbaum, M. (2011). *Creating Capabilities. The Human Development Approach.* Cambridge, MA: Harvard University Press.

OECD. (2011). *Demand-Side Innovation Policies.* Paris: OECD Publishing.

OECD. (2013). *Organization for Economic Cooperation and Development, "Innovation for Inclusive Growth: Conference Discussion Report".* Paris: OECD Publishing.

OECD. (2017). *Main Science and Technology Indicators.* Paris: OECD Publishing.

Ostrom, E. (1990/2008). *Governing the Commons. The Evolution of Institutions for Collective Action.* New York: Cambridge University Press.

Ostrom, E. (1996). Crossing the Great Divide: Coproduction, Synergy, and Development. *World Development, 24*(6), 1073–1087.

OXFAM. (2016). *An Economy for the 1%. How Privilege and Power in the Economy Drive Extreme Inequality and How This Can Be Stopped.* Oxford: Oxfam GB.

Papaioannou, T. (2014). How Inclusive Can Innovation and Development Be in the Twenty-First Century? *Innovation and Development, 4*(2), 187–202.

PEDECIBA. (2004). *Criterios, herramientas y procedimientos generales para la evaluación de la actividad académica de los investigadores.* Available at: http://www.pedeciba.edu.uy/docspd/CritEvalInv04.pdf. Accessed 12 July 2016.

Pérez, C. (1985). Microelectronics, Long Waves and World Structural Change: New Perspectives for Developing Countries. *World Development*, *13*(3), 441–463.

Piketty, T. (2014). *Capital in the XXI Century*. Cambridge, MA: Harvard University Press.

Pisano, U., Lange, L., & Berger, G. (2015). *Social Innovation in Europe. An Overview of the Concept of Social Innovation in the Context of European Initiatives and Practices*. ESDN Quarterly Report, 36. Vienna: ESDN.

Plaza, B. (2000). Política Industrial de la Comunidad Autónoma del País Vasco 1981–2001. *Economía Industrial*, *235*(236), 299–314.

Porter, M. (1990). *The Competitive Advantage of Nations*. New York: The Free Press.

Power, M. (1999). *The Audit Society. Rituals of Verification*. Oxford: Oxford University Press.

Ràfols, I., Molas-Gallart, J., Chavarro, D., & Robinson-García, N. (2016, June 2–3). On the Dominance of Quantitative Evaluation in "Peripheral" Countries: Auditing Research with Technologies of Distance. Paper presented at *Excellence policies in science*, Leiden.

Reay, D. (2011). Universities and the Reproduction of Inequality. In J. Holmwood (Ed.), *A Manifesto for the Public University* (pp. 112–126). London: Bloomsbury.

Reddy, P. (2011). The Evolving Role of Universities in Economic Development. In B. Göransson & C. Brundenius (Eds.), *Universities in Transition. The Changing Role and Challenges for Academic Institutions* (pp. 25–49). Ottawa: Springer.

Reich, R. (1992). *The Work of Nations*. New York: Alfred A Knopf.

Reinert, E. S. (2007). *How Rich Countries Got Rich and Why Poor Countries Stay Poor*. New York: Public Affairs.

Rhoades, G., Maldonado, A., Ordorika, I., & Velázques, M. (2004). Imagining Alternatives to Global, Corporate, New Economy Academic Capitalism. *Policy Futures in Education*, *2*(2), 316–329.

RICYT. (2001). Red Iberoamericana de Indicadores de Ciencia y Tecnología. Standardisation of Indicators of Technological Innovation in Latin American and Caribbean Countries. BOGOTA MANUAL. Available at: http://www.ricyt.org/manuales/doc_view/149-bogota-manual. Accssed 10 May 2017.

RICYT. (2017). *Red Iberoamericana de Indicadores de Ciencia y Tecnología*. Available at: http://www.ricyt.org/indicadores. Accessed 10 May 2017.

Rodrik, D. (2007). *One Economics, Many Recipes: Globalization, Institutions, and Economic Growth*. Princeton: Princeton University Press.

Rodrik, D. (2011). *The Globalization Paradox: Democracy and the Future of the World Economy*. New York/London: W.W. Norton.

Rogers, E. M. (1995). *Diffusion of Innovations* (4th ed.). New York: Free Press.

Roper, C. D., & Hirth, M. A. (2005). A History of Change in the Third Mission of Higher Education: The Evolution of One-Way Service to Interactive Engagement. *Journal of Higher Education Outreach and Engagement*, *10*(3), 3–21.

Rose, H., & Rose, S. (1972). *The Radicalization of Science. Socialist Register, 9,* 105–132.

Rosenberg, N. (1976). Technological Change in the Machine Tool Industry, 1840–1910. In N. Rosenberg (Ed.), *Perspectives on Technology* (pp. 9–31). Cambridge: Cambridge University Press.

Roser, M. (2015). Life Expectancy. *Published online at OurWorldInData.org.* Accesible at: http://ourworldindata.org/data/population-growth-vital-statistics/life-expectancy/. Accessed 10 May 2017.

Roser, M., & Ortiz-Ospina, E. (2016). Literacy. *Published online at OurWorldInData.org.* Available at: http://ourworldindata.org/data/education-knowledge/literacy/. Accessed 10 May 2017.

Rothwell, R., Freeman, C., Horlsey, A., Jervis, V., Robertson, A., & Towsend, J. (1974). SAPPHO Updated. Project Sappho Phase II. *Research Policy, 3,* 258–291.

Rüegg, W. (1992). Foreword. In H. d. Ridder-Symoens (Ed.), *A History of the University in Europe, Volume 1: Universities in the Middle Ages.* Cambridge: Cambridge University Press.

Ruger, J. P. (2006). Ethics and Governance of Global Health Inequalities. *Journal of Epidemiology and Community Health, 60*(11), 998–1002.

Sabato, J. (Ed.). (1975). *El pensamiento latinoamericano en la problemática ciencia – tecnología – desarrollo – dependencia.* Buenos Aires: Editorial PAIDOS.

Sabato, J., & Botana, N. (1968). La ciencia y la tecnología en el desarrollo futuro de América Latina. *Revista de la Integración* 3 (Buenos Aires).

Sarewitz, D., & Pielke, R. A. (2007). The Neglected Heart of Science: Reconciling Supply and Demand for Science. *Environmental Science and Policy, 10,* 5–16.

Sartori, G. (1987). *The Theory of Democracy Revisited.* New Jersey: Chatham House Publishers.

SCB. (2015). Statistics Sweden, *Research and Development in Sweden 2013.* UF 16 SM 1501 (in Swedish).

Schmoch, U. (2011). Germany: The Role of Universities in the Learning Economy. In B. Göransson & C. Brundenius (Eds.), *Universities in Transition. The Changing Role and Challenges for Academic Institutions* (pp. 261–282). Ottawa: Springer.

Schot, J., & Kanger, L. (2016). Deep Transitions: Emergence, Acceleration, Stabilization and Directionality. *SPRU Working Papers,* 2016–15.

Schot, J., & Steinmueller, E. (2016). Framing Innovation Policy for Transformative Change: Innovation Policy 3.0. SPRU Draft. Available at: http://www.johanschot.com/wordpress/wp-content/uploads/2016/09/Framing-Innovation-Policy-for-Transformative-Change-Innovation-Policy-3.0-2016.pdf. Accessed 10 May 2017.

Schroeder, R. (2007). *Rethinking Science, Technology, and Social Change.* Stanford, CA: Stanford University Press.

Schwandt, T. A. (2012). Quality, Standards and Accountability: An Uneasy Alliance. *Education Inquiry, 3*(2), 217–224.

Schwartzman, S. (2008). Introducción. Educación Superior, Investigación Científica e Innovación en América Latina. In S. Schwartzman (Ed.), *Universidad y desarrollo en Latinoamérica: experiencias exitosas de centros de investigación* (pp. 1–25). Bogotá: IESALC-UNESCO.

Sen, A. (1999). *Development as Freedom.* New York: Anchor Books.

Sen, A. (2000). Social Exclusion: Concept, Application and Scrutiny. *Social Development Papers, 1,* Asian Development Bank.

Sen, A. (2013). The Ends and Means of Sustainability. *Journal of Human Development and Capabilities, 141,* 6–20.

Shapira, P., Smits, R., & Kuhlmann, S. (2010). An Outlook on Innovation Policy, Theory and Practice. In R. Smits, S. Kuhlmann, & P. Shapira (Eds.), *The Theory and Practice of Innovation Policy* (pp. 449–466). Cheltenham, UK: Edward Elgar.

Singer, H., Cooper, C., Desai, R. C., Freeman, C., Gish, O., Hill, S., & Oldham, G. (1970). *The Sussex Manifesto: Science and Technology to Developing Countries During the Second Development Decade, IDS Reprints, 101.* Brighton: Institute of Development Studies.

Slaughter, S., & Leslie, L. (1999). *Academic Capitalism. Politics, Policies and the Entrepreneurial University.* Baltimore/London: Johns Hopkins University Press.

Slaughter, S., & Rhoades, G. (2004). *Academic Capitalism and the New Economy: Markets, State, and Higher Education.* Baltimore/London: Johns Hopkins University Press.

Smith, A., Fressoli, M., Abrol, D., Around, E., & Ely, A. (2017). *Grassroots Innovation Movements.* New York: Routledge.

Srinivas, S. (2014). Demand and Innovation. Path Towards Inclusive Development. In S. Ramani (Ed.), *Innovation in India: Combining Economic Growth with Inclusive Development* (pp. 78–106). India: Cambridge University Press.

Srinivas, S., & Sutz, J. (2008). Developing Countries and Innovation. Searching for a New Analytical Approach. *Technology in Society, 30*(2), 129–140.

Stiglitz, J. (2007). *Give Prizes Not Patents.* Available at: http://www.project-syndicate.org/commentary/prizes--not-patents. Accessed 4 Jan 2017.

Stiglitz, J. (2012). *The Price of Inequality.* New York: Norton.

Stiglitz, J., Sen, A., & Fitoussi, J. (2010). *Mismeasuring Our Lives: Why GDP Doesn't Add Up.* New York: The New Press.

Stirling, A. (2013). "Pluralising Progress: From Inclusive Innovation to Innovation Democracy", Contribution to the Dig-IT Workshop on Inclusive Growth, Innovation and Technology: Interdisciplinary Perspectives, University of Sussex.

Sutz, J. (1997). The Third Role of the University. In H. Etzkowitz & L. Leydesdorff (Eds.), *Universities and the Global Knowledge Economy* (pp. 11–20). London: Cassell.

Sutz, J. (2005, April). The Role of Universities in Knowledge Production. SciDevNet, Policy Briefs. Available at: http://www.scidev.net/global/policy-brief/the-role-of-universities-in-knowledge-production-.html. Accessed 10 May 2017. Published also in *Journal of Himalayan Science*, 3(5), January–June 2005, 53–56.

Sutz, J. (2012). Measuring Innovation in Developing Countries: Some Suggestions to Achieve More Accurate and Useful Indicators. *International Journal of Technological Learning, Innovation and Development (IJTLID)*, 5(1/2), 40–57.

Teferra, D., & Altbach, P. (2004). African Higher Education: Challenges for the 21st Century. *Higher Education*, 47(1), 21–50.

The Atlantic. (2017). *Why Is Sweden so Good at Pop Music?* Available at: https://www.theatlantic.com/entertainment/archive/2013/10/why-is-sweden-so-good-at-pop-music/280945/. Accessed 10 May 2017.

The Mercury News. (2007, May 31). *Hillary Clinton Brings Innovation Agenda to Silicon Valley.* http://www.mercurynews.com/2007/05/31/hillary-clinton-brings-innovation-agenda-to-silicon-valley/

The UTOPIA Project 1981–1986. Available at: http://www.nada.kth.se/cid/utopia/quality.htm. Accessed 10 May 2017.

Tilly, C. (2005). *Identities, Boundaries, and Social Ties.* Boulder: Paradigm Publishers.

Tran Ngoc Ca. (2016). The National Innovation System in Vietnam and Its Relevance for Development. In B. Göransson, C. Brundenius, & C. Aguirre-Bastos (Eds.), *Innovation Systems for Development—Making Research and Innovation Matter in Developing Countries* (pp. 138–183). Cheltenham: Edward Elgar.

Tran Ngoc Ca, & Nguyen Vo Hung. (2011). Vietnam: Current Debates on the Transformation of Academic Institutions. In B. Göransson & C. Brundenius (Eds.), *Universities in Transition. The Changing Role and Challenges for Academic Institutions* (pp. 119–142). Ottawa: Springer.

Trencher, G., et al. (2013). Beyond the Third Mission: Exploring the Emerging University Function of Co-creation for Sustainability. *Science and Public Policy*, 41(2), 151–179.

Tsounta, E., & Ouseke, A. (2014). *What Is Behind Latin America's Diminishing Income Inequality?* International Monetary Fund Working Paper 14/124.

Turkle, S. (2016). *Reclaiming Conversation. The Power of Talk in a Digital Age.* New York: Penguin Books.

UNDP. (2011). *Human Development Report 2011, Sustainability and Equity: A Better Future for All.* New York: United Nations Development Program.

UNESCO. (2017). *UI Statistics.* Available at: http://data.uis.unesco.org/Index.aspx. Accessed 10 May 2017.

van Dalen, H. P., & Henkens, K. (2012). Intended and Unintended Consequences of a Publish-or-Perish Culture: A Worldwide Survey. *Journal of the American Society for Information Science and Technology*, 63(7), 1282–1293.

Vérez-Bencomo, V. (2007). Interview. *MEDICC Review*, 9(1), 14–15.

Vincenti, W. (1990). *What Engineers Know and How They Know It. Analytical Studies from Aeronautical History.* Baltimore: John Hopkins University Press.

von Hippel, E. (1988). *The Sources of Innovation.* Nueva York: Oxford University Press.

Wallerstein, I. (1969). *University in Turmoil. The Politics of Change.* New York: Atheneum.

Weerts, D. J., & Sandmann, L. R. (2008). Building a Two-Way Street: Challenges and Opportunities for Community Engagement at Research Universities. *Review of Higher Education, 32*(1), 73–106.

Weiss, L. (2014). *America Inc.?: Innovation and Enterprise in the National Security State.* Ithaca/London: Cornell University Press.

Weiherl, J., & Frost, J. (2016). Professional and Organizational Commitment in Universities: From Judgement to Developmental Performance Management. In J. Frost, F. Hattke, & M. Reihlen (Eds.), *Multi-Level Governance in Universities. Strategy, Structure, Control* (pp. 173–192). Switzerland: Springer.

Weizenbaum, J. (1976). *Computer Power and Human Reason. From Judgement to Calculation.* San Francisco: Freeman, and Co.

Wennerås, C., & Wold, A. (1997). Nepotism and Sexism in Peer-Review. *Nature, 387,* 341–343.

Whitley, R. (2010). Reconfiguring the Public Sciences: The Impact of Governance Changes on Authority and Innovation in Public Science Systems. In R. Whitley, J. Gläser, & L. Engwall (Eds.), *Reconfiguring Knowledge Production: Changing Authority Relationships in the Sciences and Their Consequences for Intellectual Innovation* (pp. 3–47). New York: Oxford University Press.

Wilkinson, R. (1996). *Unhealthy Societies. The Afflictions of Inequality.* New York: Routledge.

Woelert, P. (2015). The 'Logic of Escalation' in Performance Measurement: An Analysis of the Dynamics of a Research Evaluation System. *Policy and Society, 34,* 75–85.

Woolthuis, R., Lankhuizen, M., & Gilsing, V. (2005). A System Failure Framework for Innovationpolicy Design. *Technovation, 25,* 609–619.

Zarei, A. E., Almehdar, H., & Redwan, E. M. (2016). Hib Vaccines: Past, Present, and Future Perspectives. *Journal of Immunology Research.* Available at: https://www.hindawi.com/journals/jir/2016/7203587/. Accessed 10 May 2017.

Ziman, J. (1994). *Prometheus Bound: Science in a Dynamic 'Steady State'.* Cambridge: Cambridge University Press.

Ziman, J. (1996). 'Postacademic Science': Constructing Knowledge with Networks and Norms. *Science Studies, 9*(1), 67–80.

INDEX

A
academia, 70, 149, 167, 188, 190, 196, 208, 209
academic evaluation, 5, 168, 175, 177, 193–9, 201, 205, 208, 212, 234, 235
academic institutions, 5, 144, 149, 159–63, 185
advanced life-long learning, 5, 232
alternative models, 174, 230
Argentina, 56, 146, 247
autonomy of the university, 5, 144, 172–4, 183, 188, 236, 241

B
basic research, 124, 144, 145, 201, 216, 219
Bolivia, 118
Brazil, 54, 56, 102, 110, 122, 123, 164, 166

C
capitalism, 23, 30, 31, 45, 73, 85, 244
capitalist, 20, 29, 48, 73, 85
Chile, 54, 108, 161
China, 15, 19, 23, 24, 41, 49, 54, 58, 146–8, 160, 161, 205, 246, 248
computers, 40, 43, 44, 51, 148, 192
connected autonomy, 5, 188–93, 241
Cuba, 109, 246

D
Denmark, 46, 54, 98, 111, 226, 228, 232, 233, 238, 240
development
    approaches to, 32, 168
    concept of, 3, 9–32, 64
    problems, 4, 9–12, 86, 146, 195
    studies, 9, 10

© The Author(s) 2018
R. Arocena et al., *Developmental Universities in Inclusive Innovation Systems*, https://doi.org/10.1007/978-3-319-64152-2

Printed by Printforce, the Netherlands